Examine circ stances in which P.Ref act was ✗
passed. assess significance. of crisis?

EDWARDIAN ENGLAND 1901-15
SOCIETY AND POLITICS

MR. ASQUITH IN OFFICE

"Come one, come all, this rock shall fly
From its firm base as soon as I."

EDWARDIAN ENGLAND 1901-15
SOCIETY AND POLITICS

Donald Read

READER IN MODERN ENGLISH HISTORY
UNIVERSITY OF KENT

HARRAP   LONDON

For Fergus

First Published in Great Britain 1972
by GEORGE G. HARRAP & CO. LTD:
182-184 High Holborn, London WC1V 7AX

ISBN 0 245 51053 x (Boards)
0 245 51064 8 (Paper)

*Composed in Baskerville type by
Rolfe Typographics Limited, Hockley, Essex and
printed by Redwood Press Limited, Trowbridge,
Wiltshire*

Made in Great Britain

Acknowledgments

The author is grateful to the following for permission to quote from some of the many contemporary documents of the Edwardian period: Mrs George Bambridge, Methuen & Macmillan Co. of Canada; Miss D. E. Collins and Methuen & Co; Constable & Co., Ltd; The Hamlyn Publishing Group Ltd; the London School of Economics and Political Science; Mr Peter Newbolt; *Punch;* and the Joseph Rowntree Charitable Trust.

Contents

Plates

Acknowledgments are due in each case to those named.

(b) George V
The Mansell Collection

XXI. (a) Old Age Pensioners
Headley Brothers
(b) Lloyd George and Winston Churchill 1916
Illustrated London News

Illustrations within the text

We are uncertain whether civilization is about to blossom into flower or wither in ruined tangle of dead leaves and faded gold.
(C. F. G. Masterman, 'What the Age Looks Like', in *The Nation*, 26th December, 1908)

We want to have our young people filled with a new realization that History is not over, that nothing is settled, and that the supreme dramatic phase in the story of England has still to come. It was not in the Norman Conquest, not in the flight of King James II, nor the overthrow of Napoleon; it is here and now. It falls to them to be actors not in a reminiscent pageant but a living conflict, and the sooner they are prepared to take their part in that the better our Empire will acquit itself.
(H. G. Wells, 'What Must be Done Now', in *What the Worker Wants* (1912), 29–30)

Are there not enough of the signs that have been always heralds of the dissolution of empires with us now to give us pause? Towns instead of country, pasture instead of tillage, machinery instead of men, imported food supplies and exported harvest hands, a mercenary army, a navy withdrawn from the frontier of the Empire to defend its heart, crushing taxation on the producers of wealth, faith dim and luxury gross—are not these enough to send us to the old paths and seek the Ark of the Covenant on our knees?
(K. G. Feiling, *Toryism, a Political Dialogue* (1913), 153–4)

CHAPTER ONE

Introduction: Period and Problems

Queen Victoria died, and in a strict chronological sense the Edwardian era began, on 22nd January 1901. The death of the Queen, the start of the twentieth century, and the impact of the Boer War (1899–1902), which had shattered complacency about the invulnerability of the British Empire, combined to give a strong sense of end and beginning to the year 1901. The nineteenth century, which economically and politically had been the British century, the age when the 'Pax Britannica' had brought peace and order to large areas of the globe and when Britain had served as 'the workshop of the world', had now given place to a new century in which British predominance was contested from the very outset. Economically the United States and Germany had caught up, and even overtaken, Britain in many fields. Both, moreover, possessed greater manpower and natural resources than the United Kingdom. In the twentieth century it was plain that the mother country would need increased support from her Empire if she were to survive as a world power. But always in the past empires had decayed and disintegrated. Would the British Empire 'decline and fall' like the Roman Empire? Had the British people the moral fibre or the physical energy to prevent this? Crowded into towns and cities as never before, was the British race degenerating? Some Edwardians gave optimistic answers to these and other disturbing questions; many contemporaries were more gloomy. Most agreed that a new vigour was needed in numerous areas of British life, but there was wide difference over the choice of policies to promote such vigour.

In the early weeks of 1901 *The Times* reflected both the optimism and the pessimism of the period. On the very first day of the new century it wrote hopefully of British prospects: 'with a people prosperous, contented, manly, intelligent, and self-reliant, we may look forward with good hope.' Three weeks later, after Victoria's death, it was less confident: 'The command of natural forces that made us great and rich has been superseded by newer discoveries and methods, and we may have to open what may be called a new chapter.' Young Winston Churchill (1874–1965), however, placed himself among the optimists who felt little regret for the past. 'Edward the VIIth—gadzooks, what a long way that seems to take one back! I am glad he has got his innings at last, and am most interested to watch how he plays it.' With characteristically large phraseology Churchill was nevertheless to admit in a speech eight years later that 'the wonderful century was over'; a new time of 'strange methods, huge forces, larger combinations—a Titanic world' had arrived. 'We must go forward . . . to renew through the generations which are to come the fame and the power of the British race.'[1] The distance between Edwardian optimism and Edwardian pessimism is measured in the three quotations which precede this chapter. The words of H. G. Wells (1866–1946), the novelist and social prophet who looked towards a socialist millenium, were appropriately confident; K. G. Feiling (b. 1884), a Tory historian, aware of the cause of the fall of Rome, was much more gloomy. Between them stood C. F. G. Masterman (1873–1927), a radical member (1908–15) of the Liberal Government; his uncertain language matched the uncertain midway position between socialism and toryism of the Edwardian Liberal Party.

'The Victorian Era has definitely closed', Masterman had written in 1901; and the rapidity of social and economic change was more easily recognized 'now that the death of the Queen and of the century have reminded us all that nature and time spare nothing'. On the very last day of the same year R. D. Blumenfeld (1864–1948), a leading Edwardian journalist, touched in his private diary on various aspects of this sense of alteration:

Queen Victoria's death alone will ever mark 1901 in the history of the nation. With her departed, perhaps, the most

glorious era of English history. The end of the Boer War,
which was so confidently assumed with the fall of Pretoria,
is not yet. . . . Trade has been only fair. We are on the eve of
great electrification movements. The automobile has come
to stay, and there are even some people who predict that in
another generation our traffic will be horseless. . . . Women
are coming more and more in competition with men in
business, and even well-to-do girls are devoting themselves
to callings other than nursing.[2]

Were such changes to be feared or to be welcomed? The
Victorians had tended to equate alteration with progress
because for them, on the whole, change—political, economic
and social—had worked to advantage. Revealingly, they had
often spoken not of change but of 'improvement'. Edwardian
pessimists were frequently men who, unlike their fathers or
grandfathers, had realized that change need not always mean
advance. It could mean difficulty and even retrogression. Havelock Ellis (1859–1939), the pioneer sexologist, himself neither
an optimist nor a pessimist but a scientific social realist, noted
in his diary in 1913 how 'the Pessimist is often merely an
impecunious bankrupt Optimist', who had imagined 'that the
eminently respectable March of Progress was bearing him
onwards to the social goal of a glorified Sunday School.
Horrible doubts have seized him. Henceforth, to his eyes, the
Universe is shrouded in Black.' In 1910 the Liberal radical
weekly *The Nation* had denounced what it dubbed 'The Cant
of Decadence', while in its 'Outlook for 1914' *The Times* likewise published a long attack upon the contemporary excess
of self-depreciation.[3] *The Times* was right to deplore the
'perpetual chorus of disparagement'. In the war which was to
begin a few months later the resilience of the British people
and of their institutions was to be strikingly demonstrated.
Much was wrong with Edwardian England, but its Jeremiahs
went too far. It was not a society in fatal decay.

Nevertheless, by 1901 Victorian certainty had been seriously
undermined. *Efficiency and Empire*, published in that year by
Arnold White (1848–1925), a popular Edwardian polemicist,
listed in a series of propositions 'the accepted creed of the
average Englishman'—'Britannia rules the waves', 'One

Englishman can beat two foreigners', 'The British Empire, on which the sun never sets, is the greatest the world has ever seen, and being free from militarism is safe against decay', 'The English fiscal system is the best in the world', 'Our system of finance is the strongest and best in the world', 'Our men of business, when they take the trouble to excel, are without rival in the world'. But now, White concluded gloomily, all these propositions were disputable: 'many of them are falsehoods'. At its most extreme this new uncertainty became conscious anti-Victorianism. An article on 'The Early Victorians and Ourselves' in 1906 attacked their confidence in themselves and 'in their eternal fame'. At the 1911 centenary of the birth of John Bright (1811–89), who had been one of the great Victorian worthies, Augustine Birrell (1850–1933), a Liberal Cabinet Minister, admitted that Bright-like 'raptures about progress' were now 'voted middle-class—a dreadful thing to be—awful, vulgar, early Victorian'. Birrell himself was dismissed as 'decidedly a Victorian product' by Lytton Strachey (1880–1932), who was to become the arch-exposer of Victorian failings. The outbreak of war in 1914, which Strachey regarded as the natural consequence of nineteenth-century complacency, was to intensify his desire to debunk sham Victorian reputations; but the first idea for *Eminent Victorians* (1918) had come to him as early as 1912.* Among Strachey's contemporaries questioning was widespread. J. A. Hobson (1858–1940), a leading Edwardian economic and political writer, noted in *The Crisis of Liberalism* (1909) how more and more men (and women) were 'possessed by the duty and the desire to put the very questions which their parents thought shocking, and to insist upon plain intelligible answers'.[4] In consequence, politics after 1901 were increasingly dominated by controversies about matters which most Victorians had regarded as settled and closed to dis-

---

* *Times Literary Supplement* review of *Eminent Victorians* (16th May 1918): 'so strangely different a world do we live in now that an air of remoteness has already settled on that recent epoch, and even those who spent part of their maturity in the time of Queen Victoria look back on her reign with a kind of wonder. If to them it now seems an odd almost incredible epoch, what appearance must it wear in the eyes of those who know it only from childish memory and from books and hearsay? The answer—well, the answer is to be found in Mr Strachey's book; surviving Victorians will read it with what is called "mixed feelings".'

cussion. This Edwardian reaction against the economic, social and political certainties of the Victorians revealed itself notably

in continuous discussion, both by social and political theorists and by practising politicians, of the proper relationship between the state and the individual;

in the attack upon free trade, launched by the 'tariff reformers' from 1903;

in new attitudes to the Empire emerging after the costly and tardy British victory in the Boer War (1899–1902);

in the introduction of the 'social service state' by the Liberal Governments from 1906;

in the unprecedented trade union unrest of 1911–12;

in the increasingly militant demand for 'votes for Women' voiced by the suffragettes from 1905;

in the resurgence of the Irish Question, culminating in the threat of civil war in Ireland in 1914;

and in the acceptance of novel, even though vague, commitments towards France and Russia in their rivalry with Germany and Austria, underlying the British declaration of war on 4th August 1914.

These eight reactions provide in turn the essence of chapters 3–10 of this survey. But it is right to begin with the social and political background as outlined in chapter 2. Who *were* the Edwardians? How were they socially connected and contrasted? How did they communicate? How did they amuse themselves? How did they regard their God and their King? Was Edwardian England a democracy? This last question leads on naturally to a consideration in chapter 3 of Edwardian political ideas, political parties and political personalities. A key problem for Edwardians was the redefinition of the limits of government intervention. The evil of mass poverty was now widely acknowledged. Could it be overcome only through full socialism, state and municipal? Such was the claim of Keir Hardie (1856–1915), the Labour pioneer. Or did the 'new Liberalism' of Lloyd George (1863–1945) represent a successful blend of idealism and practicality? These were pressing political questions for Edwardians, and they provide the central questions of chapter 3.

After much hesitation, tariff reform, devised by Joseph Chamberlain (1836–1914) from 1903, became the main Conservative alternative to Liberal social reform. It meant abandonment of the great Victorian economic dogma of free trade. The fluctuating fortunes of the tariff reform movement are considered in chapter 4. In the face of intensifying foreign commercial rivalry and deepening German power-political hostility, the tariff reformers promised both steadier work and wages and a stronger more united British Empire. 'Will the Empire live?' was a persistent Edwardian question. How could the self-governing white colonies be persuaded to give effective moral and material support to the 'Imperial idea'? How could the defeated South African Boers be reconciled to membership of the Empire? How could the allegiance of the overwhelming coloured majority within the Empire, especially in India, be retained, and their advancement be encouraged? These are questions for chapter 5. How fit was the recently urbanized mass of the English people, physically and mentally, to possess and to protect a world-wide Empire? This great question for Edwardians, and for historians, is considered at the beginning of chapter 6. Imperial considerations led even Balfour's Conservative Government (1902–5) to promote the major Education Act of 1902. This measure became an important element in the developing Edwardian 'social service state', explored through the rest of the chapter. But the main architects of the new system were the Liberals, in power between 1905–15. Old-age pensions, labour exchanges, unemployment insurance, health insurance and other innovations may seem in retrospect to have had a greater inevitability and pattern about them than was in fact the case at the time of their inception. The Liberals were sometimes halting, and Conservative opposition was often bitter, culminating in the 'peers versus people' crisis of 1909–11. This started with the Lords' rejection of Lloyd George's 1909 budget, a measure intended to provide finance for social reform. In such a context the 1911 Parliament Act, which severely limited the powers of the upper house, becomes part of the story of the progress of social reform.

Why were the Edwardian working classes themselves not especially enthusiastic about most of the social benefits enacted during these years? Many of them had become disillusioned with politics and politicians, preferring to turn to 'direct' trade union strike action. The aspirations and limitations of the 'industrial warfare' of the years from 1911 are discussed in chapter 7. And while some Edwardian workmen were displaying a new restlessness (and recklessness), so were some Edwardian women, led by the suffragettes (chapter 8). During the Edwardian years suffragette demands grew increasingly strident and their activities increasingly violent. Moreover, the violence, actual and anticipated, of the strikers and suffragettes continued alongside a still greater threat of violence coming from Ireland. The slogan 'Ulster will fight and Ulster will be right' is assessed in chapter 9. The attempt of the Liberal Government to impose Home Rule upon the Northern Irish Protestants had brought Ireland to the brink of civil war by the end of July 1914. Then suddenly the whole Irish crisis was temporarily ended by the outbreak of the First World War. Chapter 10 does not seek to explore the intricacies of Edwardian foreign policy; it concentrates instead upon asking how Edwardians regarded (or disregarded) foreign affairs. Did many of them realize that they were heading towards the 'deluge' of 1914–18? And when war came, how long did it take the English people to understand that they had become involved in a terrible, enveloping war of attrition? In other words, when did the Edwardian era finally end?

The answer to this last question is—within about a year of the outbreak of war. 1915 proved to be the twelve months of awful realization, a full five years after the death of Edward VII himself on 6th May 1910. To the end of 1914 the cry 'business as usual' had sustained some of the pre-war atmosphere. Mary Gladstone (1847–1927) noted at Christmas 1914 how Chester was still filled with light-hearted people, 'laughing, talking, shopping, shops crowded. They don't realize a bit yet.'[5] We shall see how the onset of 'total' war during 1915 completed the submergence of Edwardian society, though we shall see also that there were signs of change before the war, of 'post-war' symptoms even in 'pre-war' England.

The war was to prove a traumatic experience for all who

lived through it, not least for contemporary historians. 'La guerre paralyse toute pensée', confessed the anglophile French historian, Elie Halévy (1870–1937), in 1916. In 1926 and 1932, when he was growing increasingly pessimistic about the post-war world, Halévy published two notable volumes on the history of Edwardian England; but, revealingly, both books were permeated by a sense of what he accepted as the 'decadence' of a country heading towards the miseries of war, wider state interference and the collapse of Gladstonian Liberalism. Halévy was happy to return in the mid-nineteen thirties to writing the history of Gladstone's England. 'Je me sens anachronique, mais non pas malheureux pour cela. Car je ne suis pas un fils de la guerre; et le siècle qui commence sous mes yeux à sortir de l'enfance m'etonne mais ne m'enchante pas.'6 Only since the Second World War have historians and biographers emerged who, because they were either children or unborn before 1914, never experienced the sensation of their world collapsing about them. Moreover, such historians have enjoyed access to the private and secret records of the time, enabling them to make discoveries beyond the knowledge of the Edwardians themselves. They can now reveal, in the words of G. M. Trevelyan (1876–1962), himself a leading Edwardian historian, 'more in some respects than the dweller in the past himself knew about the conditions that enveloped and controlled his life.'7 The work of many post-Edwardian historians and biographers of the Edwardian period has been distilled and developed in the following survey.* 'What will the future make of the present?', asked Masterman in 1909.8 Here is one answer.

*Notably, E. H. Phelps Brown (b. 1906) on industrial relations, A. J. P. Taylor (b. 1906) on foreign affairs, Randolph Churchill (1911–68) on his father, Max Beloff (b. 1913) on Imperial policy, Robert Blake (b. 1916) on Conservative politics, Roy Jenkins (b. 1920) on Liberal politics, Henry Pelling (b. 1920) on Labour politics, F. S. L. Lyons (b. 1923) on the Irish question, and B. B. Gilbert (b. 1924) on social reform.

CHAPTER TWO

Social and Political Background

Population, Occupation and Urbanization

There were about 32,500,000 Edwardians in England and Wales in 1901, almost 41,500,000 in the United Kingdom. Ten years later these numbers had risen to just over 36,000,000 and almost 45,250,000 respectively.[1] Population was still increasing, but this gave little satisfaction to the Edwardians, for it was no longer growing at the fast pace of early- and mid-Victorian times. The birth-rate had first begun to fall in the eighteen seventies, from 36.3 per 1000 population for England and Wales in 1876 to 28.5 in 1901 and 24.1 in 1913. In 1881 for every million people in England and Wales there had been 135,857 children under five, by 1901 this figure had fallen to 114,262 and by 1911 to 106,857. Articles on the declining birth-rate in *The Times* of 1906 by Sidney Webb (1859–1947), the socialist planner and wirepuller, were widely noticed. A low-grade or foreign 25 per cent of all parents, concluded Webb, was producing one-half of the next generation. 'This can hardly result in anything but national deterioration; or, as an alternative, in this country gradually falling to the Irish and the Jews.' But even these prolific races were beginning to reproduce less quickly. 'The ultimate future of these islands may be to the Chinese!' Webb hoped that this 'yellow peril' (a persistent Edwardian bogey) would stimulate public opinion to support socialist welfare policies, especially in medical and educational provision. He believed that such policies would encourage the better-off and more intelligent who, because of their high economic and social aspirations, were now choosing to produce fewer children, to revert to having large families. Choice was at the heart of the problem, for family limitation was now widely practised among the upper and middle classes and was extending among the more prudent sections of the working class. The 1911 census confirmed that since the eighteen fifties, when fertility had not been greatly less within well-to-do marriages compared with the marriages of the poor (14 per cent below average for the middle classes, 5 per cent above for unskilled labourers), an important fertility change had occurred. By 1891-6 middle-class married fertility was 30 per cent below average, in contrast with the fertility level among the unskilled which was now 16 per cent above average. This marked new contrast was partly caused by later marriages among the middle classes, but more especially by the widespread adoption among them of methods of family limitation.[2]

Plain evidence survives from the private diary of W. T. Stead (1849-1912), the notable journalist, of late-Victorian family planning in practice. One night in 1889 Stead and his wife deliberately refrained from practising 'withdrawal', and a future Edwardian was conceived. 'So this night we shall have uninterrupted intercourse for the first time for five years, in the hope of getting a daughter who may, I hope, be the Lord's from her conception. . . . Perhaps by the time she comes to womanhood, the lot of women may not be so hard as heretofore.'[3] This lot was especially hard in Edwardian childbirth, especially for poor women. Hannah Mitchell, a Manchester working-class wife, recalled the birth of her baby in 1898 after twenty-four hours' painful labour: 'my strength was gone, and I could do no more to help myself, so my baby was brought into the world with instruments, and without an anaesthetic. . . I felt it impossible to face again either the personal suffering, or the task of bringing up a second child in poverty. Fortunately, my husband had the courage of his socialist convictions on this point, and was no more anxious than myself to repeat the experience.' The Mitchells may have had recourse to mechanical means of contraception which were coming into increasing use among the working people of the North during the Edwardian period. This was revealed by an elaborate survey sponsored by the Galton Eugenics Laboratory of London University, the results of which were published in 1914. The national extent of family limitation, by one means or another, was confirmed in the report of the semi-official National Birth-Rate Commission, set up in 1913 and reporting three years later. The Commission firmly rejected alarmist theories about a racial decline in national fertility. But the prospect remained, as the 1911 census report emphasized, of Britain following the contemporary French example, the seeming likelihood of a stationary or even a declining population later in the twentieth century.[4]

Admittedly, a rapidly falling death-rate was partly counteracting this trend. The rate for England and Wales dropped from 16.9 per 1000 population in 1901 to 13.8 per 1000 in 1913. Improving standards of medicine, hygiene and housing were also sharply reducing the infant mortality rate (151 per 1000 live births in England and Wales in 1901, 108 in 1913), as well as raising the expectation of life (from 46 years for men and 50 for women in 1900–2 to 52 and 55 years respectively in 1910–12). 552,000 people died in England and Wales in 1901, only 505,000 in 1913. But these 47,000 less deaths were matched by a similar reduction (930,000 to 882,000) in births. Moreover, emigration was creaming off an increasing number of the best younger people, driven out by the uncertainty of finding steady work and wages in Edwardian Britain. This exodus reached a high point in the immediate pre-war years, an annual average of 284,000 for 1901–10 rising to 464,000 in 1911–13. The numbers going to the Empire increased from only 25,000 in 1900 to 250,000 in 1912, as the United States ceased to be the main magnet, especially for unskilled labourers. This shift was some consolation to Edwardians who 'thought imperially' and believed that such emigrants could still contribute from overseas to the maintenance of British strength.[5]

But the steady subtraction of numerous young emigrants was helping to raise the average age of the population of the mother country. The people of Edwardian England were an ageing, or at least a middle-ageing, community. In 1841 a little less than half the inhabitants of England and Wales had been aged under 20; by 1911 such young people comprised less than one-third of the total. This ageing trend was apparent even within the short span of Edwardian years. Between 1901 and 1911 the number of people in the 40–44 age group passed two million for the first time. Whereas in 1901 people under 30 comprised 60.8 per cent of the population, ten years later they comprised only 57.4 per cent. Conversely, in the same period the 30–60 age group rose from 31.7 to 34.4 per cent, and people over 60 from 7.5 to 8.2 per cent. This trend, if continued, was bound to produce weakening economic and social effects. At first the consequences of the late-Victorian decline in the birth-rate had even been advantageous, in that the economy was required to support a smaller proportion of unproductive children while still benefiting from the high birth-rate in the previous generation. But by 1911 this temporary advantage had passed, and the census report warned of the economic consequences of a declining proportion 'of workers at the most economically efficient ages', and also of its military and naval implications in terms of the future supply of recruits.[6]

Alongside the late-Victorian decline in the birth-rate, the pattern of employment and residence in England and Wales had also been changing strikingly. More and more people were living and working in towns, more and more were quitting the countryside and abandoning work in agriculture. Between 1841 and 1901 over four million people left the rural areas for the towns or to emigrate. Whereas in 1851 the number of inhabitants of the rural and of the urban districts had been approximately equal at 9,000,000 each, by 1911 only one person in four (7,900,000) lived in the country. The 'great depression' of the last quarter of the nineteenth century had damaged agriculture more than any other major occupation. A massive inflow of cheap American corn had destroyed the livelihoods of the corn-growing landlords and farmers of southern and eastern England, the core of the old landed interest. A shift to meat and dairy farming had gradually followed, but this transition was often painful. The expanding towns, meanwhile, were offering a rival prospect (not always confirmed in actuality) of steadier work, higher wages, and greater independence for migrating agricultural labourers. More appealing still, the towns offered gregariousness instead of rural isolation. Under the pull of these attractions, from the eighteen seventies onwards young countryfolk flocked to the urban centres, drawn (in the words of an official observer in 1894) 'above all things, for the sake of being more in the stream of life'.

During the Edwardian years, between the 1901 and 1911

censuses, this downward trend in rural population was indeed checked. The number of agricultural labourers stabilized itself at about 750,000, while the number of farmers, graziers, market gardeners and others rose with new prosperity to give a grand total approaching 1,250,000 engaged in agriculture. An observer in 1916 noted how the 'degradation' of nineteenth-century grain farming was now long past. Labourers left on the land enjoyed protection against accidents (1900) and insurance against sickness (1911). Compulsory elementary education (1880) had helped to make them less dependent in spirit upon their employers. 'In villages imbued with the modern spirit the labourer was no longer a drudge, with no views outside his work. He studied his weekly paper and took an interest in national politics.' 'Bastard feudalism' was giving way to 'a new era'.

Yet hopeful though these trends were in the last Edwardian years, much further improvement was needed. Rural housing conditions remained generally poor, often squalid, while wages stayed below the poverty line, averaging only 17s. 6d. for English labourers in 1907. Edwardian reformers hoped to overcome such poverty and to secure the independence of the rural labourers by giving them a stake in the land. Smallholdings Acts were passed in 1892 and 1908, and the number of such holdings grew; but the necessary funds and personal qualities for successful small-scale cultivation were not widely found. Undeterred, however, right up to 1914 reformers continued to speak of the 'land hunger' of the agricultural labourers.[7]

In the quarter-century before 1907 the contribution of agriculture to the national product fell by almost half, from 11.9 per cent in 1865–84 to 6.6 per cent in 1900–9. Meanwhile, the contribution of manufacturing, coal-mining and building had remained constant, though with some change between industries. The textiles industry, for example, which had accounted for about 10 per cent of the national income in 1881, provided only 4.5 per cent by 1907. These old industries were still important, but they were now being rivalled by other occupations. In 1911 cotton manufacture employed 605,000 people, woollen and worsted manufacture 223,000, building 946,000, and coal mining 874,000; but metal working and machine making were now occupying 1,578,000 persons, transport 1,424,000, commerce (of many sorts) 790,000, the paper and printing trades 341,000, and the chemical industry 172,000. At the same date the preparation and sale of food, drink and tobacco and the provision of lodging now together gave work to 1,388,000 people. But the largest of all Edwardian occupations was domestic service. In 1911 nearly 2,600,000 people were engaged as servants, over 2,100,000 of these being women. 'Service' was much the largest field of female employment.

Most of this activity was town-centred. The growth of the service industries and of transport was particularly related to rapid urban expansion. By the beginning of the twentieth century Britain's towns and cities had reached novel proportions, creating an urban crisis of scale and of quality of life which the Edwardians were the first people to encounter. G. M. Young (1882–1959), the distinguished historian of Victorian England, remarked that 'the town . . . was the great and almost insoluble problem of Victorian statesmanship'.[8] Certainly, their manifest and manifold urban problems were never solved by the Victorians; yet most of them had persisted in regarding their towns as challenges rather than burdens. They pictured themselves as living in an advancing 'age of great cities'. A book with this title, published in 1843, asserted that the principle of progress was association and that cities were the natural centres of such contact.[9] Joseph Chamberlain (1836–1914), as Mayor of Birmingham 1873–6, had shown what could be achieved. He had muncipalized the gas and water supplies, cleared slum property to build a fine city centre, and given the town a 'civic gospel' and an international reputation for enterprise. But Chamberlain's work was undertaken just before a great acceleration of urbanization, which by the opening of the twentieth century had transformed the whole scale of English urban problems. In 1871 64 per cent of the people of England and Wales still lived in towns, villages and hamlets of less than 50,000 people. There were only thirty-seven towns larger than this, and even Chamberlain's city (population 344,000 in 1871) could still be described as a 'great village'.[10] Urban and suburban sprawl was only just beginning, and Birmingham still possessed topographical and social unity. But by 1901 the number of towns with populations over 50,000 had doubled, and by 1911 the population of England's five main conurbations (significantly, a word coined at this time)[11] had likewise come near to doubling. The growth of London had been especially striking in absolute terms, its population in 1911 exceeding the combined populations of the next two largest conurbations:

	Greater London	S.E. Lancs.	W. Midlands	W. Yorks.	Mersey-side
1871	3890	1386	969	1064	690
1901	6586	2117	1483	1524	1030
1911	7256	2328	1634	1590	1157

(× 1000)

This prolonged rapid rate of growth produced very high urban population densities, with consequent overcrowding on a scale unknown to the early Victorians, even though urban sanitary improvements did now avoid the very worst forms of squalor to be found in the earlier period. In 1901 London possessed 38,795 inhabitants per square mile, the other great towns 18,435 per square mile. The Edwardian census reports defined overcrowding as an average of more than two persons per room per tenement; by such a standard 3,258,000, 11.2 per cent of the total population, were overcrowded in 1891, and 2,668,000, 8.2 per cent, ten years later.[12]

The town, the city, the conurbation were now the preponderating features upon the map of England. The urban problem, which, for all its difficulties, their grandfathers had accepted as a stimulating challenge, had come to present itself to the Edwardians as more burdensome than stimulating. 'The sphinx of the twentieth century propounds to us the riddle as to what England will do with this town population, or perhaps more truly, what this town population will do with England.' So exclaimed a book on *The Town Child*, published in 1907.[13] The influx of healthy country people into the towns had been like a blood transfusion; but now a generation of young people was growing up *born* in the towns, whose whole lifetimes had been spent in a debilitating urban situation. Though poverty and bad housing had always been, and were still, widespread in the country districts, such features were much more damaging in the new crowded and almost inescapable urban environment. By the turn of the century, elaborate and disturbing evidence about life and work in the capital had been collected in Charles Booth's (1840–1916) monumental *Life and Labour of the People in London*, issued in seventeen volumes between 1889 and 1903. Booth's survey was followed in 1901 by B. Seebohm Rowntree's (1871–1954) *Poverty, a Study of Town Life*, which showed from the example of York how the situation which Booth had revealed in London was not exceptional, how even an ancient cathedral city of some 75,000 inhabitants was in the grip of poverty and misery. Having found York as bad as London, Rowntree concluded, 'we are faced by the startling probability that from 25 to 30 per cent of the town populations of the United Kingdom are living in poverty'. He also showed how this poverty problem was closely linked to the urban housing question and to the problem of the health of the people. Because of poverty, 6.4 per cènt of the inhabitants of York lived more than two to a room, while the number who lived, and slept, in rooms which provided inadequate air space was very much greater. Rowntree noted the low physical quality of intending army recruits in York, Leeds and Sheffield; between 1897 and 1901 nearly one half were rejected on medical grounds. Urban life was thus creating a direct threat to future national and Imperial security. Britain's declining competitiveness in world trade could also be related to the poor health of her urban population. Rowntree emphasized the superior physical fitness of American workers. 'The question of efficiency—mental and physical—has become one of paramount importance'; 'the widespread existence of poverty in an industrial country like our own must seriously retard its development'.[14]

The effects of the Edwardian urban crisis thus spread wide. So did the cities themselves. In spite of their very high population densities, they were also suffering from the contrasting problem of urban sprawl, which was further damaging the quality of urban life. London, in particular, was edging out further and further. Between 1881 and 1891 the three English counties with the largest population increases were the Home Counties of Middlesex (51 per cent), Essex (38 per cent), and

Surrey (24 per cent). In the next ten years the towns with the largest rates of growth were nearly all on the edge of great cities—East Ham, Walthamstow, Leyton, West Ham, Willesden, Hornsey, Tottenham, and Croydon (round London), King's Norton, Handsworth, Smethwick (round Birmingham), and Wallasey (near Liverpool). The coining in the eighteen nineties of the word 'suburbia', with particular reference to London, was revealing. London's suburbs were now so extensive that they were losing proper contact with their metropolitan heart. They were developing instead a separate and uniform half-life of their own, and so acquired a quasi-proper name of their own.[15] In the mid-Victorian period Charles Kingsley (1819–75), the clergyman novelist and social reformer, had looked hopefully upon 'the rise of the suburbs' to produce 'a complete interpretation of city and country . . . a combination of the advantages of both'. But by Edwardian times this combination was proving hard to find. Vigour had been withdrawn from the centres of cities often only to destroy the character of once rural and now suburban districts through unplanned and monotonous over-building. As *The Times* remarked in 1904, in the redbrick rows of Edwardian terraces (so characteristic of the age and mostly still standing seventy years later), 'the town is reproduced in its least interesting or stimulating form'.[16]

The lower middle-class inner suburbs constituted a new environment which enjoyed neither the advantages of city concentration nor the peace of rural dispersion, and so could not hope to combine them. The energies of many suburbanites were wasted in commuting, and in pursuit of trivial excitement and of a superficial social round. A scathing indictment called *The Suburbans* appeared in 1905:

It is fair and reasonable to call Clapham the capital of Suburbia . . . . If you walk down the Clapham Road, from the end of the Common to Clapham Road Station, with your eyes open, you will have seen the best part of all that Suburbia has to show you. You will understand, as it were, intuitively and without further ado, the cheapness and out-of-jointness of the times; you will comprehend the why and wherefore and *raison d'être* of halfpenny journalism . . .

you will perceive that whizzers, penny buses, gramophones, bamboo furniture, pleasant Sunday afternoons, Glory Songs, modern language teas, golf, tennis, high school education, dubious fiction, shilling's worth of comic writing, picture postcards, miraculous hair-restorers, prize competitions, and all other sorts of twentieth-century clap-trap, have got a market and a use, and black masses of supporters.

In his widely read book *The Condition of England*, published in 1909, C. F. G. Masterman offered a more balanced but still searching analysis of the climate of opinion in the suburbs. Suburbanites, argued Masterman, succeeded commendably in winning the 'struggle to live', but then too often pursued false values in the subsequent 'struggle to attain'. Their children grew healthy in the fresh air of the suburbs, and this was a great national gain; but the mental climate of suburbia was ennervating for their parents. The superficial chatter of the commuter trains and of suburban tea parties touched on great and small matters without any sense of 'which are the heroic, which the trivial'. Local government was largely neglected, or translated into terms simply of keeping down the rates. In politics suburban seats were solidly Conservative, 'not because the Conservative creed is there definitely embraced, but because Conservatism is supposed to be the party favoured by Court, society, and the wealthy and fashionable classes'. L. T. Hobhouse (1864-1929), another Edwardian Liberal, even went so far as to declare that politically the suburbs constituted a greater national danger than the slums. Both Hobhouse and Masterman emphasized the psychological and political significance of the increasing topographical separation of different classes in different localities, the working classes in the slums, the lower middle classes in the inner suburbs, the middle classes in the outer suburbs. The social conscience of the average suburbanite had now no chance of being stimulated by close contact with his poor neighbour:

Every day, swung high upon embankments or buried deep in tubes underground, he hurries through the region where the creature lives. He gazes darkly from his pleasant hill villa upon the huge and smoky area of tumbled tenements which stretches at his feet. He is dimly distrustful of the forces fermenting in this uncouth laboratory. Every hour he anticipates the boiling over of the cauldron.[17]

The wealthy upper-middle classes had indeed passed beyond even such hillsides distantly overlooking the hovels of the poor. They had withdrawn to towns and villages entirely separate from the main urban complexes, commuting by train from the Home Counties into London, from Cheshire into Manchester, from Wharfedale into Leeds. 'Like the Arab', exclaimed the *Birmingham Mail* in 1903, 'they are folding their tents and stealing silently away in the direction of Knowle or Solihull . . . a little revolution is in progress.'[18]

The whole suburban revolution had been made possible by a transport revolution. During the late-Victorian period suburban surface railway services and facilities, including the provision of cheap workmen's fares, had been greatly extended. The world's first underground railway, the Metropolitan Line, had been opened in central London in 1863, developing into the 'Inner Circle' by 1884. In 1890 the first electric 'tube' line was built, free from the smoke of the underground's steam-engines and destined within the next twenty years to extend as far as Shepherd's Bush, Hampstead, Finsbury Park, and Clapham. Perhaps a quarter of a million rail commuters were flocking daily into London by the start of the new century. The demand for these improved services was also increasingly sustained by growing crowds of off-peak visitors to the new department stores, exhibitions, music halls and football matches. A hundred thousand spectators attended Edwardian F.A. Cup Finals at the Crystal Palace. 'How the railway companies get them all there from the city is a mystery.' Off the railway routes the Victorians had depended upon horse buses or trams, both slow, and the horse buses expensive and therefore patronized only by the middle classes. But the intro-duction of electric trams—in the provincial cities from the eighteen nineties, in London from 1901—rapidly transformed the situation, for they were faster, wider ranging and cheap. Clanking about the city streets, the trams gave a new mobility to the Edwardian working class, becoming (in one sociologist's striking phrase) 'the gondolas of the people'. Gross tramway receipts rose from £6,320,000 in 1901 to £15,638,000 in 1913. Nevertheless, by this last date the motor bus was already emerging as a strong rival. The London General Omnibus Company developed the reliable 'B' type bus from 1910. By this year horse and motor bus receipts were already almost equal (£1,941,000 to £1,863,000): only three years later motor bus receipts had jumped to £5,197,000, and horse bus receipts slumped to £382,000. Thus swiftly was the horse bus finally driven from the London streets. The tramcar itself was now plainly threatened. In 1914 *Punch* carried a cartoon, 'Beaten on Points', showing a London tram, pictured with a boxer's arms, derailed by a motor bus likewise sporting boxing gloves. 'Hard lines on me!', exclaims the tram. 'Yes, it's always hard lines with you, my boy', answers the bus. 'That's what's the matter; you can't side-step.'

The lead in the development of motor transport had come from the Continent. 'Britannia's task of ruling the seas', complained the first number of the *Daily Mail* (4th May 1896), 'has left her a little careless of the rule of the road.' Till that year the road speed limit for powered vehicles (fixed with only threshing and ploughing machines in mind) had been a mere four miles per hour. The speed limit was then raised to twelve miles per hour, and in 1903 to twenty, when car registration was also introduced. Thereafter Edwardian motoring progressed rapidly. In 1901 only 15,000 cars had been bought, average price £390 per car, whereas in 1913, 338,000 were purchased, average price £340. The age of mass motoring still lay in the future, but car ownership had progressed from being a novelty for a handful of enthusiasts to acceptance as a convenience for the well-to-do. The famous Rolls-Royce partnership began in 1907. For most Edwardians, however, their first experience of motor car travel came not in a private car but in a taximeter car, soon abbreviated to 'taxi':

Oh, the car! the taximeter car!
It's better than taking a trip to Spain,
Or having your honeymoon over again.

So ran a music-hall song of 1907. The first London taxi-cabs ran in 1903, growing rapidly thereafter in reliability and

Army recruits 1900. Would there always be enough fit men?

Sir Cosmo Duff-Gordon gives evidence at the Titanic inquiry.
Should fewer first-class and more third-class passengers have survived?

III   *Providence Place, Stepney* c. *1909. An Edwardian slum.*

Lord and Lady Howe at home. Providence favoured the few.

numbers. By 1914 receipts from motor cabs passed those from horse cabs for the first time, and in London the horse-drawn hansom cabs and growlers were gradually disappearing from the streets.

Motor traffic, faster and heavier than horse-drawn vehicles, threw up clouds of dust from soft road surfaces made for horse traffic. Gradually, action was taken to provide hard tarred roads, but the Edwardians did little more to meet the present and future needs of motor transport. The famous 1909 Budget set up a Central Road Fund and a Road Board, but the influence of vested interests and of divided authority allowed only a relatively small amount of road construction and re-aligning. The number of road accidents increased rapidly as cars 'scorched' (the Edwardian word) along narrow and winding roads, destroying the peace and safety of town and country alike. The police soon had recourse to speed traps, disregarding complaints that they were 'un-English'. By 1912 the motor bus was killing one person every other day in London, and feelings ran high against its 'murderous invasion of our streets and its specially destructive career along our suburban thoroughfares'. A Royal Commission on London traffic had reported in 1905 in favour of an overall road and rail transport policy to meet the daily flow to and from the suburbs. It wanted an advisory Traffic Board and some consolidation of railway and tramway management. But Edwardian opinion was not ready to accept even this limited degree of control. By 1914, however, commercial pressures had created virtually one motor bus network in London, with management of the tramways concentrated in the hands of local authorities.

Indication of how road transport, already driving out the horse and threatening the electric tramcar, would one day undermine the position of the train, was first given during the great railway strike of 1911. In that year a significant number of middle-class people, unable to travel by train, set out on their holidays for the first time by motor car. The number of railway passengers was, admittedly, still rising: 1,142,000 in 1900, 1,455,000 in 1913; but the railways were no longer undisputed masters in the provision of longer distance transport. The transport revolution was, indeed, entering upon a new phase by these last Edwardian years, with major international as well as national effects. At sea huge turbine-driven luxury liners like the *Titanic* (46,000 tons) aimed to average twenty-five and more knots across the Atlantic. In the air the dream of centuries had at last been realized: the Edwardians could fly. The significance of the American Wright brothers' first flight in a heavier-than-air machine in 1903 was fully brought home to the Edwardian public in 1909 when the Frenchman Louis Blériot (1872–1936) flew the Channel from Calais to Dover. A hundred and twenty thousand people queued to see his plane on exhibition in London. H. G. Wells quickly drew the power political implications of the Frenchman's feat: Britain was no longer an island. A year later he also pointed out some social consequences of recent dramatic progress in transport.

1900

1910

Nationally and internationally, concluded Wells, man was 'off the chain of locality for good and all'.[19]

Some of Wells's conclusions were, indeed, overdrawn. He envisaged men entirely abandoning attachment to one place, which agricultural tillage had imposed upon them, and returning in a new guise to a migratory existence. Edwardians enjoyed reading such forecasts, but they were not quite so restless as Wells suggested. Though they were moving out from their cities, and were worried about urban trends, they had no wish to abandon city life entirely. On the contrary, they were turning to fresh approaches to urban problems. In particular, they discovered 'town planning'. Significantly, this new term was coined about 1906 and quickly adopted thereafter.[20]

The advance guard among the town planners were the 'garden city' enthusiasts. The Victorians had built a number of paternalistic planned 'company towns', notably the Cadbury family's Bournville, near Birmingham (1878), and Lever brothers' Port Sunlight in the Wirral (1887). Both were flourishing by the Edwardian period, when the Rowntree family added Earswick, near York, to the number (1904). At the turn of the century, however, Ebenezer Howard (1850–1928) had come forward with a bolder town-building scheme than any of these, bolder both in its economic basis and in its physical layout. He wanted to build a model 'garden city' (as he called it) which would avoid dependence upon the benevolence of any one firm by standing on its own as a sound commercial enterprise. His ideas were first announced in a book called *Tomorrow*, published in 1898 and re-issued in 1902 as *Garden Cities of Tomorrow*. Howard's book made an immediate impression, partly because it was engagingly written, partly because it appeared at a time when, as Howard himself remarked, leaders of opinion—politicians, labour leaders, scientists, and newspaper writers—were all becoming deeply concerned at the continuing inflow of population from the countryside into the towns. Howard offered a scheme which, in one move, might check the townward rush and its associated rural depopulation. His garden cities, sited in open country, aimed to attract people back from the overcrowded conurbations into a planned environment which would combine the best of both town and country, urban community with rural healthiness. Howard's most original suggestion was that when a city had grown to full size (about 32,000 inhabitants) further development should be switched to a nearby new city; in time a cluster of cities, separated by rural zones, would thus be created. He also recommended permanent municipal ownership of land, which was to be leased to private developers but with the unearned increment arising from city prosperity reserved to the community. He hoped, too, that industries would be attracted to the garden cities, thereby providing local employment for the greater number of the inhabitants.

In 1899 the Garden City Association was formed to discuss and publicize Howard's ideas. Four years later the first garden city was started at Letchworth in Hertfordshire. Within a few years, despite some financial difficulties, it was apparent that Letchworth was a success. By 1914 9000 people were living where only 400 had lived before, and over £600,000 had been spent on new buildings. The best Letchworth working-class houses comprised a kitchen and living room on the ground floor, three bedrooms and a combined bathroom and w.c. on the first floor, plus an outside coal shed and earth closet. Howard had proved that better living and working conditions could be provided for poorer people, and that this could be done by private enterprise on a profitable basis. The town so built, moreover, was a balanced community, ranging over social classes and providing a high proportion of local employment. 'We must be ready with our ideal of the small town of the future', exclaimed *The Times* in 1908. That ideal was Letchworth.

The success of Letchworth did not lead, however, to any attempts in the Edwardian period to copy it elsewhere. Howard's hopes of a rapid direct influence in this sense were disappointed. The immediate influence of the garden city idea came through a growing acceptance of land-use control by local authorities, in more concern for street layout, and in greater emphasis upon good housing design. This new spirit found physical expression in the 'garden suburbs' first built by the Edwardians. These were not brand-new towns, but planned extensions of existing ones, the most notable being Hampstead Garden Suburb, started in 1907. Its architect was Raymond Unwin (1863–1940), who had drawn the first plan for Letchworth. He was an able writer and lecturer, and became a leading propagandist for town planning. Hampstead's promotors emphasized how they wished 'to do something to meet the housing problem' by providing cottages with gardens only a 2d. bus ride from central London. They hoped, also, to encourage social integration by building residences for wealthy people on 'some of the beautiful sites round the Heath'. Alongside this planned building they promised to preserve natural beauty by keeping every tree and by retaining 'the foreground of the distant view'. The Hampstead estate quickly prospered, attracting international notice, though socially it disappointed one of the hopes of its founders by becoming a mainly middle-class district.

By 1914 town planning was thus accepted as a vital function, and the Town Planning Institute was founded in that year as a joint professional organization for architects, engineers, surveyors and lawyers engaged in this new activity. Their separate work was not, of course, new; but the idea of carefully linking it was potentially creative in a new way. The Victorians had tended to be satisfied with piecemeal remedies, whereas the Edwardians began to see the value of overall urban thinking, both in the present and for the future. Unwin contrasted Victorian 'sanitary reform' with Edwardian 'town planning': 'endless rows of brick boxes, looking out upon dreary streets and squalid backyards, are not really homes for people, and can never become such, however complete may be the drainage system. . . . There is needed the vivifying touch of art which would give completeness.'

This was not a case, however, of art motivated solely by social benevolence. International politics exerted an important influence. The Edwardians, anxious about the declining competitiveness of British industry, discovered a connection between the apparently superior efficiency of German workers and the success of German town planning. Unwin recorded in 1909 how great an impetus had been given to the British town planning movement by the publication in 1904 of a book by T. C. Horsfall (1841–1932), a Manchester social reformer. This was called *The Improvement of the Dwellings and Surroundings of the People, the Example of Germany*. Horsfall emphasized how the Germans had realized that the housing problem could only be solved by measures which ensured not only an adequate supply of cheap wholesale dwellings, 'but also that both the immediate and the more distant environment of these dwellings shall be pleasant, and, in all other ways also, conducive to good health of body and mind'. Four years later Horsfall published a pamphlet on *The Relation of Town Planning to the National Life*. It asked if a nation which was 'unable or unwilling to create for its own people conditions fit for human beings' was 'worthy to be allowed to hold so large a proportion of the most desirable parts of the earth's surface'?

> Unless we at once begin at least to protect the health of our people by making the towns in which most of them now live more wholesome for body and mind, we may as well hand over our trade, our colonies, our whole influence in the world to Germany without undergoing all the trouble of a struggle in which we condemn ourselves beforehand to certain failure.

In 1909 the Liberal Government responded to the new mood by promoting the Housing and Town Planning Act. This was a pioneering, yet inadequate measure, for which the President of the Local Government Board, John Burns (1858–1943), made large claims. Its purpose, he announced, was to secure 'the home healthy, the house beautiful, the town pleasant, the city dignified, and the suburb salubrious'; it aimed to 'abolish, reconstruct, and prevent the slum'. Yet on the town-planning side the act was very limited. It concerned itself only with the development of new suburbs, not with existing built-up areas or with towns as a whole. A town-planning scheme might be prepared with respect to any land undergoing building development or likely to be so developed; but previously developed land or land unlikely to be developed could only be included in a scheme when it was unavoidably involved with development already occurring or likely to occur. By 1915 74 local authorities had been empowered to prepare 105 schemes under the town-planning provisions of the Act covering less than 168,000 acres.

The housing aspects of the 1909 Act were an extension of the principles of the 1890 Housing of the Working Classes Act.

Some twenty-eight measures relating to housing had been passed between 1851 and 1903, as the Victorians hesitantly gave increasing powers to local authorities to secure healthy standards of accommodation and sanitation. Local councils were at first only allowed to build houses in order to rehouse families displaced by slum clearance; but later-Victorian legislation did allow municipal construction of workers' dwellings without this limitation. The 1909 Act rendered obligatory the adoption by local authorities of the housing provisions of the 1890 Act. Nevertheless, by the end of 1913 fewer than 200,000 houses had been rendered fit for habitation under the 1909 measure, and less than 50,000 had been closed or demolished. House-building loans for only 6,355 properties had been sanctioned, and only one-fifth of these had been built. By 1914 a 'house famine' prevailed, a shortage (according to one contemporary estimate) of at least 120,000 houses. 95 per cent of working-class housing was still being provided by private speculative builders. Only a few councils (notably Liverpool) were active house-builders; most still regarded municipal action of any sort as a last resort. Birmingham, for example, showed enterprise in town planning under the 1909 Act, producing the first suburban scheme to be accepted; but it hesitated over municipal landownership. As Neville Chamberlain (1869–1940), soon to be Lord Mayor (1915–16) and later to become Prime Minister (1937–40), admitted in 1914, the best choice of sites and streets, and ideal standards of housing density were 'often thwarted and checked in town planning, because we find that what would be best for the community would involve injustice or hardship to individuals'. It was a reflection of Edwardian uncertainty about interference with private property rights that even such a limited measure as the 1909 Act could be presented as an adequate instrument for solving the whole problem of urban planning and housing.

A building boom had persisted during much of the first decade of the new century, but the number of houses constructed for the working class declined markedly just before 1914. Builders of small houses, whose profit margins on the houses themselves were tiny, found the 1909 budget threatening the compensating profit which they had been making by the increment on land. The number of new houses built in Great

Britain, after fluctuating about 150,000 per annum between 1898 and 1903, had fallen some two-thirds by 1912–13. At the same time population was still increasing. Consequently, over-crowding was actually on the increase during the last Edwardian years. The outbreak of war in 1914 thus found Britain with a housing shortage, and also with a town-planning programme only just beginning to be formulated. Historians have blamed the Edwardians severely for their slowness in putting into practice their new good intentions in housing and planning. This uncertain pre-war situation was destined to form the basis of the great post-war housing and planning crisis. After 1918 too much which the Edwardians had only begun to do slowly had to be skimped in a hurry. The result was that the urban and rural reality has never yet approached the ideal as first pictured by Edwardian enthusiasts.[21]

Class and Behaviour

In his novel *Tono-Bungay* (1909) H. G. Wells described the inner suburbs of London: 'Endless streets of undistinguished houses, undistinguished industries, shabby families, second-rate shops, inexplicable people who in a once fashionable phrase do not "exist".' Wells knew that the struggle for 'existence' in Edwardian England was not only economic, it was also social. Society was split by deep, self-conscious class divisions. 'Baths for working people, 1d. cold and 2d. hot', so ran the notices in London's bath-houses; 'Baths for any higher classes, 3d. cold and 6d. hot,' England enjoyed liberty, observed one leading Nonconformist clergyman, 'but equality and fraternity are hardly understood'. In 1910 *Punch* carried a cartoon showing a 'lady' asking a little girl what she was reading: 'Shakespeare! Ah! What a wonderful man! And to think he wasn't exactly what we would call a gentleman.'[22]

There were three basic Edwardian social classes—the working class, the middle class, and the upper class. But at the very bottom of society, below the working class, stood the un-employables, the misfits, the tramps, the destitute. In the mid-Victorian period John Bright had given these people the opprobrious name of 'the residuum', persons 'of almost helpless poverty and dependence'. Though Bright had been a radical in politics he had firmly opposed their enfranchisement, in the belief that they lacked the independence necessary to resist corrupting influences. The same sector had been described with more compassion by William Booth (1829–1912), the founder of the Salvation Army, as 'the submerged tenth'. Both Bright's and Booth's expressions enjoyed wide currency among Edwardians. Winston Churchill, for example, pressing in 1908 for the de-casualization of labour through the establishment of labour exchanges, concluded that 'the resultant residuum must be curatively treated exactly as if they were hospital patients'. Yet there were still Edwardians who did not share Churchill's social conscience, who, in words taken from E. M. Forster's *Howards End* (1910), tried to be 'not concerned with the very poor'. They were 'unthinkable, and only to be approached by the statistician or the poet'.[23]

As we have seen, statisticians such as Charles Booth and Seebohm Rowntree had indeed been approaching the problem of the poor, revealing the deep suffering which extended over a quarter or a third of the population. The poor just above the level of the residuum comprised the core of the Edwardian working class; not quite destitute but always in fear of destitution through illness, accident or old age, not unemployable but always in danger of unemployment, not without homes but often living in slums. In 1886 W. E. Gladstone (1809–98), the great Victorian Liberal, had contrasted these 'masses' with the 'classes' above them. He spoke of opponents and supporters of Irish Home Rule as 'class against the mass, classes against the nation . . . all the world over, I will back the masses against the classes'. The Edwardians continued to think in terms of this Gladstonian contrast. 'If the masses and, for that matter, the classes, wish to retain their right to drink what suits them', argued a critic of teetotalism in 1907, 'they will have to assert it.' The 'classes' were defined by one writer as persons enjoying a competence to whom, on balance, life was a pleasure: the 'masses', on the other hand, had 'to strive in order to procure for themselves the bread which perisheth, as well as the amount of leisure time which enables them to rise to anything above mere animal employments and enjoyments'. In manners, modes of life, clothes, interests and accent working people were marked off as inferior to the 'classes'. The latter regarded the poor as 'beings of a totally different order from themselves.'[24]

Skilled craftsmen, earning upwards of 40s. per week, who were better housed and often better educated than ordinary working men, formed an elite at the top of the working class, comprising some 10–15 per cent of the population. These artisans had provided leaders through the nineteenth century for many reform movements, both political and religious, men such as William Lovett (1800–77), the cabinet maker and Chartist. In the Edwardian period individuals of the same type were active within the rising Labour movement, though there were also others, content with their lot, who were socially and politically conservative.[25] Above the skilled artisans stood the clerks and shop assistants. These constituted an especially significant group because, though perhaps earning less than many artisans, they were granted a higher social standing. They were addressed as 'Mr' or 'Miss' by employers, not, like domestic servants or factory workers, merely by their surnames. They stood within the middle class, albeit the 'lower middle class'. 'Bow, bow, ye lower middle classes! Bow, bow, ye tradesmen, bow, ye masses.' So ran the social rollcall in *Iolanthe* (1882). Here was a critical Edwardian social line, which many sons and daughters from aspiring working-class families might cross. This was the social area to which H. G. Wells's shop assistant Kipps (1905) belonged, and through which Wells himself had passed. It was also the area of Mr Pooter, a head clerk, who was the pretentious yet engaging hero of *The Diary of a Nobody* (1892). Admittedly, shop assistants worked very long hours for low wages, making theirs a 'sweated' trade; and few clerks were as fortunate as Mr Pooter who received a £100 rise as a reward for over twenty years' faithful service. Charles Booth noted 'the pinched and pathetic lives of some of the lower middle class, who are struggling to maintain a social position they cannot afford'. But nearly all preferred to struggle —to keep, for example, at least one female servant—rather than to sink into the working class below.[26]

Taking shop assistants as the starting level, the employed middle-class population of the United Kingdom comprised about 4 million in 1901 and almost 5 million in 1911. At the

same dates the employed working-class population totalled
some 13.8 and 14.7 million respectively. The Edwardian middle
ranks were thus increasing in proportionate as well as in
absolute numbers. The solid middle class consisted of families
with incomes in or beyond the £700–£1000 range. A four-
figure income was a high aspiration in Edwardian England.
Alfred Harmsworth (1865–1922) deliberately aimed the most
successful newspaper of the period, the *Daily Mail*, at lower
middle-class readers who, though not earning £1000 a year,
cherished the continuing hope of one day doing so. The number
of Edwardian income tax payers in the £700–£1000 category
was in fact relatively small, only some 60,000 in 1911–12.
Arnold Bennett (1867–1931), the novelist, believed that his
readers came especially from this sector; but, born himself into
the lower middle class, he was sharply critical of them. 'Their
assured curt voices, their proud carriage, their clothes, the
similarity of their manners, all show that they belong to a caste
and that the caste has been successful in the struggle for life.'
John Galsworthy (1867–1933), who came from this class,
showed in *The Forsyte Saga* (1906–22) and elsewhere how
shallow its family 'success' might be. 'I hate to see dead people
walking about', exclaimed Bernard Shaw (1856–1950) in his
preface to *Fanny's First Play* (1911); 'it is unnatural. And our
respectable middle-class people are as dead as mutton.'

The further a family's income fell below £700 per annum the
more it depended upon aspiration to support its middle-class
status. From his own experience George Orwell (1903–50), the
social novelist, remembered the atmosphere of Edwardian
family life on £400–£500 per year:

> I was born into what you might describe as the lower-upper-
> middle class. . . . People in this class owned no land, but
> they felt that they were landowners in the sight of God and
> kept up a semi-aristocratic outlook by going into the pro-
> fessions and the fighting services rather than into trade. . . .
> To belong to this class when you were at the £400 a year level
> was a queer business, for it meant that your gentility was al-
> most purely theoretical. . . . Theoretically you knew how to
> wear your clothes and how to order a dinner, although in
> practice you could never afford to go to a decent tailor or a

decent restaurant. Theoretically you knew how to shoot and ride, although in practice you had no horses to ride and not an inch of ground to shoot over.[27]

As Orwell suggested, the professions were an important middle-class preserve, extending from the heights of the Church, the services, the law and the administrative civil service down to elementary schoolteaching. The increasing complexity and sophistication of Victorian society had produced a great expansion of the professions. As one Edwardian writer explained, 'our so-called "middle class" is of comparatively modern growth, and corresponds to a development of the professions and of the organizing branches of industry'. The 1911 census placed 413,000 men and 383,000 women in professional occupations and their subordinate services, compared with 113,000 and 49,000 respectively seventy years earlier. Industry and commerce had become dependent upon growing numbers of engineers (of various types), accountants, solicitors, architects, surveyors, and the like. In 1917 the Webbs published a special *New Statesman* supplement on 'Professional Associations', analyzing their novel influence and proliferation. Two years earlier in the same journal they had discussed 'English Teachers and their Professional Organization'. Teaching was much the largest single Edwardian profession, the 52,000 teachers of 1841 multiplying some fivefold by 1911. Elementary schoolteachers alone numbered 190,000 by 1909, three-quarters of these being women earning an average of only £75 per annum but assured of their middle-class status by their professional function. At the other end of the professional middle class were families such as the Hopkinsons, whose head was a Cambridge-trained engineer, one of the chiefs of a nationally important Manchester firm (Mather and Platt). Lady Chorley, a daughter of the family, has given a sensitive account of its life in Alderley Edge just before 1914, emphasizing how Edwardian material well-being did not everywhere produce shallow self-indulgence, as many contemporary critics too readily assumed. There was a *douceur de vivre* about the ordered round of work and play, entertaining and churchgoing. 'It is certainly not the exclusive art of living of an aristocracy, nor need it depend on luxury, although it is nourished best by the conditions of a certain kind of leisure and a certain amount of money, a sense of security and a prized tradition.' In their extreme old age in 1948 Dean Inge (1860–1954), a leading Edwardian Churchman, reminded Bernard Shaw of this high quality of Edwardian professional life. 'I do not think that anywhere in the world has there been a happier condition than that of the comfortable professional class in England before the two wars. "Neither poverty nor riches"; interesting work; a large measure of security. If we did not recognize that we were very lucky, it was our fault.'[28]

The professional classes certainly made a valuable contribution to Edwardian life. More blameworthy were those Edwardians who enjoyed great material wealth without making any equivalent social contribution. At the head of this category stood the 'plutocrats', thus opprobriously named by the late-Victorians. The wealth resulting from late-nineteenth century commercial and Imperial expansion had produced a cluster of rich and very rich families. 'Thirty or forty years ago millionaires were somewhat of a rarity', remarked one observer in 1914, 'and were spoken of with a certain amount of wonder, if not of awe. Now they are counted by the score, if not by the hundred, and even multi-millionaires are looked on as a matter of course.' The Times in 1913 attacked 'that modern class—the waste products of prosperity'. Many millionaire nouveaux riches, and others who were wealthy though not millionaires, felt a need to display their material goods in order to gain and to retain high social recognition. This activity was found in the United States as well as in Britain, and was described in a famous phrase by Thorsten Veblen (1857–1929), the American sociologist, in his Theory of the Leisure Class (1899) as 'conspicuous consumption'. Down the Edwardian social scale among the lower middle classes the more modest equivalent of 'conspicuous consumption' was 'keeping up with the Joneses', another American expression, coined in 1913. Confident upper-middle class families, such as the Hopkinsons, felt no wish to buy themselves into the aristocracy or gentry. But plutocrats such as 'Sir Gorgius Midas', depicted by George Du Maurier (1834–96) in Punch, made this their main objective in life. Philanthropist plutocrats such as Andrew Carnegie (1835–1919), the steel magnate, Sir Thomas Lipton (1850–1931), the grocer and friend of Edward VII, or Sir Julius Wernher (1850–1912), the diamond king, showed some sense of social obligation amidst their great wealth. But many others did not, yet were still admitted to 'society'. One octogenarian aristocrat, Lady Dorothy Nevill (1826–1913), complained in her reminiscences (1906) how 'society' had changed and wealth 'usurped the place formerly held by wit and learning. The question is not now asked, "Is So-and-so clever?" but, instead, "Is So-and-so rich?"' Lady Dorothy remembered how when Samuel Warren (1807–77) wrote his popular novel *Ten Thousand a Year* (1839) such an income was considered princely. 'What is it to-day? Why, your modern millionaire gives as much for a single picture, whilst up-to-date entertaining on such a sum is hardly possible.' Members of the old landed gentry and aristocracy had often been hard hit by the late-Victorian depression in agriculture, and many of them switched to living on investments and City directorships. By 1896 167 noblemen, a quarter of the peerage, were directors of companies. This meant, however, a growing identification of interest between this old upper class and the new City-centred plutocracy. 'I am told', remarked Lady Dorothy, 'that there are now many scions of noble houses who exhibit nearly as much shrewdness in driving bargains in the City as a South African millionaire himself.' The millionaires, for their part, encouraged this process of assimilation by buying country estates in order to bolster their social pretensions. Wernher bought Luton Hoo, while Carnegie's Skibo Castle in Scotland was described as 'a royal place' outshining Balmoral. A few fortunate landowners were able to more than hold their own in such ostentatious living because their estates yielded valuable coal or iron royalties, or because they owned land in the centres of expanding cities. Five square miles of inner London were owned by nine families, headed by the Duke of Westminster (1879–1953), who possessed four hundred acres, including Belgrave Square and much of Knightsbridge. Ducal 'conspicuous consumption' had about it a confident display which the plutocrats could never quite rival. 'Good God!', exclaimed one new guest on reaching the vaulted breakfast room at Eaton Hall, the Duke of Westminster's great house; 'I never expected to eat bacon and eggs in a cathedral!'

Bacon and eggs was, indeed, a decidedly modest ducal dish. Elaborate over-eating was one of the most noticeable Edwardian vices, extending from the aristocracy and plutocracy well down the middle class. Edward VII himself set the pace, annually retiring to the Continent to take the waters and reduce his ample figure. But any customer of the Army and Navy Stores could order a thirteen-course dinner from its 1907 catalogue. A guest described the dinner ritual at one great house. 'A footman to every square yard and the most heavenly ices. Last night we had clear soup with custard shapes, sole all dressed up with lobster sauce, a mousse of ham with a sauce with cherries in it, roast lamb and all kinds of vegetables, partridges, an ice which was made to look like a melon, and a mushroom savory, and, of course, lots of wine and always champagne.' Another guest at a dinner party for twenty-four counted 362 plates and dishes in use, plus 72 wine glasses.

Alongside such increasingly intensive eating went increasingly intensive playing of games by the men (and to a lesser extent by the younger women) of the upper and middle classes. During the Edwardian period golf, in particular, came into great vogue, an especially 'conspicuous' form of sporting indulgence, demanding the exclusive allocation of much land for the enjoyment of relatively few people. 'Golf, of course, had long been a fashion', explained *Punch* in its 1911 survey of the previous decade, 'but it was only now that not to play put one outside the pale.' Even Lloyd George, the scourge of the aristocracy, played golf regularly.

Yet with increasing indulgence went increasing restlessness, at least among the very rich. Improvements in transport now made it easy and comfortable for them to be frequently on the move. 'What is the life of the rich man of today?', asked Lady Dorothy Nevill. 'A sort of firework! Paris, Monte Carlo, big-game shooting in Africa, fishing in Norway, dashes to Egypt, trips to Japan.' The ill-fated *Titanic* was a luxury liner especially built for such plutocratic globe-trotters, and the ship's sinking on its maiden voyage with a quartet of multi-millionaires aboard was seized upon by many social critics as a fitting judgment upon contemporary materialism. The *Manchester Guardian* had described the vessel before the tragedy as built for 'cosmopolitan millionaires' who regarded the sea as merely 'a dreary slum surrounding a Grand Babylon Hotel'. Left-wing commentators were unsurprised but angered to note how a much greater proportion of first-class than of third-class passengers had been saved. Over 1500 drowned, 706 survived. H. G. Wells wrote scornfully of the rescue of Bruce Ismay (1862–1937), chairman of the shipping company. 'His class thinks it was right and proper that he did escape. . . . He was a rich man and a ruling man, but in the test he was not a proud man.' How rich could a man be and retain a clear conscience, asked one book published in 1908. The answer was left to 'individual conscience'; but 'no arguments drawn from deserts or requirements of efficiency or powers of appreciation can justify the selfish expenditure of the millionaire or of the idle rich or of the very rich'. £3000–4000 per year, the author concluded, was probably the justifiable income limit.[29]

The expression just quoted, 'the idle rich', had become (complained the aristocratic *Queen* magazine) 'a byword of the moment'. 'It is the fashion today to talk of social duty and the right to live.' The *Queen* preferred *noblesse oblige* to social equality. L. G. Chiozza Money's (1870–1944) *Riches and Poverty* (1905) which became a popular socialist textbook, was frontispieced with a striking scale representation of the uneven spread of wealth in 1904. 'The Aggregate Income of the 43,000,000 people of the United Kingdom is approximately £1,710,000,000. 1¼ million persons take £585,000,000; 3¾ million persons take £245,000,000; 38 million persons take £880,000,000.' Socialists contended that the rich were actually getting richer, as did radicals such as Winston Churchill. In fact, income seems to have been distributed in much the same proportions as in mid-Victorian times. In the decade 1860–69 wages and salaries had absorbed 48.5 per cent of the national income, rents 13.7 per cent, and profits, interest and mixed incomes 38.9 per cent. For the years 1900–9 these proportions were little changed at 48.4 per cent, 11.4 per cent, and 40.2 per cent respectively.

Edwardian working men were probably the more ready to believe that the rich were getting richer because, in general, their own incomes had become stationary. This was in dispiriting contrast with the late-Victorian period when between 1880 and 1895–6 real wages had grown by as much as 40 per cent. Thereafter, however, though money wages continued to

A family living in one room 1912.

IV

V   *The upper and lower classes at Ascot. But the middle-class nonconformist* Manchester Guardian *did not carry racing results.*

A skilled worker with his family. The elite at the top of the working class.

increase at about 1 per cent per annum up to 1914, commodity prices, which in the earlier generation had been
falling, tended to rise in step with (and in some years faster
than) money wages. In consequence, with some exceptions
(notably among coal miners and cotton workers, who continued to improve their standards of living), Edwardian workmen found themselves marking time in terms of the purchasing
power of their wage packets.

A QUIET SUNDAY IN OUR VILLAGE.

Yet during these very same years they were being made
increasingly aware of upper-class wealth. The new motor cars
of the wealthy rushed noisily and dustily along the roads. The
new popular press gave the possessions and activities of the
rich continuous publicity. 'They read of costly menus, and they
know their own outlay on bread and dripping—if that—for
their children. They see the pictures in the papers, which love,
both from interest and inclination, to chronicle the doings of

the financially famous. They even witness the actual portrayal of it all in the cinematograph shows which are springing up.' These mass media were themselves adding to the daily costs which working men felt they must meet—a point made by the Labour politician Philip Snowden (1894–1937) in his book *The Living Wage* (1913):

> There has been an advance in the cost of living in another sense than by the increase in the price of commodities. New expenses have come into the category of necessities. The development of tramways, the coming of the halfpenny newspaper, the cheap but better-class music hall and the picture palace, the cheap periodicals and books, the very municipal enterprise which was intended to provide free libraries, free parks, free concerts, has added to the expenditure of the working classes, who cannot take advantage of these boons without incurring some little expense in sundries. The features of our advancing civilization are always before the eyes of the working classes, and they fall into the habit of indulging in the cheaper ones. People cannot see tramways without wanting to ride sometimes; they cannot see newspapers without at least buying one occasionally; they cannot see others taking a holiday into the country or to the seaside without desiring to do the same. These additional items of working class expenditure, coming out of wages which are stationary, make the struggle to live more intense, and compel a lessening of expenditure on absolute necessaries.

Relatively few Edwardian working men followed the lead of the extreme socialists in demanding the destruction of the rich, and the equalization of incomes. Though wanting to narrow the gap between themselves and the wealthy, they looked much more to pulling themselves up than to pulling the rich down. In the labour unrest of the last Edwardian years they were pressing for higher wages not merely to live but to live well; seeking in some small measure to emulate the good life of the rich, aspiring, in other words, towards the 'affluent society' which their grandchildren were finally to reach some fifty years later.[30]

Unsympathetic members of the upper and middle classes were always ready to assert that working men only wanted more money in order to waste it on drink and gambling. These were certainly the two chief vices of the Edwardian working class. Heavy drinking was related to the depressing quality of much working-class life. Hard labour for long hours left men with little energy for the more elevating forms of recreation; over-crowded homes tempted husbands to retreat to the public house, which served as the working man's sitting room. Drinking brought conviviality, and if that were not enough it could also bring oblivion. In the words of a revealing contemporary expression drink was 'the shortest way out of Manchester'. Nevertheless, the volume of consumption was declining throughout the Edwardian period. Hours of work were being reduced somewhat, and the range of popular interests was widening. From 1870 to 1900 total sales of beer grew more or less in proportion to population; but after 1900 consumption per head showed a definite fall. Spirits drinking reached a peak in 1900, falling by one-quarter by 1913. In 1900 approximately £195 million was spent on alcoholic drinks (including £112 million on beer), by 1913 the total had fallen to £182 million (including £115 million on beer). What Edwardian men saved on alcohol they tended to spend on tobacco, especially upon cigarettes. Between 1900 and 1913 the weight of cigarette tobacco consumed increased fourfold, from over 11 million lbs. to over 45 million lbs. Convictions for drunkenness in England and Wales fell from 207,000 in 1905 to 162,000 in 1910. Here was a marked improvement, though the number of drunks on the streets, especially in working-class districts, was still dis-gustingly high by later twentieth-century standards (75,000 convictions in 1968).

Temperance campaigners, who had been very active during the Victorian period, continued busy in the new century. Hall Caine's (1853–1931) novelette *Drink, a Love Story on a Great Question*, was a best-seller in 1907, telling how a girl from a good family cursed by alcoholism was cured by the love of her fiancé. 'Is it a sign of national old age', asked Caine in a note to one reprint, 'that the great spirit of our people seems power-less to meet the tragic situation of the curse of intemperance, and that, all the efforts at licensing legislation notwithstanding,

Drink is a dark cloud that enshrouds our country and seems never to lift?' Caine, and the extreme wing of the temperance party, the teetotallers, were vigorously answered by T. W. H. Crosland (1868–1924), a leading Edwardian polemicist, in a book called *The Beautiful Teetotaller* (1907). Crosland attacked the United Kingdom Alliance and the Band of Hope for threatening Englishmen's liberty of choice. 'When they say they desire to banish drunkenness from the country, they mean that they desire to banish drink.' Nonconformist teetotallers, to Crosland's alarm, were influential within the Liberal Party, and he feared that the Liberal Government would attempt to pass prohibitionist legislation. In fact, the Liberal Governments of 1904–14 never sought to do so, knowing the popular uproar that would result. The party leaders, moreover, were not themselves abstainers. They did hope, however, to reduce drunkenness by reducing the excessive number of public houses. A Conservative Licensing Act of 1904 with this same purpose had enraged temperance reformers because it provided compensation, out of a fund levied on the trade, for brewers and publicans whose licences were withdrawn. Temperance enthusiasts objected to financial support being offered to men who, they contended, had already made large profits by debauching the poor. In 1908 the Liberals introduced a Licensing Bill intended to supersede this earlier measure, speeding up closures by providing for the compulsory reduction of the number of licensed premises by about one-third (30,000–32,000) over a period of fourteen years. 'Too many pubs' were Asquith's only legible notes on the back of an envelope for a public speech explaining the Bill. Compensation would continue to be paid, but would cease at the end of the fourteen-year period. Hours of Sunday opening in provincial England were also to be severely limited, and local option, a favourite temperance panacea, was to be permitted. The Liberal measure was, however, rejected by the House of Lords. This angered the Liberals even more on constitutional than on temperance grounds. Nevertheless, under the 1904 Act (and even before it) the number of on-licenses was falling steadily, from 102,000 in 1900 to 92,000 in 1910.

Heavy gambling was second only to heavy drinking as a working-class vice. A House of Lords Select Committee re-

ported in 1902 that betting was not confined to horse-racing
but was also prevalent at athletics meetings and at football
matches. Street betting had become common. About £5 million
was known to be spent annually on gambling at the beginning
of the Edwardian period, rising to about £5.5 million at its
end. In 1905 Seebohm Rowntree edited a volume called
Betting and Gambling, a National Evil. He emphasized the link
between betting and the 'monotony of life' for both rich and
poor. Lively counter-attractions were needed to draw the poor
away—clubs, concerts, allotments. But the most fundamental
need, concluded Rowntree, was for improved working-class
housing, higher wages and better education, which would
combine to encourage higher standards of interest.[31]

Some such widening of working-class interests was, indeed,
already beginning to take place, even though it was not so
directly elevating as Rowntree desired. Though working men
placed bets on football matches, the rapid late-Victorian spread
of enthusiasm for watching the play of local professional soccer
teams was socially beneficial. Whereas interest in horse-racing
was largely a gambling interest, working men were able to
attend football matches regularly as spectators and in that
sense to participate. This gave a point of colourful focus and
excitement to otherwise drab urban lives. Working men began,
too, to travel to watch away matches, thereby broadening their
experience. One observer remarked in 1898 how on a night
walk round an industrial town almost every fragment of over-
heard conversation was a 'piece of football criticism or
prophecy'. The Football Association had been formed in 1867,
and from the eighteen seventies working-class supported teams
of professional soccer players were formed extensively throughout the industrial Midlands and North. These sides soon began
to outclass the older-established amateur and middle-class old
boys' clubs of the South. As already noted, by Edwardian times
100,000 spectators were attending Cup Finals at the Crystal
Palace. Among many middle- and working-class people interest
in politics, except at crisis periods, was now being overshadowed
by interest in sport—soccer and 'Northern Union' (Rugby
League) for the 'masses', golf and Rugby Union for the
'classes', cricket for both. 'Even in England', remarked G. K.
Chesterton (1874–1936) in 1904, '. . . where we have some love

of politics . . . we have a much greater love of cricket, and C. B. Fry represents us much better than Mr Chamberlain.' Expenditure on sports and travel goods grew from £7 million per annum in 1901 to almost £12 million by 1913. Critical observers, such as Mr Punch, saw this new interest as entirely frivolous, dangerously threatening the quality of political discussion and even undermining readiness to do a good day's work. After payment of Members of Parliament had been introduced in 1911, *Punch* carried a cartoon showing a working man indicating his Member of Parliament, speaking in the market place, with the remark that 'the likes of Hus . . . 'as to pay him £400 a year. It makes me that wild to think as we could 'ave two first-class 'arf-backs for the same money.' But this new interest was more social gain than political loss for Edwardian England.[32]

Edwardians of all classes were making it increasingly plain that they regarded the quality of life as all-important. 'Our forefathers were content with a Heaven after death; we demand a Heaven here.' In the towns a majority of working men and women did not attend church or chapel. A religious census taken in 1902–3 by the *Daily News* in metropolitan London counted only some 830,000 worshippers compared with 1.4 million non-attenders, persons who were available to attend divine service but did not do so. In outer London there were 420,000 worshippers compared with 460,000 non-attenders, the higher proportion here of attenders reflecting the greater practice of religious observance among the middle classes. Attendance figures, by denomination, for the whole of London were: Church of England 538,000; Nonconformist 545,000; Roman Catholic 96,000; others 72,000. Working-class children usually went to Sunday School—parents were glad to get them out of the house—but (as Charles Booth observed) 'the very choir boys when their voices crack promptly claim the privileges of men and give up churchgoing'. Booth suggested that one reason why working men were suspicious of the churches was a deep desire not to be thought to be seeking charity. The Salvation Army, founded by William Booth in the eighteen seventies, had contrived to avoid overtones of condescension in its charitable work, and this was one major reason for its social success. But it was clear long before Booth's death in 1912 that the

Army was achieving much less in terms of religious conversion. Another reason why working men separated themselves from the churches was what they took to be the exacting standards of religious obligation. 'They expect a religious man to make his life square with his opinions', noted Charles Booth. 'They like their club with its pot of beer, its entertainments . . . and a bet on tomorrow's race, but they look on these things as inconsistent with all religious profession.' Many of those working-class Edwardians who were practising Christians were Nonconformists, especially Methodists of various sects. In 1906 Wesleyan Methodism reached a height never touched before or since, with about half a million adherents. Methodists were prominent within the Edwardian Labour and trade union movement. Keir Hardie (1856–1915), the Labour pioneer, was an undogmatic Nonconformist who believed that 'the only way to serve God was by serving humanity'. The desire to link Christianity and politics underlay the Labour Church movement of the eighteen nineties; but this experiment was already failing by the beginning of the twentieth century. One reason for this was the convivial success in the North of England of the Clarion Cycling Clubs, encouraged by Robert Blatchford (1851–1943), the influential Labour journalist, who at the beginning of the century ostentatiously abandoned all religious faith. His book *God and My Neighbour* (1903) caused much controversy in socialist circles. Many early Labour leaders, such as George Lansbury (1859–1940) and Arthur Henderson (1863–1935), remained convinced Christians; but increasingly this was treated as a personal preference quite apart from Labour's quest for social justice.

The middle classes were much more inclined to attend church or chapel than were the working classes. Middle-class people were not inhibited by any working-class scrupulousness about matching the practice of their daily lives to their religious precepts. They felt it important, moreover, to set an example to the lower classes. Such observance did not necessarily imply any deep religious conviction. Church attendance, too, was a pleasant way for the middle classes to enjoy social contact and social display:

The Church Parade beats everything,

The Church Parade when in full swing
Is a thing to see and wonder at,
For, oh, the wealth displayed,
Of the millinary art,
And costumes smart,
In the Church Parade.

So ran one popular song of 1904. Social mixing at church with such working people as did attend was hardly expected, at least in Anglican circles. Though the Church of England was beginning to make efforts to improve its contact with the masses, this proved difficult for the gap was wide. As Conrad Noel (1869–1942), a rare combination of socialist and Anglican clergyman, exclaimed in 1906, 'we Anglicans are often charged with being a sleepy, unprogressive lot. Well, we never made much progress towards Manchester, nor sang with any enthusiasm "Our Feet shall Stand in Thy Gates, O Sheffield".' The very eagerness of some clergymen to treat the working class as a mission field carried with it self-defeating overtones of condescension. On the other hand, the Archbishop of Canterbury, Randall Davidson (1848–1930), gave great offence in 1905 when he refused to receive a deputation of unemployed headed by a Leicester Anglican cleric. The Archbishop expressed Christian sympathy, but he coldly declined to attempt 'rough and ready solutions of far reaching and complicated economic problems'.

Younger middle-class Edwardians were losing interest even in the outward observance of religion. Less of them were seeking ordination, so that by 1908 the Church of England was already short of over five thousand clergy. The young of all classes were beginning to break up the deadness of the Victorian Sunday by playing games, cycling, taking trips by rail and road, and (among the upper and upper-middle classes) by 'week-ending' at one another's houses. Only a relative few of these young people were deliberately rejecting religion; the majority remained vaguely Christian. But they were unobserving Christians, even though many of them might still practise the Christian virtues. Here already forming was the spirit which has proved to be the predominant English attitude towards Christianity during the twentieth century.[33]

Mass Communication and Mass Entertainment

Though the religious life of Edwardian England was suffering from failures of communication, in other spheres contact
between minds was extending as never before. 1896 had been a
crucial year in the history of the mass media. Guglielmo Marconi (1874–1937) had come to England to give a demonstration
of signal-sending by 'wireless'; the first moving-picture show
had been presented in London; and on 4th May Alfred Harmsworth (1865–1922), later Lord Northcliffe (1905), had published the first number of the *Daily Mail*.

A combination of conditions—social and technological—
was now favouring the rapid development of a mass audience
for both information and entertainment. Population had become concentrated in towns on a novel scale, and real wages
had risen markedly during the previous generation. Hours of
work were still long, but leisure time was gradually increasing.
In 1909, for example, over half a million coal miners had their
worktime reduced by four hours per week by Act of Parliament.
Bank holidays had been instituted in 1871, a Saturday half-
holiday was becoming common even without legislation, and a
half-day for shop assistants was enforced by the 1911 Shops
Act. It was now easy to travel to and from places of entertainment within towns on greatly improved public transport. The
same new technology which had developed the town tramcar
had also invented the cinematograph and the gramophone,
and had transformed newspaper production. 'It is no secret',
proclaimed the first number of the *Daily Mail*, 'that remarkable
new inventions have just come to the help of the press.' Use
of mechanical type-setting, and of presses capable of printing
ten or twelve-page newspapers (compared with eight as
previously) at a new high rate of 20,000 per hour, cut the
Mail's costs by a quarter or a half. It appeared as 'a Penny
Newspaper for One Halfpenny'. Yet even at this low price it
could carry more and bigger advertisements. A periodical
article of 1897 on 'The March of the Advertiser' remarked how
splash advertising had suddenly become ubiquitous. The
demand for such display was a result of the mass marketing of
branded retail products (such as Pear's Soap, Player's
Cigarettes, or Bovril) and of the establishment of large depart-

ment stores in London and other cities. On its opening in 1909 Selfridge's store took six whole pages and three quarter pages in the *Daily Mail* within nine publishing days. The pressure of the advertiser on the hoardings and in the press was becoming increasingly hard to escape in Edwardian England.

The *Daily Mail* led the way not only in newspaper advertising but in most things journalistic. The classified newspaper advertisements of earlier days had been aimed at small groups: the appeal of the new display advertising was to a wide general public. The *Daily Mail* was the first British daily paper to secure such a readership, access to which was sold to advertisers at high rates and great profit. *Mail* readers were not working-class. A fallacy circulating even in Edwardian times was that Harmsworth's publications catered only for working people newly taught in the Board Schools created under the 1870 Education Act. This fallacy was doubly incorrect. It assumed not only that ordinary working men were the main readers of the *Daily Mail*, but also that before the late nineteenth century they had been largely illiterate. The success of the Chartist *Northern Star* (selling 50,000 copies weekly at its peak in 1839) had shown how this was far from the case. Yet Victorian working men were not, in the mass, readers of morning daily papers. They read halfpenny local evening papers and penny Sundays, such as the *News of the World*; and their Edwardian sons and grandsons inherited this preference. In the very year of the *Daily Mail*'s commencement *Lloyd's Weekly News* was the first newspaper to achieve a million sale. Such Sunday prints concentrated on violent or salacious crime and law court news, while the local evening papers specialized in racing and football news and results.

Before 1896 Harmsworth had already made a reputation as the founder of *Answers* (1888), a weekly compilation of miscellaneous information, *Comic Cuts* (1890) for children, *Forget-Me-Not* (1891) for women, and several other weeklies with a total sale by 1892 of over a million copies per week. The market for all these publications centred upon the lower-middle and artisan classes. And the *Daily Mail* was designed to give these same people a daily newspaper suited to their tastes and aspirations, deliberately written, as we have already remarked, not for real £1000 a year men but for men (and their wives) who vaguely hoped one day to reach £1000 a year. The *Mail* announced itself as 'The Busy Man's Daily Journal'. Harmsworth realized what no one had realized before, that the busy lower-middle classes wanted a 'bright' newspaper which they could enjoy in the train or the tram. The *Mail*'s especial strength lay in its news coverage. Harmsworth discerningly separated news into two categories: 'actualities' and 'talking points'. The first, he explained to one employee, 'is news in its narrowest and best sense—reports of *happenings*, political resignations, strikes, crimes, deaths of famous people, wrecks and railway smashes, weather storms, sporting results, and so on. The second is getting the topics people are discussing and developing them, or stimulating a topic oneself.' The most extreme way of stimulating a topic was to run a stunt, which the *Mail* did frequently. Some stunts were beneficial, like the large prizes offered to encourage aviation progress, culminating in the £10,000 London-Manchester air race of 1910. Others were harmless, like the agitation for *Daily Mail* Standard Bread. A few were ridiculous, like the campaign for the *Daily Mail* hat. But all made news, and news (not all serious) from far and wide was what the lower-middle class loved to read. Long-winded leading articles were rejected by the *Mail* in favour of short leaders. Political matters were noticed when important, but politics, Harmsworth ruled, had no 'divine right' to newspaper space. The long, even verbatim, reports of politicians' orations found in the traditional penny papers were not copied in the *Mail*. On the other hand, a lively political speech from a personality such as Lloyd George or Winston Churchill was likely to receive an appropriately lively summary.

The danger of Harmsworth's method was that it seemed to elevate the trivial, thereby running the risk of corrupting the judgment of his readers. Harmsworth denied that giving trivia more space meant that he was giving them more importance. Trivia were included, he would argue, only for balance. 'Make the paper a happy one, fresh and free from dullness, and with plenty of contrast in the news.' Triviality, moreover, never meant a lowering of tone. Harmsworth was particularly watchful against 'indecent' material. 'The modern newspaper has many faults', he wrote in 1905, 'but it is at least decent, and it does not give the rest of the world the impression that English life largely centres round the Divorce Court and the prize ring.'

Harmsworth's successful wooing of the lower-middle class gave the *Mail* in its first decade the highest circulation ever attained by a daily newspaper. Boosted to almost a million during the excitement of the Boer War in 1900, sales averaged rather over three-quarters of a million during the Edwardian years, finally passing the million mark in 1915, with the renewed wartime demand for news. Yet despite the success of the *Mail*, the older-established papers survived, albeit with some loss of circulation and some brightening of presentation, proving how Harmsworth had found a new reading public. The number of daily newspaper readers has been estimated to have doubled between 1896 and 1906, and to have doubled again by 1914. Spending on newspapers increased from less than £8 million in 1901 to well over £13 million in 1913. This increase largely resulted from the appeal of three new journals, the *Daily Mail* and the *Daily Mirror*, and their chief rival, the *Daily Express*.

The *Daily Mirror* had been started by Harmsworth in 1903 as a paper written by gentlewomen for gentlewomen, price one penny. It was an immediate failure, but was saved by transformation in 1904 into a daily illustrated paper at a halfpenny, the first to make regular use of half-tone photographs. These could now be (rather blotchily) reproduced in newspapers. The *Mirror* eventually overtook the *Mail* in circulation, becoming in 1912 the first daily paper to reach a million sale. The *Daily Express* had been started in 1900 by Arthur Pearson (1866–1921). It was the first British daily to print news on its front page, but up to the First World War it could never quite match the magnetism of the *Mail* or *Mirror*, even though it sold some 300,000 copies per day.

In 1908 Harmsworth made an acquisition which no rival could hope to match. He bought *The Times*. Since the retirement of J. T. Delane (1817–79) in 1877 *The Times* had gone down steadily, its influence and circulation undermined by editorial blunders and internal disputes. But it remained a national institution, and Harmsworth was proud to use his wealth to restore its success. He gradually achieved this without, as was feared, changing the tone of the paper or weakening the editor's independence. Sales rose from only 38,000 daily in 1908 to over 150,000 just before the outbreak of the First World War, especially after price reductions from threepence to twopence in 1913 and then to a penny in March 1914.

Harmsworth's other 'quality' newspaper was the Sunday *Observer*, which he acquired in 1905. Under the editorship of J. L. Garvin (1868–1947), beginning in 1908, the *Observer* quickly achieved great influence within the Conservative Party, its circulation rising twelvefold to reach 60,000 weekly in 1911. But Garvin's *Observer* was predominantly a paper of opinion, and (*The Times* apart) Harmsworth was not really interested in journals of this type. In 1911 he therefore sold out. The Edwardian press included several other publications of strong opinions but limited circulations. The most successful Edwardian weekly was the Conservative *Spectator*, edited by St Loe Strachey (1860–1927), selling 22,000–23,000 copies in 1903. Two weeklies which lost money were the radical *Nation* (1907), edited by H. W. Massingham (1860–1924) and subsidized by the Rowntree family, and the socialist *New Statesman* (1913), launched by the Webbs and their political friends with a sale of 3000–4000 copies. Influential were a quartet of London evening papers—the *Pall Mall Gazette*, the *Westminster Gazette*, the *St James's Gazette*, and the *Globe*—written for a well-connected but small West End/Whitehall public, and surviving only so long as they were subsidized by a succession of wealthy proprietors. One daily newspaper which managed to combine significant political influence on the Liberal side with some commercial success was the *Manchester Guardian*, edited by C. P. Scott (1846–1932). The *Guardian* was especially strong in its advocacy of free trade, radical social reform, and internationalism.

The 'quality' publications had a low opinion of the lively *Daily Mail* and the illustrated *Daily Mirror*. 'The first', it was said, 'was designed for those who cannot think, and the second for those who cannot read.' One *Nation* journalist irritatedly noted in 1913 how 'fact, or what passes for fact, often has more influence upon opinion than the most skilful and persuasive arguments'. Harmsworth's 'facts' were sometimes important, sometimes trivial; but he must be given credit for being the first daily journalist to address the new urban and suburban lower-middle class public. The 'serious' Edwardian press ignored this important audience, or even treated it with contempt. This was the more odd in that most of the 'serious' journals were professedly on the popular side in politics. But their journalism was arid and intellectual. 'The real tragedy of that time', concludes a modern journalist and historian of journalism, 'if tragedy indeed it was, lies not in the Northcliffe revolution but in the *trahison des clercs* that allowed it so easy and so complete a victory'.[34]

A handful of men of letters, who were also busy journalists, enjoyed a flattering intensity of interest among the enlarged Edwardian reading public—H. G. Wells (1866–1946), George Bernard Shaw (1856–1950), Arnold Bennett (1867–1931), John Galsworthy (1867–1933), G. K. Chesterton (1874–1936); and Hilaire Belloc (1870–1953). The years before 1914 witnessed the peak of the influence of the written word, read by a mass audience not yet distracted by the less demanding media of radio or television. Traditionalist critics complained indeed that contemporary writing was distorted by its popularity. 'Our ablest men today are, with few exceptions, able as journalists, not as men of letters . . . They do not talk over their ideas with us as did the elder writers . . . They think it better to spring at our throats.' Galsworthy, quipped Max Beerbohm (1872–1956), had 'sold his literary birthright for a pot of message'. Yet a work such as Wells's novel *Tono-Bungay* (1909) succeeded in both passing judgment upon the world of Edwardian business and in reading like a good novel. Similarly, Shaw's best plays of the period, such as *Man and Superman* (1903), *The Doctor's Dilemma* (1906), or *Pygmalion* (1913) were well constructed to hold as well as to lecture his audiences. Shaw, Granville Barker (1877–1946), and a few others brought English play-writing back to a level of creativity not known since the eighteenth century.

The most popular literary figure of the eighteen nineties had been Rudyard Kipling (1865–1936). In the new century, however, though still widely read, he was no longer in touch with the trend of opinion. Kipling's imperialism had begun to seem dated. He remained politically on the right when Edwardian England was moving (however hesitantly) to the left. 'It has been too plain now for years', explained Arnold Bennett in 1909, 'that he is against progress.' Bennett and most of the foremost names in Edwardian literature were advocates of social reform. The fantasies of Chesterton and the satires of Belloc linked the Anglo-Catholicism of the one and the Roman Catholicism of the other to a version of social criticism akin to that of the syndicalists. Galsworthy's plays and novels never seemed quite at ease in their attacks upon the upper-middle class from which he sprang, or in their advocacy of the working class for which he felt sympathy; but at least (as was said of him in 1911) he was salving his conscience as a citizen. Wells and Shaw, by contrast, were almost excessively self-assured in their advocacy of their own brands of socialism. Shaw attached long prefaces to many of his plays. Wells gloried in 1912 in 'the incoming tide of aggressive novel-writing'. Unfortunately, he ultimately went too far, when in his last Edwardian novels—*Marriage* (1912), *The Passionate Friends* (1913), *The Wife of Sir Isaac Harman* (1914)—social argument did begin to submerge literary form.[35]

Edwardian poetry was much slower than Edwardian play or novel writing to show a spirit of innovation. For long the most popular type was not lyric poetry but narrative, notably that of John Masefield (1878–1967). Then in 1912 appeared the first volume of *Georgian Poetry*. This collection was motivated by a spirit of reaction against Victorian romanticism, which had collapsed in the preciosity of the nineties. Sincerity, announced one critic, 'is the goal of the modern quest; to be a poet is to be frank even unto brutality'. Poetry now sought to be realistic, just as the novel and drama had become realistic, both in subject and language. The refreshment of this new approach gave the Georgians a sense of elation and perspective. Rupert Brooke (1887–1915), destined through his war poems to become the best known of all the Georgians, described himself as 'given to the enchantment of being even for a moment alive in a world of real matter'.

D. H. Lawrence (1885–1930) contributed to *Georgian Poetry*, but he really belonged to no school. Amidst all the reformers on the literary scene Lawrence was the one revolutionary. In 1913 were published both his *Love Poems* and the novel *Sons and Lovers*. In 1915 *The Rainbow* caused a stir on account of its alleged indecency. But Lawrence's work was of the future more than of the present. When in 1914 a literary periodical polled its readers to discover their choice of the greatest living novelist the winner was the late-Victorian Thomas Hardy (1840–1928). Wells came second, and Joseph Conrad (1857–1924) third. Conrad's *Chance* was the novel of the year, his

An Edwardian music hall.

first popular success, full of reflections upon life and especially upon the role of women, a particular Edwardian preoccupation. 'All of it about a girl and with a steady run of references to women in general', explained Conrad himself. 'It ought to go down.' And so it did, the last major Edwardian novel before the outbreak of war.[36]

As in drama so in the composition of serious music Edwardian England saw a burst of creativity after a long Victorian period of small achievement. 'The land without music', as Britain had become known on the Continent, now produced four composers of significance—Sir Edward Elgar (1857–1934), arguably at his best a truly great figure, Frederick Delius (1862–1934), Ralph Vaughan Williams (1872–1958), and Gustav Holst (1874–1934). Elgar's *Pomp and Circumstance* marches (1901–7), the first of which was soon given the words of 'Land of Hope and Glory', became Elgar's best-known, though not his best, work. 'We are a nation with great military proclivities', he explained in 1904, 'and I did not see why the ordinary quick march should not be treated on a large scale'. At his most profound, as in *The Dream of Gerontius* (1900), or his violin concerto (1910), Elgar composed music sounding highly personal to himself yet appropriate to an end period in history, 'the last twilight', in the words of a modern critic, 'of a symphonic tradition that never happened'.[37]

The music of Holst and Vaughan Williams was influenced by traditional English folk songs. The systematic recording of these was undertaken from 1904 onwards by Cecil Sharp (1859–1924). But the Edwardians' own folk songs were being written for musical comedy and for the music hall. They enjoyed a long stream of musical comedy successes, with leading ladies such as Gertie Millar (1879–1952), star of *The Quaker Girl* and *Our Miss Gibbs*, who (such was the social acceptability of musical comedy) eventually became Countess of Dudley. Even the rough past of the music hall was being forgotten, and (as Charles Booth recorded) its social tone rising. Moss Empires opened a chain of halls fitted with plush seats and no bars so that respectable matrons could enjoy the show without fear of impropriety, watching Marie Lloyd (1870–1922), Dan Leno (1860–1904), or Harry Lauder (1870–1950) at the main theatres, though only lesser performers elsewhere. In 1913

Florrie Forde (1874–1941) introduced a new song about an Irish boy in London beginning 'It's a long way to Tipperary'. At first 'Tipperary' made little impression, but by August 1914 it was the marching song of the expeditionary force to France, and on Harmsworth's orders the *Daily Mail* printed the music 'so that everybody shall know it'. Edward VII had visited the music halls incognito, but in 1912 George V formally attended the first Royal Command Variety Performance. With this event the music hall had finally achieved recognition as a national institution.[38]

Yet already a rival was appearing. Charles Booth noticed in 1902 how restricted was the range of 'variety' offered, especially in the lesser music halls. Jugglers, tumblers, dancers, comedians, male impersonators, female impersonators, soubrettes, ventriloquists, the possible permutations were not many. By the turn of the century, music-hall proprietors were countering the danger of monotony by introducing the novelty of short cinematograph shows. 'At the moment of writing', recorded one Middlesbrough observer in 1911, 'there are ten music halls in full swing, at all of which Moving Pictures are shown on the Cinematograph, and at seven of which a variety entertainment is given as well.' In other words, by this date three of Middlesbrough's 'music halls' were attracting audiences without offering any form of live performance. They were not music halls at all but 'cinemas', a very new word obviously still unknown in Middlesbrough in 1911. Fifteen years had passed since the first film exhibition in England, at the Empire Music Hall in London. The first building specially constructed for film shows was apparently not opened until 1908, at Colne in Lancashire. But thereafter progress was very rapid. Big business in the shape of Provincial Cinematograph Theatres Limited entered the field in 1909, and by 1914 at least 3500 cinemas were in existence.

Edwardian cinema audiences were youthful and predominantly working-class, the middle classes exhibiting the same attitude of superiority towards the new medium which they were to show towards television in the early nineteen fifties. Many working-class cinema-goers had never been regular habitués of theatres or music halls. They constituted a brand new public for which the cinemas were the first and only medium of mass entertainment. For courting couples a new experience could now be shared, not only in watching the screen but also in sitting together in semi-darkness in the cinema back-seats.

The earliest films were short sketches, often knockabout comedy. 'The curious fact that, in almost any social circle, it makes people laugh convulsively to see any one tumble down, is kept well in view.' Newsreels, too, were popular, showing such events as the Shackleton and Scott expeditions to the Antarctic. By the last Edwardian years, with the cinema network established, full-length films had become popular and film stars were emerging. These were mostly American, for in 1913 only some 15 per cent of films shown were British-made. Charlie Chaplin, though London-born (1889), achieved international fame from Hollywood, where he made his first film early in 1914.[39]

Edwardian films were, of course, silent. But recorded sound was adding its impact to the communications revolution. The phonograph, or speaking machine (1877), and the motion picture camera (1889), were both inventions associated with the American Thomas Edison (1847–1931). Phonograph performances were, according to Charles Booth, one of the 'varieties' resorted to by early-Edwardian music hall proprietors. Gradually the phonograph was transformed into the gramophone, able to reproduce vocal music with fair authenticity, though orchestral music only tinnily. Two outstanding singers, Enrico Caruso (1873–1921) and Nellie Melba (1861–1931), were among the pioneers of recording, demonstrating its capacity for spreading enjoyment of the work of great composers and performers far beyond the concert halls. As usual, many older people remained disdainful of the new channel of communication, and a few, such as Stopford Brooke (1832–1916), a Nonconformist minister and literary critic, even found the gramophone un-Christian. Brooke objected to reproductions which 'violate the sacred silence of the dead'; he also disliked recordings of music-hall songs. The gramophone was, in short, 'a vile concoction of the scientific people'.[40]

Certainly the concoctions of the scientists were vastly extending the range of mass communication and mass entertainment in Edwardian England. Comic-song records or custard-pie-throwing films may have been childish, and much of Harmsworth's new journalism may have been trivial. Yet all were cheering and in demand, and they helped to broaden (however superficially) the extent of popular awareness. This broadening process was a pleasing feature of the Edwardian scene. 'The masses spend less on drink and more on drama', remarked one observer in 1910. 'The national habits are changing. Recent years', he concluded, carefully not claiming too much, 'have seen the rise of amusement and in some way, too, of culture.' Though still naive and ignorant when compared with their mid-twentieth century grandchildren, the Edwardians were better informed and better entertained than any previous generation.[41]

King, Government and People

The two Edwardian kings, Edward VII (1841–1910) in his reign from 1901 to 1910, and George V (1865–1936), his son and successor, fulfilled two very different roles. On the one hand, royal court functions formed the apex of 'society' life: on the other hand, the monarch traditionally comprised in his own person one whole estate of the realm. Edward VII revivified court routine, which had become emasculated and dull during Queen Victoria's long widowhood. 'He loved ceremony', it has been remarked, 'but he seldom stood on it.' George V, though less sociable than his father, conscientiously continued an elaborate court round up to the outbreak of war in 1914. In June of that year the United States Ambassador, W. H. Page (1855–1918), despatched some penetrating descriptions of great court occasions to his President. Nobody knew that the 'deluge' of war was only weeks away, but Page did sense an autumnal tone surrounding all the apparently confident ceremony: 'the sunlight falls on our New World. Here we are very gay but—in the shadow.'

Page noted how much the poor man paid for the pageantry of privilege. 'If he knows that he is "worked", he can hardly hope for relief in his lifetime, and he goes sadly on, doing the best he can and drinking the King's health as an expression of pride in the Empire.' Good-humoured Edward VII was popular with all classes, though personally known only to a select few and never even seen by the vast majority of his subjects. Press publicity was growing, but it was still restrained, and his relationships with women remained unknown to the middle and working classes. George V, on coming to the throne in 1910, introduced a new spirit of sober dedication and service into the Monarchy, which has done much to ensure its survival in the twentieth century. 'He leads a regular life', reported the American Ambassador. 'He grinds away at his job . . . Everybody agrees that an indiscreet or openly dissolute King would come to grief.' George V was deeply disturbed by the fierce industrial unrest and working-class bitterness of the first years of his reign, and he began the practice of making frequent royal tours of the industrial districts, with the aim of combatting the progress of 'socialism' by gaining acceptance for the Crown as a national symbol above class antagonisms. His straightforward manner was quickly noticed and welcomed by the public. After one West Riding tour in the summer of 1912 he wrote with satisfaction in his diary how at least three million of his subjects must have seen him. A week later, by contrast, a state ball was held at Buckingham Palace. 'Thank goodness!', the King now wrote, 'the last Court function this year!'

This new and important role for the Sovereign as a reconciler of classes was paralleled by the new role of the Crown as the one common link between the self-governing colonies. The Monarch had become the Imperial lynch-pin. 'The King is the typical and the only recognized representative of the whole Empire', remarked A. V. Dicey (1835–1922), a leading Edwardian jurist. These important symbolic functions of monarchy were developing just as the last remains of real royal political power were fading. Queen Victoria's uncle, William IV, had been able to dismiss a Ministry in 1834; but her grandson was twice warned by his Prime Minister (in 1910 and 1913) of the unconstitutionality of such action. The famous formula laid down by Walter Bagehot (1826–77) in the eighteen sixties was that the Sovereign, though now without executive powers, still possessed the right to be consulted by Ministers, to encourage and to warn them. Queen Victoria in her later years was usually referred to in this spirit, but her successor was less certain of such consideration. He grumbled to his private secretary about the Liberal Education Bill of 1906 'excluding teaching religion in our schools. Do they wish to copy the French? I look with considerable alarm to the way the Prime Minister is going on, and needless to say he never brings anything before me.' In certain areas, however, such as the conduct of foreign policy, the King could still expect to be more in the picture. He was related to most of the crowned heads of Europe; he visited the Continent regularly (though this was one reason why he grew more out of touch with domestic affairs than his mother), and he spoke German (like a native), French, Italian and Spanish. All this gave him a good sense of the atmosphere of European diplomacy. Foreign rulers, moreover, always dealt with him on the assumption that he could powerfully influence British foreign policy (just as they could influence their own policies), and this made it desirable for him to be informed and consulted. Gradually, he was able to secure the appointment of individuals congenial to himself in certain key diplomatic posts, notably the placing of Sir Charles Hardinge (1858–1944) as Permanent Under-Secretary at the Foreign Office (1906–10). Hardinge, like his Sovereign, viewed the drift of German policy with increasing concern. Yet the King's influence was never so strong that he could be called one of the architects of the ententes with France (1904) and Russia (1907), with their ultimate implications of opposition to Germany. The reputation which he began to acquire after his successful state visit to Paris in 1903 as 'Edward the Peacemaker', seeking security for Britain and peace for Europe, was not justified by his limited activity. In 1908 he met the Russian Emperor at Ravel. Before their first meeting the King asked the British Ambassador to Russia 'to explain the present nature and purposes of Russian policy; the exact names and past records of the Tsar's staff; the prospects of agriculture in Russia; the personal relations between M. Iswolsky and M. Stolypin, as well as the personal relations between them and the Empress; the exact provisions and scope of the Anglo-Russian Convention and the Franco-Russian Alliance . . .'— and so on. These were not the queries of a monarch who had directed Anglo-Russian diplomacy, simply of one anxious (at the last moment) to inform himself about policy and willing to use his personal contacts to further it.

Foreign policy could be seen as outside party politics, and therefore a proper field for royal interest. National defence could be similarly regarded, and both Edwardian Kings took careful notice of military and naval matters. Edward VII gave keen support both to R. B. Haldane's (1856–1928) army reforms and to Sir John Fisher's (1841–1920) naval revolution. The royal veto still survived to the extent that George V could refuse to allow the name *Oliver Cromwell* to be given to one of His Majesty's ships. All important naval, military and Church of England appointments, and the award of honours, could not be made without the opportunity for royal comment, not always favourable. Peerage creations especially had to be made with royal knowledge and at least acquiescence. Edward VII and George V, though both in favour of some Lords reform, were dismayed by the idea of a drastic reduction in the power of the House of Lords as eventually enacted by the Parliament Act of 1911. Edward VII complained several times about the bitterness of Lloyd George's attacks on the peers. 'Mr Lloyd George has made another indecent attack on the House of Lords', the King's secretary wrote to the Prime Minister in 1906. 'Mr Lloyd George is very anxious that the King and Queen should go to Cardiff next summer to open some new docks there . . . the King says that nothing will induce him to visit Cardiff unless Mr Lloyd George learns how to behave with propriety as a Cabinet Minister holding an important Office.' The petty nature of this threat showed how limited were the punishments now exercisable by Kings of England. Nevertheless during the 'Lords versus Commons' crisis of 1909–11 both Edward VII and George V were seriously tempted to assert the survival of major prerogative rights in relation to the dissolution of Parliament and to a possible mass peerage creation intended to swamp the Conservative majority in the Lords. In the end, however, George V had to give way. To have done otherwise, to have forced the resignation of the Liberal Government, would have brought the Crown into party politics. A similar situation arose in 1913–14 over the possibility of a royal veto of the Irish Home Rule Bill, or a possible dismissal of the Liberal Administration. George V was not totally opposed to Home Rule, but he believed that Liberal tactics were precipitating civil war in Ireland. Conservative Opposition leaders when consulted by the Monarch found plausible grounds for the exercise of a royal veto; but as Asquith, the Liberal Prime Minister, explained to the King, intervention would have meant that the Crown had 'become the football of contending factions'. The Edwardians witnessed important constitutional changes; fortunately they escaped what would have been (in Asquith's phrase) 'a constitutional catastrophe'.[42]

The two Edwardian kings were popular with the masses. So, as individuals, were the more than six hundred Edwardian peers. The spirit of 'deference' in British society detected by Bagehot in mid-Victorian times was still very strong, even though the composition of the peerage had changed. With the decline of the agricultural interest, noted A. L. Lowell (1856–1943), the American author of a major contemporary survey of Edwardian government, 'respect for the old territorial aristocracy has been replaced by a veneration for titles, and this has inured to the benefit of the peerage'. All Edwardian politicians in the Lords and most in the Commons belonged to the upper or upper-middle classes. 'Gentlemen' were usually preferred by the electorate as Commons candidates for either the Conservative or Liberal Parties. The stratum from which Ministers usually came was still more restricted—'the few thousand representatives of the nobility, landowners, capitalists, and leading professional men, who make up London society'. In the 1905 Liberal Cabinet, however, politicians from upper-middle class backgrounds finally outnumbered those drawn from the aristocracy. John Burns (1858–1943) was a working man, and Lloyd George's background was humble. But this was still not 'government of the people by the people': rather (as one contemporary observer remarked) it was 'government of the people, for the people, by the best of the people'. Socialists denounced such exclusiveness, but there was no widespread demand for government by working men. Lowell indicated the advantages of a system whereby both main parties chose their leaders from the same social circle. It meant that Edwardian major party politics never split along class lines. Moreover, in the hands of men of substance reform was unlikely to become revolution. 'To entrust a man of conservative traditions with the execution of a radical programme is a

safe and sometimes a wise proceeding. Such a condition does
not obviate pressure for democratic class legislation, or
prevent it from being effective, but it does act as a moderating
force.'[43]

'The personal influence of the Lords', commented Lowell,
'is far greater than their collective authority.' The limitation,
after a prolonged constitutional crisis, of the power of the upper
house by the 1911 Parliament Act was the biggest constitutional change of the Edwardian period. In late-Victorian
times the upper chamber had become too decidedly one-party
Conservative in political character. This bias had developed
notwithstanding a large infusion of new blood from fresh
backgrounds. 246 fresh titles were created between 1886
and 1914. One-third of these new peers came from commerce and industry; another third from the professions
(especially the law) or from the diplomatic, colonial and armed
services. But many Whigs had left the Liberal Party even before
Gladstone first proposed Irish Home Rule in 1886. His 1893
Home Rule Bill was overwhelmed in the Lords by 419 votes
to 41. The politics of the peers' resistance first to the 1909
budget, and then to the Home Rule Bill of 1912–14, will be
discussed later. Between these two episodes the Parliament Act
deprived the Lords of all power over finance; but (as in the
case of their resistance to the Home Rule Bill) it left them still
able to delay non-financial legislation for two years. A measure
sent up by the House of Commons in three successive sessions
could now become law on the third occasion regardless of
continuing Lords objection. The Parliament Act thus severely
restricted the powers of the peers, but it did not reform the
composition of their chamber. This had been under discussion
even before the defeat of Gladstone's 1893 Home Rule Bill.
Many schemes for Lords reform were aired during the Edwardian years, some abolishing hereditary membership entirely, some restricting the number of hereditary peers, many
suggesting the introduction of life peers, some wanting the
upper house to include representatives of outside bodies such as
county councils. In 1908 a committee of the House of Lords
itself proposed a membership reform scheme, but one too
limited to begin to satisfy advocates of change. Before the
passing of the Parliament Act, action tended to be inhibited by

fear that a properly reconstructed upper house would expect almost an equality with the House of Commons. Then after 1911 it seemed to matter much less who were (or were not) members of a body with such reduced powers. The promise in the preamble to the Parliament Act of 'a Second Chamber constituted on a popular basis instead of hereditary basis' therefore remained unfulfilled. As one commentator remarked in 1913, 'why go to the trouble of elaborating a new upper chamber or senate to exercise such a paltry vestige of power!'

Yet this vestige of power was enough to sorely disturb Anglo-Irish politics in the years 1912-14. And if the peers' political powers were diminished, their high social standing remained. From the eighteen nineties both the Conservative and Liberal Parties unashamedly exploited this social appeal by virtually selling peerages in return for large contributions to party funds. The expense of conducting politics for an enlarged electorate was proving very high. A general election meant a charge on Conservative central funds of between £80,000 and £120,000. Liberal headquarters probably spent about the same amount. One rich Conservative was reported in 1914 to have even offered money to the Liberals in return for a title, on the ground that the Conservative leaders, if they won the next election, had already been paid for as many peerages as they could reasonably hope to offer in the lifetime of one Parliament.[44]

The 1884 Franchise Act had been enacted in an atmosphere of political compromise, and it had left an eccentric registration system unreformed. As a result, the parties found themselves spending an estimated £500,000 a year in placing favourably disposed voters on the electoral registers. The Edwardians often spoke of their Parliamentary franchise as 'democratic', but this was an exaggeration. It stopped well short of 'one man one vote', and had no place at all for 'one woman one vote'. Over 40 per cent of men and all women were unenfranchised in 1911. On the other hand, of the 7,700,000 men (mostly householders and occupiers of property valued at £10 a year or above) who did enjoy the suffrage, over 500,000 could cast plural votes. These plural votes tended to favour the Conservatives, and in 1906, 1912 and 1913 Bills to abolish plural voting were passed by the Liberal majorities in the Commons only to be rejected in the Lords. The peers were able to argue with some plausibility that a redistribution of seats should accompany franchise reform, and that the cry 'one man one vote' was meaningless without the corollary of 'one vote one value'. The 1885 Redistribution Act had never intended to produce precise mathematical equality of representation in relation to population, but by Edwardian times population changes had produced excessive variations. Ireland had been unduly favoured from the start, returning 103 Members of Parliament compared with Scotland's 72 even though the Scottish population and electorate were larger. But from 1910 the Liberal Government depended for its Commons majority upon the votes of Irish Nationalist members, and the Liberals were unwilling to allow a reduction of Irish representation at Westminster except as part of a Home Rule measure.

Paradoxically, both the middle and working classes were more continuously interested in politics under this still limited franchise than under the genuine democracy of the later twentieth century. Rival attractions to politics—sport, travel, the music hall and cinema—were growing rapidly, but the strong political feelings of Victorian times were not yet forgotten. Victorian Nonconformists, for example, had campaigned persistently and with much success from within the Liberal Party against Anglican privileges and against their own position as second-class citizens, notably in relation to education. Their prolonged opposition to the 1902 Education Act was the last major expression of this feeling. Denunciation of this measure formed part of the 1906 Liberal general election programme. Such 'programmes' were late-Victorian innovations, framed to win the votes of the new large electorate. In the eighteen eighties and nineties both the National Liberal Federation and the National Union of Conservative Associations had aspired to impose constituency opinion upon their party leaders in Parliament, endorsing programmes at annual conferences. But by the Edwardian period these extra-Parliamentary organizations had lost their momentum, and in 1906 the Liberal programme was simply that put forward by Sir Henry Campbell-Bannerman (1836–1908), the party leader, in his speeches. Voters now expected to be given an outline of policies for consideration, giving the successful party a 'mandate' for action. Elections were no longer conducted as in mid-Victorian times simply to choose individual Members of Parliament, who were then left largely free to make or unmake both measures and Ministries. 'Strictly speaking', remarked the *Daily News* in 1901, '. . . there is no such thing in England as a mandate. Lord Salisbury was the first to introduce into English politics that essentially Jacobinical phrase.'[45]

The Edwardian House of Commons contained 670 members spread among the constituencies as follows:

	England	Wales	Scotland	Ireland
Counties	234	19	39	85
Boroughs	226	11	31	16
Universities	5	—	2	2

Exactly equal numbers of Conservative and Liberal candidates (272) were elected in December 1910, facilitating comparison between the economic interests of members on the two sides. Liberal landowners totalled only 38 compared with 123 Conservatives, but 12 Conservatives with brewery connections were matched by only 1 Liberal. Links with heavy industry and with transport were evenly shared between the two parties, but 40 Liberals had merchanting interests compared with only 20 Conservatives. 15 Liberal members were connected with the textile trades, against only 5 Conservatives. Yet clearly it could no longer be said that, while the Conservatives represented only 'land', the Liberals alone represented 'business'. The Conservatives were now closely connected with urban business, perhaps with bigger business than the Liberals: 124 Conservative members had links with the financial world compared with 92 Liberals. Occupationally, much the largest group in all Edwardian Parliaments was formed by the solicitors and barristers: 66 Conservatives in December 1910, 62 Liberals, and 20 Irish Nationalists. Both major parties were well educated, reflecting the voters' preference for electing 'gentlemen'. 196 Conservatives had attended public schools (90 at Eton), and 104 Liberals (23 at Eton). 87 Liberals had been educated at secondary schools, but only 23 Conservatives. Among Labour members only 2 had enjoyed any secondary education.[46]

Standards of personal morality instilled at Victorian public schools had helped to spur Members of Parliament to eliminate corruption from late-Victorian and Edwardian politics. Under the Corrupt and Illegal Practices Act of 1883, corruption—defined as bribery, treating, undue influence, assault or abduction, impersonation or perjury—was made punishable by up to two years' imprisonment. Tight statutory limits were also set upon election expenses. Disreputable practices common-place in early-Victorian times now disappeared with re-markable suddenness from the electoral scene. But if electors could no longer receive money, in 1911 Members of Parliament began to do so. Payment of members had begun to be discussed in the late-nineteenth century, and the Liberals came to favour it. Campbell-Bannerman argued in the Commons in 1906 that a salary would enhance the quality of members by widening the range of choice, and also their independence once elected. But the Liberals long hesitated to act, believing that a decision by politicians to pay themselves would be unpopular, even though the £252,000 needed was no more than the cost of one battle-ship. In the end, however, the Osborne Judgment (1909), forbidding expenditure by trade unions for political purposes (such as payment of union members in Parliament), virtually forced the Liberals to act. From the beginning of the financial year 1911–12 all members of the Commons became entitled to £400 per year, a quarter of this allocated for necessary Parliamentary expenses free of income tax. Conservative critics grumbled that this would encourage 'professional politicians'. But Campbell-Bannerman had answered this complaint. 'What do you mean by professional politics? If you take a man who devotes himself to his work, to the study of public affairs, in order to qualify himself here, and contrast with him a man who came here as a pastime or a means of social advancement, which of the two is the better man?' Traditionalists feared that the House of Commons would lose its character as 'the best club in London'. Labour representa-tives (29 in number by 1906), who were not 'gentlemen', were most suspect in this context. But the fears proved groundless, for most Labour members came to accept not only the written but also the unwritten rules of the House. Churchill was soon praising them as 'a stable and not an unstable element', who had 'added greatly to the wisdom and the earnestness and consequently the dignity of the House'.[47]

Labour remained a small minority party in the Edwardian Parliaments. The main struggle for office lay between the Liberals and the Conservatives, the latter supported by the Liberal Unionist group originally organized in opposition to Gladstone's 1886 Home Rule Bill. The Liberal Unionists were becoming increasingly absorbed into the Conservative body, which in Edwardian times preferred to call itself simply 'Unionist' in order to underline its support for the territorial unity of the United Kingdom including Ireland. During the later nineteenth century voting along strict party lines had increased steadily in the House of Commons. Ministers carrying out 'programmes' expected steady support from their back-benchers rather than idiosyncratic voting or frequent expressions of opinion. 'The old judicial type of Member', Lord Salisbury (1830–1903) told Queen Victoria in 1889, 'who sat rather loose to his Party . . . has disappeared. They are all partisans.' When Government supporters in the Commons felt dissatisfied with Cabinet policy they now explained their doubts, not on the floor of the House, but in private to party Whips or to Ministers. If such representations were numerous, back-bench opinion could still exert an influence, party leaders accepting that 'our fellows won't stand it'. But open voting in opposition to one's party was not expected. In the eighteen fifties and sixties governments lost ten or fifteen Commons divisions each year, whereas by the first years of the twentieth century they were defeated perhaps once a session. The parliamentary sitting had lengthened to an average of 140 days, but Private Members were allowed only about 14 of these on business of their own choosing, for the Government was itself short of time. In the ten years ending 1909, 388 Government Bills passed the Commons in 483 days, the 10 most important measures occupying 207 of these days.

The Cabinet, described by Bagehot as 'a hyphen which fastens the legislative part to the executive part of the state', now held the initiative in relation to politics both in Parliament and in the country. Joseph Chamberlain's resignation from the Cabinet in 1903 to conduct the 'tariff reform' campaign was a last attempt to create a 'movement' of the type which (as with the Anti-Corn Law League) had been highly influential in early-nineteenth century politics. Within the Edwardian Cabinet the Prime Minister was tending to become more than 'the first among equals'. Significantly, the existence of the office was given belated formal recognition in 1905. The number of other Cabinet Ministers was increasing, thereby enhancing the Prime Minister's uniqueness. He was developing, too, a special function as the chief adviser of the Crown on Imperial matters. And he possessed the final right of deciding when to advise a dissolution of Parliament. As party leader he then led his side's general election campaign. Dicey was already forecasting the day when a British general election ('a popular election of a particular statesman to the premiership') would compare with an American presidential election. This tendency was delayed only because none of the Edwardian Prime Ministers possessed mass appeal as personalities. But the opportunity for such an approach to the voters was now open, as Lloyd George was to show as Prime Minister at the 1918 election.[48]

The Edwardian electorate had the first and the last word, but its power was spasmodic, exercised only at general elections. Under the Parliament Act the maximum duration of a Parliament was reduced from seven to five years, but this still did not give the voters a continuous direct involvement. Edwardian political theorists and politicians discussed at length whether between elections it would be desirable to introduce appeals to the electors by referenda on specific issues. This discussion was stimulated not so much by ultra-democratic feeling as by concern about the role of the House of Lords. Before the passing of the Parliament Act, while the Lords were rejecting major Liberal Bills on the ground that there was no popular demand for them, it was argued that this could be tested by referendum. After 1911 it began to be contended that use of the referendum would provide a substitute for the reduced power of the House of Lords as a check upon governments. 'The real control of our legislation is in the hands, not of the body of elected representatives, but in those of a small Cabinet, selected mainly out of a little aristo-plutocracy with a leaven of successful lawyers, and of a powerful bureaucracy whose class sympathies are natural and notorious. The Referendum must be recognized not indeed as a substitute for, but as a necessary supplement to, representation in any nation aiming at popular self-government.'

So argued J. A. Hobson in 1909. But did the enlarged Edwardian electorate want to be so frequently consulted on specific measures? Edwardian electors certainly enjoyed conferring a 'mandate' upon Ministers at election times, usually involving support for some specific legislative proposals. But this did not mean that the voters were aspiring continuously to govern themselves. As early as 1889 R. B. Haldane, one of the leaders of Edwardian Liberalism, had penetratingly summed up the new role of Government in relation to the enlarged electorate:

> What we have to do at home is to try to gain the confidence of the electors and to mould their opinions . . . a democracy has not got, as is assumed in practice, a body of definite opinions, for the expression of which in Parliament it seeks .delegates . . . it is an assembly of human beings earnestly seeking guidance from those of whose sympathies it is sure.

Joseph Chamberlain had thought along similar lines in 1886:

> The problem is to give the democracy the whole power, but to induce them to do no more in the way of using it than to decide on the general principles which they wish to see carried out and the men by whom they are to be carried out. My Radicalism, at all events, desires to see established a strong government.

The progress of reform in the late-Victorian and Edwardian electoral situation therefore demanded not weak government, shifting before every change of public opinion, but strong government giving a lead. Though the great Liberal social reforms had long been under public discussion, they were finally passed not in response to any immediate popular demand but upon Government initiative. 'While public opinion by a sort of volcanic process upheaves and hurls forth one problem after another, the party leaders who alternately come into office, the rulers, fasten on those problems the solution of which appears to them necessary and possible.'

To assist in shaping the increasing volume of legislation and to administer it once passed was the function of the Edwardian civil service. This bureaucracy had been growing steadily in size since its great mid-Victorian reorganization. By 1914 it was divided into three main non-industrial categories: administrative, 'intermediate' (executive), and clerical. Permanent non-industrial civil servants numbered about 165,000 in 1914 compared with 133,000 in 1911 and 106,000 in 1901. 124,000 of the 1914 total were employed in the Post Office, over 12,000 in the defence departments, some 12,000 in tax collection. Numbers engaged in administering the social services (including education) almost doubled between 1911 and 1914 (2800 to 5300), largely because of the introduction of social insurance. On 1st April 1914 *Punch* carried a cartoon satirizing 'the craze for salaried officials', suggesting additional appointments as 'Wardens of Reputations to suppress scandal' or 'Censors of Phraseology to restrain bad language'. 'The professional administrator, of one kind or another', concluded an analyst of British government in the same year, 'is a characteristic product of modern conditions like the professional politician.'

The most comprehensive of the welfare services was also the oldest, the Poor Law, reorganized after 1834. It provided payments to paupers in money or in kind plus the spartan facilities of the workhouse. The local Poor Law Guardians were responsible to the Local Government Board, established in 1871. The same Board also had oversight of local authority public health services. State education was another responsibility of the local authorities, in this case under the guidance of the Board of Education, formed in 1900. Old age pensions, instituted in 1908, were administered by the Board of Customs and Excise, while the Board of Trade handled unemployment insurance and the provision of labour exchanges. Finally, health insurance was organized through four new Insurance Commissions for each country of the United Kingdom. [50]

Before 1914 central government was thus beginning to exert a novel and important influence upon local life. Growing activity by both central and local authorities was reflected in greatly increased expenditure. Between 1890 and 1910 the amount of money spent centrally and locally rose from £131 million per annum to £305 million. In 1900, inflated by the military costs of the Boer War, total expenditure had temporarily reached as high as £281 million. Peacetime spending in 1914 was therefore well past this wartime level. In other words, the extra money which the late Victorians had found to spend on armaments the late Edwardians chose to continue to spend partly still on armaments but partly also on domestic services. Defence costs grew from under £35 million in 1890 to over £91 million in 1913. But social service spending grew even more markedly: centrally from under £8 million in 1890 to nearly £55 million in 1914, and locally from over £19 million to over £46 million.

Increasing expenditure by national and local government meant increasing taxation. United Kingdom income tax (at 6d in £) produced £12 million in 1890, £18.9 million (at 8d in £) in 1900, £43.5 million (at 1s 2d in £) in 1914. English and Welsh local rates raised £27.7 million in 1890, £40.7 million in 1900, £71.3 million in 1914. Total local authority receipts from rates, loans, trading profits and government grants rose from £57.3 million in 1890 through £100.6 million in 1900 to £168.3 million in 1914. Exchequer grants played a growing part in local finance, totalling only £6.5 million in 1890 but £22.6 million by 1914. These grants were made to help local authorities bear the increasing costs of certain services which they were now required to provide, especially in education. The Treasury preferred to make specific grants, linked to particular services, rather than to give non-specific grants available for general support of rate-fund expenditure. Such specific grants tended to entail more detailed central supervision.

At the opening of the century, however, municipal freedom and enterprise was at a peak. The late Victorians had introduced a long overdue reform of the local government system, reversing the earlier Victorian preference for ad hoc authorities by creating a network of popularly elected multi-purpose authorities: county councils (1888), county borough councils, municipal borough and district councils (1894). Borough and county electorates were rather broader than Parliamentary electorates, the difference being made up mainly of female voters, spinsters or widows but not married women. The first women to hold local office appear to have been members of the school boards elected after 1870. Two ladies returned to the new

London County Council in 1889 were disqualified by the courts, and women were not finally given the right to sit on county and borough councils until 1907.

Many Edwardian councils were increasingly busy not simply with local administration but also with municipal trading, especially with the provision of water, gas and electricity, with municipal transport, and (in a few places) with housing for the working classes. Receipts from these main trading sources rose from £6.5 million in 1890 through £15 million in 1901 to £33.6 million by 1914. Within these totals, receipts from municipal transport services sprang from a negligible figure in 1890 to £10.3 million by 1914. It was argued in favour of municipal provision of water, gas and electricity that, to be efficient, they needed to be local monopolies, and monopolies should not be controlled by private profit-seekers who might exploit the public. The same argument was used in favour of municipal tramways, with the additional justification that they involved disturbance of the public highway. The case for municipal house-building—that slum clearance must be undertaken to a local plan, that private builders did not find it sufficiently profitable to undertake redevelopment themselves—ran closer to 'socialism', as did municipal employment of 'direct labour'. Conservative critics, indeed, were fiercely distrustful of what they preferred to call 'municipal socialism'. It was a subject, noted Lowell, 'more controversial than any other English question not strictly a matter of party politics'. *The Times* in 1902 carried a long series of articles entitled 'Municipal Socialism' alarmedly reiterating that 'the primary duty of a local governing body is to govern and not to trade.' The anonymous author was disturbed that local electors, without ever electing socialist representatives, seemed to be unconsciously repudiating private enterprise. Sir Charles Dilke (1843–1911), a radical supporter of the new trend, remarked in 1901 how in France 'the electors of certain cities return Socialist municipal councils. They are all but absolutely powerless. We, on the other hand, elect Tory or Whig municipalities, and they do the best of Socialist work.' Avowed socialists, such as Bernard Shaw, author of *Commonsense of Municipal Trading* (1904), were enthusiastic about this 'highly desirable and beneficial extension of civilisation'. The mass of local electors, drawing their water, lighting their gas, or catching their trams enjoyed the benefits of 'municipal socialism' and ignored the political ideology, desirable or dangerous, lying beneath.

Was the promotion of such trading services asking too much from unpaid local councillors? *The Times* thought so, and used this as an argument against municipal trading. 'The idea of "governing" their fellow-citizens may well have appealed to their higher instincts, but the idea of keeping shop for them is quite a different matter.' *The Times* claimed this as one major reason why leading local figures seemed to be increasingly reluctant to participate in local government. This reluctance was widely observed by commentators of all political shades. Beatrice Webb (1858–1943), the Fabian socialist, discussing the character of Manchester City Council in 1899, noted how its leading members were all older men, also how membership was predominantly lower-middle class, few leading business and professional personalities participating. A *Birmingham Mail* article in 1907 asked 'Has the City Council Deteriorated?' It noticed the relative fewness of young business and professional men coming forward, partly because they preferred golf or motoring to national or local politics, partly because their energies were absorbed by intensified business competition, partly because they disliked submitting themselves to contested elections, partly because they were discouraged by the operation of the party system within the council, and not least because they now lived in distant suburbs. Analysis of membership of Birmingham, Liverpool and Leeds councils revealed how 'gentlemen' comprised 19.3 per cent of council members in 1870, only 7 per cent by 1910; 'merchants' had dropped from 11.4 per cent to 6.2 per cent, 'manufacturers' from 18.2 per cent to 15 per cent. 'The men of wealth, of large affairs', explained Lowell, 'the leading citizens, have been gradually replaced by people with perhaps as much public spirit and good intentions, but with an experience less broad and of a smaller calibre.'

But though enthusiasts for municipal trading might agree with *The Times* critic that there had been a decline in the calibre of council personnel they did not agree that this required the abandonment of municipal enterprise. Some reformers began to advocate the introduction of long-serving paid council leadership on the German burgomaster model. Enthusiastic young Winston Churchill asked in 1908 'about the proposal to have skilled professional mayors on the German plan instead of our present happy-go-lucky amateur system . . . the times are now coming when active and increasing social construction and reconstruction will be the order of the day.' Another proposed reform under discussion urged the reshaping of local government into larger regional units. These would be more efficient for municipal trading purposes. The Fabian Society issued a report in 1905 called *Municipalization by Provinces*, recommending a 'new heptarchy', seven or eight regional boards elected by local authorities to handle functions requiring large-scale operation. The boundaries of the new provinces were to be defined to best meet the needs of the water, electricity, housing and transport services.

One virtual region already existed as an Edwardian local government unit—London. The Fabians were very active within the London County Council, first elected in 1889. When late Victorians began to speculate about 'the politics of the future' they usually referred to London, where until 1907 the 'Progressives' (mainly Liberals) enjoyed a majority and which promised to become a laboratory for social experiment. The Fabian *London Programme* (1890) advocated municipal socialism, and much (though not all) of the Fabian policy was put through by the Progressives. Municipalization of the cemeteries and free burials were recommended, for example, with the tart observation that 'communism in funerals' was unlikely to lead to 'reckless increase in the demand for graves'. But the Fabians failed to persuade the Progressives to extend municipal intervention into non-monopolistic activities, such as baking, milk supply, the sale of intoxicating liquors, pawnshops, or fire insurance. The Progressives were too middle-class to become securely the party of the London masses, and finally in 1907 they fell from power, never again to secure a majority.

'Municipal socialism' in London and elsewhere was losing momentum by this date. Central government was developing its own rival 'state socialism'. The new social services introduced by the Liberals were national in scope, control and finance. With the unemployed, the elderly and the sick partly taken off poor relief, and with the increasing importance of specific Exchequer grants, local initiative began to count for less and central direction for more. Around 1905 local authority spending had reached about one-half of all public spending, but thereafter the proportion slowly declined. At the beginning of the century the Association of Municipal Corporations had been pressing for wider local powers, more flexible procedure, and longer time for loans, all with a view to expanding municipal activities. But by the immediate pre-war years the character of this contact had undergone a significant change. The Association was now occupied with pressing central government for more support and finance, no longer was it seeking more independence. Within the Edwardian period there had been, in the words of one expert, writing in the nineteen twenties, an 'increasing transfer of the *thinking* from the local to the central government'. By 1914, in contrast to the position in 1889 or even 1905, it was apparent that 'the politics of the future' were now centred round, not the municipality but the state.[51]

CHAPTER THREE

The Individual and the State

Political Ideas

'While in 1864 orthodoxy meant distrust of the State, and heresy took the form of a belief in paternal government, in 1914 orthodoxy means belief in the State, and heresy takes the form of mild excursions into anarchism.' So explained Ernest Barker (1874–1960) in a Home University volume on contemporary political thought written at the very end of the Edwardian era. Growing numbers of Edwardians were consciously seeking to strike a new balance in the relationship between the individual and his government. They had come to accept that the State must increase its intervention in order to raise up the under-privileged, even though this meant exposing all citizens to greater government activity. The Victorian rule of *laissez faire* in economic and political life, which had never in fact been practised without qualification, was now becoming a rule with as many exceptions as applications.

The leading contemporary school of British philosophers, the Idealists, headed by Bernard Bosanquet (1848–1923) and F. H. Bradley (1846–1924), assisted this shift of emphasis by arguing that there need be no conflict between an active state and the enjoyment of personal liberty. T. H. Green (1836–82), the most distinguished of the British Idealists, had already emphasized the mutual inter-dependence of individuals and the State: 'without persons no society, without society no persons'. The idea of a 'fixed liberty fund', explained J. H. Muirhead (1855–1940) in Edwardian lectures favourably interpreting Green's political teaching, 'has gone the way of the wage-fund'; political interest had shifted to 'social liberty in the new and positive meaning of the word'. Such social liberty could be related to aggregates of individuals as well as to indi-viduals regarded separately. In mid-Victorian times Samuel

Smiles's (1812–1904) secular gospel of individual *Self-Help* (1859) had been widely influential. But by 1901 Sidney Webb, who had already dismissed Smiles as 'an unconscious corrupter of youth', was demonstrating how in a complex industrial society individuals were often at the mercy of forces uncontrollable by solitary effort:

> The England of this generation is changing because Englishmen have had revealed to them another new world of relationships, of which they were before unconscious. This time it is not a new continent that the ordinary man has discovered, but a new category. We have become aware, almost in a flash, that we are not merely individuals, but members of a community, nay, citizens of the world. . . . The labourer in the slum tenement, competing for employment at the factory gate, has become conscious that his comfort and progress depend, not wholly or mainly on himself, or on any other individual, but upon the proper organization of his trade union and the activity of the factory inspector. The shopkeeper or the manufacturer sees his prosperity wax or wane, his own industry and sagacity remaining the same, according to the good government of his city, the efficiency with which his nation is organized, and the influence which his Empire is able to exercise in the councils, and consequently in the commerce of the world. Hence the ordinary elector, be he workman or manufacturer, shopkeeper or merchant, has lost his interest in individual 'rights' or abstract 'equality', political or religious. The freedom that he now wants is not individual but corporate freedom—freedom for his trade union to bargain collectively, freedom for his co-operative society to buy and sell and manufacture, freedom for his municipality to supply all the common needs of the town, freedom, above all, from the narrow insularity which keeps his nation backing, 'on principle', out of its proper place in the comity of the world. In short, the opening of the twentieth century finds us all, to the dismay of the old-fashioned Individualist, 'thinking in communities'.

In other words, the quest for individual liberty often became translated into some form of group aspiration. 'If we are individualists now', explained Barker in 1914, 'we are corporate individualists. . . . No longer do we write *The Man versus the State*: we write *The Group versus the State*.' By the end of the Edwardian period trade unions had secured a high status and were seeking still higher; guild socialism, Irish Home Rule, federal government for the United Kingdom, and Welsh Church disestablishment were all under active discussion. On the one hand, concern for individual rights was being left behind by these group demands: on the other, the preponderance of the State was being challenged by them. 'We see the State invited to retreat before the advance of the guild, the national group, the Church.' Here was an important aspect of the theoretical politics behind the turbulent practical politics of the immediate pre-war years.[1]

Yet the idea of State intervention always remained a major part of the Edwardian political debate. At its most thoroughgoing this meant, if not communism, at least 'socialism'. But there were many Edwardian definitions of socialism. Among its opponents it was often a term of disparagement, 'including nearly everything to which they object in social organization or in political procedure'. Among its advocates it was 'an impeachment of the present' in an opposite sense, 'a compendious summary of all the changes they would like to see accomplished', embracing a wide variety of content, emphasis and priority. In *New Worlds for Old* (1908) H. G. Wells defined the basic Edwardian socialist idea as 'the denial that chance impulse and individual will and happening constitute the only possible methods by which things may be done in the world'. Socialists accepted that it was possible to formulate 'a general plan of social life' to produce 'equality of opportunity'. All agreed (though differing over timing) that this required collective ownership of the means of production, consumption and distribution, along with community participation in the upbringing of children to ensure their good health and education. Wells pressed only for what he called 'constructive socialism'; he came to repudiate the communistic and confiscatory proposals of some nineteenth-century socialist pioneers. Edwardian socialist propagandists echoed the arguments of the Idealist philosophers in emphasizing that increased State intervention would liberate, not restrict. 'The penniless man is in society, but not of it; none of the freedom it bestows on its more favoured members is for him'. Socialism, by placing the instruments of production under the control of the people, 'and abolishing the tributes of rent and interest, gives them the economic basis without which any freedom, in the sense of mere absence of law, would be meaningless'.[2]

Yet, fluently though Wells and many other socialist writers elaborated their creed, they made only a limited number of converts. A leading analyst of Edwardian socialism concluded in 1907 that there were probably not 50,000 electors who called themselves socialists. Many working men reacted unfavourably to the basic socialist assumption that they were 'slaves' within the capitalist system. This offended their pride. 'I don't put myself down as a slave', exclaimed one workman in *The Ragged Trousered Philanthropists*, a documentary novel of life among Edwardian building workers written by one of themselves. Another contemporary observer of artisan life remarked how the word 'socialist' was 'still a lump of political mud, handy to throw at any opponent; just as twenty years ago the word "atheist" was.' The poor were traditionally suspicious of the State, their experience of State action coming chiefly from contact with the police or the Poor Law authorities. They dumbly assumed that bureaucratic social reform would only further enable 'them' to oppress 'us'. When the *Daily Mirror* asked for a 'leading man' to stand forward as champion of the poor, Bernard Shaw replied with a pessimistic paradox. 'How many votes will he get? Our Statesmanship destroys the character of the people and so we go on helplessly in a vicious circle, made cowardly and narrow-minded by poverty, and kept poor by our cowardice and narrow-mindedness.'

Fortunately, there was one 'leading man' ready to espouse the cause of the poor in spite of their apathy—Lloyd George. 'If these poor people are to be redeemed they must be redeemed not by themselves, because nothing strikes you more than the stupor of despair in which they have sunk—they must be redeemed by others outside, and the appeal ought to be to every class of community to see that in this great land all this misery and wretchedness should be put an end to.' So exclaimed Lloyd George in 1908 at the beginning of the period of great Liberal social reforms. These reforms were enacted not in response to clamour from the 'masses', but to an important extent because of the stirrings of conscience of increasing numbers of the 'classes'. Lloyd George, supported by Winston Churchill, combined sincere social concern with the opportunistic hope that social reform would become electorally popular with working-class voters after, even though not before, its enactment.

'Let's not relax our eagerness to do something for the poor: "all the world's agin the poor!". I feel that I am not so much inclined to care or at least to break into revolt against conditions of poverty as I am to settle down in the social order . . . Pray for the fire within adequate to burn up the sins of the world.' Here in the breast of C. F. G. Masterman, recently appointed a junior Minister, was 'social conscience' at work in 1908. The history of this expression in Edwardian times is in itself revealing. A lecture of Shaw's in 1888 had spoken of 'the value of trade unionism in awakening the social conscience of the skilled workers'. 'Social conscience' in this sense meant a spur prompting working men to act for themselves. By 1914, however, its meaning was shifting. It now referred to acceptance of social responsibility by the middle and upper classes. In a public speech in 1907 Asquith, after noting the apathy of the masses, used 'social conscience' in this new sense. He admitted to being 'amazed at the patience and inertness with which the mass of mankind acquiesced in what they deemed to be their lot. No wonder that constant contemplation and reflection upon such a spectacle had driven and continued to drive some of the best and finest spirits of our race into moral and intellectual revolt. Now there was much in what was vaguely and loosely denounced as the spread of Socialism, which meant no more than this—that men's social vision was being enlarged and their social conscience aroused.' In short, the Edwardian masses having been slow to develop a 'social conscience' of their own in the sense Shaw had envisaged in 1888, the Edwardian higher classes had intervened, diverting the application of the expression to themselves.[3]

Political Parties

The one thing which might have checked this upsurge of social conscience would have been a credible threat of socialist

revolution, perhaps violent, certainly rapid and total, aimed at
the confiscation of property. But advocates of violence were very
few in Edwardian England. 'The day for physical rebellion is
perhaps past', admitted one ultra-socialist in 1908; but 'the day
of political revolt has at last come. And the symbol and practice
of revolt must take the shape of a Socialist Party that will
challenge all other species of reform.' For a generation the
Social Democratic Federation had aspired to be such a party.
It had been founded in 1884 by H. M. Hyndman (1842–1921),
a wealthy barrister and journalist. The British Marxist movement, it has been said, dated from Hyndman's reading of a
French translation of *Das Kapital* in 1880 on an Atlantic
steamer bound for North America. The SDF achieved rapid
success in publicizing the socialist message, but it was never able
to convert wide public notice into comparable public support.
Also it remained persistently lukewarm towards the trade
unions, which constituted the backbone of the British working-
class movement. The SDF was therefore followed in 1893 by the
formation of the Independent Labour Party, under the especial
inspiration of Keir Hardie. The ILP kept closer to practicalities
than the SDF, linking its socialism less with Marxist doctrine
and more with everyday working-class experience, an approach which recommended itself to trade unionists and
co-operators. These men preferred, in the words of one socialist
critic of the SDF, to be 'guided mainly by events, and not by
theories', to be moved by the 'need for mutual aid, which is at
the root of all society, enforced upon them daily by the tyranny
of modern industrial conditions, just as they would have done if
Karl Marx had never lived'. Hyndman soon came to deplore
the lack of militant class feeling among the British workers. The
SDF programme assumed that one day 'the class war will
become conscious instead of unconscious on the part of the
working classes'; because the capitalists controlled the state 'the
class war must assume a political character, and become a
struggle on the part of the workers for the possession of the
political machinery'. During the labour unrest about 1912 there
did seem some prospect that militancy might be developing,
and in that year the SDF merged into a new British Socialist
Party, which claimed some 40,000 members organized in 370
branches. By 1914, however, membership had slumped by over

a half. Hyndman and his friends had continued to be critical of trade union methods. Great strikes, they argued, might force concessions but they would not transform society. Yet the Hyndmanites were disdainful and unclear in their proposals for practical political action to begin this transformation.[4]

Hyndman dismissed the ILP as 'the Dependent Labour Party', even though its programme was as socialist as that of the SDF. Its tone, admittedly, was more conciliatory. 'It is not classes but systems which are at war', explained Keir Hardie in 1901. Capitalists and workers were equally the creatures of social accident. If the rich were willing to resign their property, Hardie was willing to welcome them in a spirit of 'fellowship with the race' which would make life a joy'. The ILP was certainly 'dependent', as Hyndman claimed, in the sense that it aimed to influence the two main political parties. Its founders had been impressed by the success of the Irish Nationalists in concentrating Liberal and Conservative attention upon the Irish question between 1886 and 1893, and they hoped to achieve the same impact for social reform. This pressure was to be exerted not only by ILP Members of Parliament, but also through Liberal and Conservative members with numerous working-class voters in their constituencies. In provincial industrial districts, such as the West Riding, ILP public meetings were often enthusiastic occasions, addressed by stirring socialist orators. Among these Philip Snowden was the foremost:

> A lecture by Mr Snowden, in a provincial town, is an event of some importance; his coming is announced beforehand on every hoarding, and his speech is well reported in the local press next day. The people who hear it are a sufficient proportion of the total population to reappear in little groups next morning in every workshop in the town; and are sufficiently delighted with what they have heard to ensure that the principal topic on Monday morning among the working classes, after Saturday's football match, shall be Sunday's Socialist lecture.

The ILP claimed about 6000 members by 1900, touching a peak of 22,000 and 887 branches in 1909. Joining the ILP, explained the sympathetic observer just quoted, was 'not to pass from Individualism to Socialism—hundreds and thousands of Trade Unionists have done that already—so much as to transcend the region of purely material Socialism, the Socialism that can be defined by formulas and set down in programmes, and to join the spiritual fellowship of Socialism itself, the fellowship that touches and colours, not politics only, but the whole of life.' In other words, the ILP (rather than the SDF for all its theory) was 'the soul of the Labour movement', 'a soul in living touch with the body of Trade Unionism'.[5]

Keir Hardie was out of Parliament between 1895 and 1900, but in those years the ILP extended its influence by securing the election of party members to local councils, school boards and boards of guardians. In the local government of London, however, the socialist lead was taken by members of the Fabian Society. This articulate group of middle-class intellectuals had been formed in 1884. By the turn of the century membership of the London Fabian Society, much the most important Fabian group, was fluctuating about the 800 mark, rising some three-fold by the late-Edwardian years. In 1913, 11 university Fabian Societies and 39 provincial branches also existed. Fabianism, noted one Edwardian critic, 'appeals greatly to school teachers of various grades, and is therefore doubly influential. . . . Civil servants of the lower grades, clerks, journalists, and "advanced" women—people with some knowledge and a bent for serious things, who at the same time have something to gain in their own circumstances—all these are attracted by the Fabian Society's lectures.' Led by Sidney Webb and Bernard Shaw, the Fabians were prolific writers and publicists. Between 1906 and 1914 some fifty Fabian tracts were published, covering a wide range of social and political questions. The Fabian watchword was 'permeation'. The aim was to coax opinion within and without Parliament into acceptance of more-or-less socialist reforms. 'Nobody now conceives Socialism as a destructive insurrection', explained Shaw reassuringly in the 1908 edition of *Fabian Essays in Socialism* (first published in 1889), 'ending, if successful, in millenial absurdities. Membership of the Fabian Society, though it involves an express avowal of Socialism, excites no more comment than membership of the Society of Friends.' Certainly, the Fabians had done much to make socialism 'respectable'. Sidney Webb, and his equally dedicated wife, Beatrice, were eager to contact and entertain leading Liberal and Conservative politicians. It is possible to exaggerate direct Fabian influence upon Edwardian legislation, exaggeration which the Fabians themselves encouraged at the time and in retrospect. The Webbs' campaign for the abolition of the Poor Law, for example, came to nothing in the short term. But Fabian (and especially Webb) ideas were always before the Edwardian public, presented with impressive expertise and frequent reiteration. In practical terms Fabian socialism sought the promotion through both national and local government of a 'national minimum' of living, working, educational and recreational standards. This required extension of the Factory Acts, control of 'sweated' trades, industrial arbitration, an eight-hour working day, a broadening of workmen's rights to compensation for accidents, provision of old-age pensions, Poor Law reform, improved working-class housing, and the development of State education:

> Outside the narrow ranks of the 'political workers' of either party, the millions of citizens are quietly pursuing their ordinary business . . . And if we now inquire what it is that comes into these men's minds when they read their newspapers, when they, in their particular callings, impinge on some corner of public administration, or when, in their own lives, some public disaster comes home to them, there is but one answer. They are not thinking of Liberalism or Conservatism or Socialism. What is in their minds is a burning feeling of shame at the 'failure' of England—shame for the inability of Parliament to get through even its routine business, shame for the absence of grip and resourcefulness of our statesmen, shame for the pompous inefficiency of every branch of our public administration, shame for the slackness of our merchants and traders that transfers our commercial supremacy to the United States, shame for the supineness which looks on unmoved at the continuing degradation of our race by drunkenness and gambling, slum life, and all the horrors of the sweated trades . . . This sense of shame has yet to be transmuted into political action.

In their quest for 'efficiency' the Fabians could thus take a detached view of political parties, Conservative, Liberal, even

Labour. The Webbs, especially, were more interested in good government than in fully democratic government. Beatrice Webb revealingly defined the role of an elected representative as 'a "foolometer" for the expert', passing on information about mass conditions and attitudes. Sidney Webb, himself a civil servant by training, often spoke of 'a discreetly regulated freedom' as the ideal. Such an attitude of superiority ensured that the Fabian Society never sought to transform itself into a popular political party. By the later Edwardian years it had grown remote from the trade unions, the trades councils, and the ILP.

A SOUVENIR FOR MAY DAY 1907

Socialists promised to solve all problems.

George Bernard Shaw and H. G. Wells. Commentators on Edwardian life.

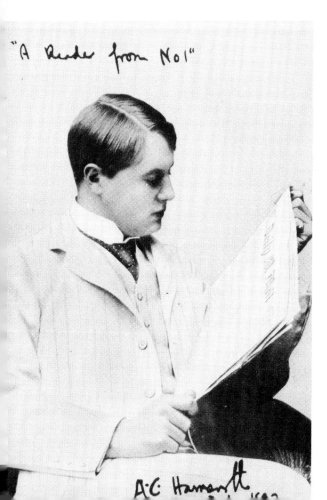

"A Duke from No1"

Alfred Harmsworth. The Daily Mail's *front page was still far from sensational.*

Shepherd's Bush Green 1903. The electric tramcar gave new mobility to the lower-middle and artisan classes.

VII   *Piccadilly Circus 1910. Horse-drawn vehicles compete with motorized traffic.*

A socialist commentator in 1908 noted how its members, living mostly in London, 'in very imperfect touch with the organised workers, taught much, but learnt comparatively little. In spite of its surface appearance of modernity, there is a flavour of the nineties about Fabianism yet.'[6]

Fabian pressure group methods had begun to seem less useful to some socialists because Labour was now an established presence in the House of Commons. In 1900 the Labour Representation Committee had been formed with the aim of uniting the efforts of the ILP, the trade unions, the trades councils, socialist societies and local Labour associations to secure the return of more representatives of the working class to Parliament. Only two LRC candidates were successful at the 1900 general election (Hardie was one); but the Taff Vale Judgment in the next year, meaning that a trade union was liable to pay damages to any amount for losses caused by a strike, greatly increased trade union interest in the new grouping. This damaging legal decision could only be overturned by new legislation. LRC constituent membership therefore grew from 376,000 early in 1901 to 861,000 by 1903. Such increasing support helped to convince the Liberals of the need to avoid splitting the anti-Conservative vote in constituencies with significant numbers of Labour electors. Accordingly, Herbert Gladstone (1854–1930), the Liberal Chief Whip, and Ramsay MacDonald, the LRC secretary, negotiated a secret agreement to enable the LRC to propose most of its candidates at the next general election without Liberal opposition in return for Labour support of Liberals in other constituencies. As a result, 29 Labour candidates were returned in the 1906 general election, only 5 of these against Liberal opposition.

The appearance in the Commons of this new group, which now took the title of the Labour Party, was hailed with enthusiasm by many advanced reformers and with alarm by many conservatives. Yet in the event up to 1914 neither these hopes nor these fears were to approach fulfilment. Only a minority of the 329,000 Labour voters in 1906 were socialists. This constrained Labour in Parliament to act with moderation, knowing its need to retain its non-socialist support. Ramsay MacDonald even emphasized in a Home University Library volume on *The Socialist Movement* (1911) how the Labour Party was in itself 'not socialist', but a federation organized 'for immediate political work'. This need for restraint made it difficult, however, for the new party to project a separate identity. Paradoxically, this difficulty increased after the 1910 general elections when the Liberals depended upon Labour and Irish support for their continuance in office. In the first 1910 general election not a single Labour candidate was returned against official Liberal opposition. Labour's own leaders could not foresee in 1914 how four years of war would undermine Liberalism and give Labour its chance to emerge as the major reform party. H. G. Wells (still in his forties) remarked a few months before the war that he had 'never believed that a Socialist Party could hope to form a Government in this country in my lifetime; I believe it less now than ever.'

We have already seen how about 1912 the socialist ultras were trying to break this stalemate by creating a British Socialist Party. They were demanding the repudiation of all electoral deals with the Liberals, followed by agitation for total socialism without qualification. They wanted, in the words of one revealingly titled book on *The Problem of Parliament* (1909), no more 'watering down of their faith to please their allies'. The trade unions, for their part, also lost confidence in the methods of the Labour Party in Parliament. We shall trace in a later chapter how in the widespread labour unrest of 1911–13 they turned to direct action on a scale never before known. During the 1912 coal strike *Punch* carried a cartoon showing Ramsay MacDonald shut out from the door of the coal conference, 'smarting under a sense of his own futility'.[7]

'The plain fact is', confessed Beatrice Webb in her diary in 1912, 'that Lloyd George and the Radicals have out-trumped the Labour Party.' So it might seem in the aftermath of the sequence of great Liberal social reforms. But was this 'new Liberalism' sufficiently defined and compelling to produce a continuing party political appeal? The problem for the Edwardian Liberal Party was to prove that it could go far down the road of social reform while still retaining its unity and its identity. It had to hold the support of its Gladstonians, preoccupied with individual liberty; it had also to avoid a virtual capitulation to socialism. Though both Gladstonians and socialists were supposedly to the left in politics, there was no hope of Lloyd George, or any other leader, bringing them together in one party, new or old. In 1903 Keir Hardie attacked John Morley (1838–1923), Gladstone's disciple and biographer, for asserting that Liberals, and even Conservatives, had been friends of the people. 'What is the outcome of their joint efforts? Of every two working men who attain the age of sixty-five one dies a pauper.' Hardie admitted that nineteen times out of twenty Liberal and Labour members voted together in the Commons; 'but the twentieth time would always be a case of vital interest to Labour, in which Liberalism would join with Toryism to secure its defeat'. In the same year Hardie publicly urged Lloyd George to leave the Liberals and to lead Labour. But Lloyd George preferred to work within the Liberal Party. Though prepared to promote socialistic measures, he was not attracted to a socialist party. He rightly saw that a reform party needed middle-class support for success. 'That is an asset brought by Liberalism to the work of progress which would never be transferred to a progressive party constructed on purely Labour lines.' Lloyd George's political temperament, moreover, disqualified him from being a socialist pioneer, for he preferred opportunism in reform to consistency. And at least up to 1914 his opportunism served the Liberal Party and the working classes well.

Yet Lloyd George's influence within the Liberal ranks only developed its full strength some time after the massive Liberal election victory of 1906. This triumph had been insecurely based mainly upon negatives and upon the mistakes of the outgoing Conservative Government, as one perceptive post-election critic emphasized:

> The old Liberal spirit animating a whole party is dead. It may seem an odd remark to make just after the late election, but the evidence is abundant and the explanation simple. Domestic reform on a large scale and on individual lines has reached its limit; but to many Liberals . . . reform on socialist lines is abhorrent . . . there is a large party called Liberal, which, through the faults of its opponents and the accidents of time, is successful and has the high spirits of success, but is no more now than it has been for twenty years a party of homogeneous confidence in domestic reform.

Liberal policy in 1906, as defined by Campbell-Bannerman, the party leader, another veteran Gladstonian, still mainly involved a pursuit of abstract liberty negatively conceived as freedom from government interference. Campbell-Bannerman defined 'freedom in all things that affect the life of the people' as freedom of conscience, freedom of trade, trade union freedom, freedom from oppressive privileges and monopolies, and freedom for individual self-improvement. To protect and promote all these freedoms he recommended 'freedom of Parliament', in other words a fully democratic franchise.

But from 1906 the radicals within the Liberal ranks were beginning to press for more positive policies in the name of liberty, policies not hesitating to use government interference where it could enlarge rather than restrict popular freedom. The *Manchester Guardian*, celebrating the centenary of Gladstone's birth in 1909, reassuringly explained to its Liberal readers how there was no real opposition between the new Liberalism and the old. 'It is a further development, not a revolution.' Gladstone had cleared the ground 'for the constructive work which is the special task of our time by the demolition of the old house of bondage'. In the same spirit L. T. Hobhouse's (1864–1929) Home University Library volume on *Liberalism* (1911) found no true opposition 'between liberty as such and control as such', only between 'the control that cramps the personal life and the spiritual order, and the control that is aimed at securing the external and natural conditions of their free and unimpeded development'. The State must ensure that 'the normal man who is not defective in mind or body or will can by useful labour feed, house, and clothe himself and his family. The "right to work" and the right to a "living wage" are just as valid as the rights of person or property.'

A key phrase in radical arguments was 'equality of opportunity'. In *The Crisis of Liberalism* (1909) J. A. Hobson accepted this objective as 'the best opening for an inquiry into the nature of the fuller and more positive liberty to which the Liberalism of the future must devote itself'. He asserted bluntly that, if their party hoped to survive, 'the majority of solid Liberals in the centre, must accept the need for social reform to promote equality of opportunity. The old Liberal cry of 'Peace, retrench-

ment and reform' was now outdated. 'Let it be clearly understood that this policy cannot consist in mere economy, in good
administration at home, peace abroad, in minor legislation for
education, temperance, or even land reform':

> Liberalism is now formally committed to a task which
> certainly involves a new conception of the State in its relation
> to the individual life and to private enterprise. That concep-
> tion is not Socialism, in any accredited meaning of that term,
> though implying a considerable amount of increased public
> ownership and control of industry. From the standpoint
> which best presents its continuity with earlier Liberalism, it
> appears as a fuller appreciation and realization of individual
> liberty contained in the provision of equal opportunities for
> self-development. But to this individual standpoint must be
> joined a just apprehension of the social, viz., the insistence
> that these claims or rights of self-development must be ad-
> justed to the sovereignty of social welfare.[8]

While Edwardian Liberals were uncertain how far to commit
themselves in favour of social reform, Edwardian Conservatives
were equally uncertain how far to commit themselves in opposing it. Paternalism had always been prominent within the
Tory creed, but this had implied acceptance of social and
economic inequality even while ameliorating some of its harsh
effects. Could Conservatives go to the point of accepting or
promoting more systematic policies of social assistance without
seeming to question this underlying inequality, and without
seeming to accept the assertions of socialism? In the eighteen
eighties Lord Randolph Churchill (1849–95), father of Winston,
had tried with his cry 'trust the people' to prove that 'Tory
Democracy' could combine a popular social reform programme
with traditional Conservative acceptance of established institutions. But Churchill's meteoric career soon came to nothing, and
at the turn of the century Conservative high policy was largely
dictated by two members of the Cecil family, Lord Salisbury
(1830–1903) and his nephew A. J. Balfour (1848–1930) who,
while not lacking paternalistic inclinations, were uninterested
in seeking popularity through social reform. Lord Hugh Cecil
(1869–1956), Salisbury's son and a prominent Edwardian

Member of Parliament, emphasized in his 1912 Home University Library volume on *Conservatism* how care for the rights of property must take precedence over social reform and even over paternalism. Conservatism, explained Cecil, had been formulated by Edmund Burke (1729–97) to defend the Monarchy, the Empire and the Established Church against the levelling principles of the French Revolution. There was still, claimed Cecil, 'a taint of Jacobinism in socialist language'. It was 'plain that to take what one man has and to give it to another is unjust, even though the first man be rich and the second man poor'. Conservatives, therefore, condemned such levelling down. But should they also condemn trade union or national insurance legislation designed to level up through the creation of immunities or privileges for special groups? Gladstonian Liberals had revelled in dismantling such privileges, and Edwardian Conservatives were able to score debating points in reminding Liberal Ministers of this fact. 'Do not let us create a privilege for the proletariat, and give a sort of benefit of clergy to trade unions.' Yet could the Conservatives themselves plainly delimit 'the duty of the State in respect to the relief of suffering'? 'A more difficult question', admitted Cecil, 'can scarcely be asked in political discussion.' He was sure that the poor had no *right* to assistance. 'The cruel State that leaves a man to starve does not actively injure him. The only question is, does it withhold from him something to which he is entitled? I find it hard to argue that it does.' The State helped the poor only for reasons of charity, gratitude for services rendered, or expediency:

And on none of the three grounds has Conservatism any reluctance to support the policy. The influence of gratitude and of expediency are felt in common by all those who wish well to their country, and the argument from charity appeals certainly not least to the party that inherits the religious tradition of Toryism. The only aspect in which these matters can bring Conservatism into conflict with other bodies of opinion is if they are made the occasion of establishing the doctrine that every one has a claim on the State in proportion to the services he has rendered to it. If only a claim of gratitude is put forward, no exactness of proportion comes in question at all. But if the claim is one of justice, and be

admitted as such, a foundation is at once laid on which the
fabric of a complete system of State socialism might be
erected.

And State socialism, in Conservative eyes, meant the end of
private property, the fall of traditional institutions, the collapse
of Christianity, and the disruption of morality and family life.

> What is a Socialist? One who has yearnings
> To share equal profits from unequal earnings;
> Be he idler, bungler or both, he is willing
> To fork out his sixpence and pocket your shilling.

Characteristically, the businessmen who were assuming increasing importance within the Conservative ranks laid heavy
emphasis upon the high expense of large-scale State activity.
One such businessman was Stanley Baldwin (1867–1947), still
an obscure back-bencher but destined to become Prime Minister. In the 1914 budget debates Baldwin answered Asquith's
claim that 'as people get clearer views of that which the State
can do' expenditure must grow. Statesmen, urged Baldwin,
should instruct the ignorant people not only in the possible
advantages of State intervention but also 'whether the expenditure the country has to undergo is justified by the benefits.'

So Christian paternalism stimulated by expediency but
restrained by cost-consciousness competed to determine the
Conservative attitude, always set against a background of first
care for property rights and established institutions. This
mixture left much room for unpredictability and even inconsis-
tency, though one voluminous Conservative publicist, W. H.
Mallock (1849–1923), in a book entitled *Social Reform* (1914)
did attempt to offer a theoretical umbrella to cover both
Conservative sympathy and reserve towards the underprivi-
leged. Conservatism, argued Mallock, 'represents the rights of
individual property as justified by their concrete results'. It
recognized that, human nature being imperfect, 'these results
will, from period to period, comprise elements of evil, but it
insists that such evils would be intensified, not remedied, by
destroying the roots of the tree with a view to improving the
general quality of the fruits.' The 'main difficulty' for Conservatives, Mallock conceded, was 'that a variety of very real evils

have been so identified by extremists with demands for impossible remedies, that the necessity for opposing and of exposing the latter gives rise to a diffidence in admitting the full seriousness of the former.' But practising Conservative politicians, such as Lord Hugh Cecil, when they came to propose or oppose specific legislation, did not recognize any need for shelter under theoretical umbrellas. Any scheme for increasing the functions of the State, concluded Cecil, must be judged 'merely on its merits without reference to any general formulae . . . Subject to the counsels of prudence and to a preference for what exists and has been tried over the unknown, Conservatives have no difficulty in welcoming the social activity of the State.'[9]

Politicians

Thus novel political ideas were in the Edwardian air; but they needed strong political personalities to translate them into action. Indeed, Edwardians gave personalities first place. 'Fidelity to persons, rather than to principles, is the spirit of our party life', admitted one leading student of Edwardian politics. 'Formal statements of doctrine' were unimportant 'compared with the utterances and assertions of influential men'. For nearly twenty years the National Union of Conservative Associations had been passing occasional resolutions in favour of protection; yet only when in 1903 a leading politician, Joseph Chamberlain, took up the cry for 'tariff reform' did it become 'practical politics'.[10]

Both the Liberal and Conservative Parties comprised various (not always harmonious) elements, each with its leader or leaders. The Conservatives almost split over tariff reform, Chamberlainites taking one side, free traders the other, with Balfourites somewhere uncomfortably in between. Similarly, during the first years of the new century the Liberals were in danger of separating into Liberal Imperialists (who supported the Boer War), radicals (who opposed it) and Gladstonians (who attempted to hold a middle position). The party chief, Sir Henry Campbell-Bannerman (1836-1908) was a Gladstonian chosen, not because he was expected to give a strong lead, but because of his genial capacity for reconciling differences. 'It is because I have no fault to find with anyone that I am where I am.' 'C-B', the son of a wealthy Glasgow wholesale draper, had served in two Gladstone Cabinets as War Secretary (1886, 1892–5), and became Liberal leader in the Commons in 1899. He narrowly kept the Liberal Party connected, even though divided, during the Boer War, and then from 1903 led it with increasing confidence in defence of free trade against tariff reform. He became Prime Minister in December 1905, firmly resisting pressure from Asquith and the Liberal Imperialists to transfer to the Lords. He soon established his authority both within his Cabinet and in the Commons. But his health began to break up, and he retired and died in April 1908. His view of social reform was narrow (chiefly land reform), and his longer continuance as leader might have begun to undermine that very party unity which he had laboured successfully to create.[11]

His successor as Prime Minister, H. H. Asquith (1852–1928) proved equally successful up to 1914 in holding the Liberal Party and Cabinet together. Though a Liberal Imperialist by origin, he made himself acceptable to Lloyd George and other 'pro-Boer' radicals by his sympathy with the progress of social reform. He had been born the son of a West Riding woollen manufacturer, but his success as a barrister had gained him entrance into the highest society. His second wife, Margot Tennant (1864–1945) was a fellow member with A. J. Balfour, the Conservative leader, of a coterie known in the eighteen eighties and nineties as 'the Souls'. In Edwardian politics both Asquith and Balfour adopted (in Asquith's phrase) 'a guise of lethargy' to reinforce an attitude which, according to circumstances, may be regarded as praiseworthy detachment or blameworthy aloofness. Asquith was never well-known to the public, always stiffly described as 'H. H. Asquith'. But in his own cool, lawyer-like way he was deeply concerned to improve the lot of the poor, striking a balance between the claims of individual freedom and the benefits of State intervention, between what he once described in Gladstonian language as 'the misdirected and paralysing activity of the State' and what in radical language he recognized on the same occasion as 'needs, services which could not be safely left to the unregulated operation of the forces of supply and demand'.

Though not a magnetic figure, Asquith was an able speaker in and out of Parliament, and during his peacetime Premiership he gained an easy predominance in the Commons. He enjoyed a similar ascendancy within his pre-war Cabinet. He let his two brilliant but restless lieutenants, Lloyd George and Churchill, have their heads, winning their respect (and asserting his primacy) by sometimes lending them support at critical moments. 'A sudden curve developed of which I took immediate advantage' was his characteristic description of the adroit solution of one Cabinet clash in 1909. Unfortunately, these Olympian methods did not qualify Asquith to be a successful wartime leader. He seemed to be insufficiently involved after 1914, and as the war dragged on the press began to complain. Again like Balfour (and quite unlike Lloyd George or Churchill), he had never cultivated a newspaper connection. His phrase 'wait and see', first used in a threatening sense during the 1910 budget debates, was now unfairly but damagingly presented as evidence of his preference for apathy and delay. His final downfall as Prime Minister in December 1916 showed party intrigue at its most distasteful, but his replacement by Lloyd George was by then clearly in the national interest. [12]

The wartime and post-war Premiership of David Lloyd George (1863-1945) does not concern us here. Though less than Asquith in intellect, Lloyd George was much better qualified as a war leader. By 1916 he had proved himself both in peace and in war as 'the man who gets things done'. He was the first man springing from the people, the first Nonconformist, and the first Welshman to become Prime Minister. His father, who came from farming stock, had died young, and the future politician was brought up by his maternal uncle, Richard Lloyd, a self-educated shoemaker and co-pastor of a strict Baptist chapel at Criccieth, Caernarvonshire. Lloyd George preached at this chapel as a young man. The local landowners were chiefly English-speaking Anglicans and Conservatives; uncle Lloyd and his nephew were Welsh-speaking Liberals. After gaining local prominence as a solicitor, Lloyd George was elected Member of Parliament for the Caernarvon Burghs in 1890, his seat for fifty-five years. During the eighteen nineties he was very much the Welsh politician, until his courageous opposition to the Boer War won him a national reputation, though at first a widely unpopular one. In 1905 he became President of the Board of Trade, and in 1908 Chancellor of the Exchequer. In both offices he displayed great enterprise and industry, leading the Liberals through a succession of major social reforms. He had been impressed by the failure of Continental Liberalism to modernize its policies:

> The Liberalism of the Continent concerned itself exclusively with mending and perfecting the machinery which was to grind corn for the people. It forgot that the people had to live whilst the process was going on, and people saw their lives pass away without anything being accomplished. British Liberalism has been better advised. It has not abandoned the traditional ambition of the Liberal Party to establish freedom and equality; but side by side with this effort it promotes measures for ameliorating the conditions of life for the multitude.

Lloyd George's acceptance of the Premiership in 1916 permanently split the Liberal Party. His Cabinet comprised fourteen Conservative members but only seven Liberals. Notwithstanding his radicalism, the idea of a coalition with the Conservatives had long attracted him. At the height of the 1910 constitutional crisis he had aired a plan for a coalition to tackle all national problems. He expected solid results from politics, and party differences for their own sake did not interest him. Lloyd George's example as wartime Prime Minister was remembered by Winston Churchill when he was national leader in the Second World War. Both men were orators who could rouse enthusiasm in peace and war, though their styles were very different. Churchill's studied manner was best on anticipated great occasions; Lloyd George was more spontaneous, able at will to inspire almost any audience.

Lloyd George fell from power in 1922, never to take office again. One reason for his fall was his deviousness. This does not mean that he was insincere in his desire for reform in peace or victory in war. But he was very ready to sacrifice individuals for the sake either of his policies or his own advantage. 'He was the flame at which all warmed, and many scorched their hands.' Asquith asserted plainly that, though Lloyd George possessed many qualities fitting him for the first place, 'he lacks the one thing needful—he does not inspire trust.' The 1913 Marconi scandal, when Lloyd George and three other Ministers were alleged to have used privileged knowledge to make profitable share purchases, might have ruined him if Asquith himself had not lent generous support; for Lloyd George had certainly acted disingenuously even though not strictly dishonestly. Asquith and others were equally unsure about the future of Winston Churchill (1874–1965), the second dynamic personality in the pre-war Liberal Cabinet. Asquith liked Churchill, but he did not foresee him reaching the top: 'to speak with the tongue of men and angels, and to spend laborious days and nights in administration, is of no good if a man does not inspire trust.' Nevertheless, much of the distrust inspired by Churchill can now be seen as less damning than that provoked by Lloyd George. Churchill was never devious. Unlike Lloyd George, he had many friends. He was distrusted mainly for what was regarded as his instability. Lloyd George himself more than once expressed this view. 'A brilliant fellow without judgment which is adequate to his fiery impulse. His steering gear is too weak for his horsepower.' Churchill had been dogged by this opinion since his first entry into the Commons in 1900. He was welcomed there as a reminder of his dead father, Lord Randolph Churchill. Lord Randolph had risen rapidly to the Chancellorship of the Exchequer in the eighteen eighties, only to shatter his brilliant career by an impatient resignation. In 1904 young Churchill's support for free trade led him to cross the floor of the Commons from the Conservative to the Liberal benches. This move could be seen either as attachment to principle or as a symptom of recklessness inherited from his father. Churchill certainly matched his father in ambition. A newspaperman, hearing him speak at the 1900 general election, divined that he would 'never be content to be a backbencher'. He was always full of schemes, some valuable, some wild, which his colleagues were expected to sift. But, unlike Lord Randolph, Winston Churchill was capable of learning from experience. In Asquith's Cabinet he was successively President of the Board of Trade (1908), Home Secretary (1910), and First Lord of the Admiralty (1911–15). At the Board of Trade he showed that he could be constructive as well as dashing. He defined the 'new

Liberalism' as 'the cause of the left-out millions'. Like Lloyd George he refused to be constricted by political theory:

> There is no necessity tonight to plunge into a discussion of the philosophical divergencies between Socialism and Liberalism. It is not possible to draw a hard-and-fast line between individualism and collectivism. You cannot draw it either in theory or in practice. That is where the Socialist makes a mistake. Let us not imitate that mistake. No man can be a collectivist alone or an individualist alone. He must be both an individualist and a collectivist.

At the Admiralty Churchill supervised the growth of the fleet to meet German naval competition. Trained as a soldier, he was fascinated by war, an interest which (especially in the nineteen thirties) caused him to be dubbed a warmonger. But in reality Churchill was horrified as well as fascinated by conflict. 'Much as war attracts me and fascinates my mind with its tremendous situations—I feel more deeply every year . . . what vile and wicked folly and barbarism it all is.' In 1915 he promoted the Dardanelles campaign, but it was not pursued with sufficient vigour and resources, and Churchill was removed from the Admiralty as a scapegoat. This and later adversity in his own career were tempering his character in preparation for his 'finest hour' in 1940. Even in these early years Churchill sensed that he had been chosen for some great role. 'Winston may in your eyes and in those with whom he has to work have faults', Mrs Churchill told Asquith in 1915, 'but he has the supreme quality . . . the power, the imagination, the deadliness, to fight Germany.'[14]

After the war Churchill was to return to the Conservative Party. Perhaps he had always remained a Tory radical, like his father, even while a leading member of the Liberal Party. Certainly he was never a socialist. 'Socialism wants to pull down wealth, Liberalism seeks to raise up poverty.' Keir Hardie, who had looked hopefully upon Lloyd George, was never attracted by what he on one occasion called Churchill's 'shameless prevarication'. James Keir Hardie (1856–1915), the founding father of the Independent Labour Party, was the best-known Edwardian socialist. Of illegitimate birth, he began work as a

Lanarkshire miner, was dismissed as an agitator, and became a miners' trade union leader. He first entered Parliament in 1892, wearing a cloth cap to emphasize the social significance of his election. He was not a deep socialist thinker, being happy, for example, to remind the founding ILP conference in 1893 how 'there were not in that meeting any of the great ones nor the learned ones amongst the masses of men and therein lay the hope of the Labour movement'. Nor was he a more than competent speaker and journalist. Yet he came to enjoy in his own lifetime a unique intensity of respect within the Labour movement, a movement often highly critical of its leaders. Hardie won this position by his single-mindedness, and by his patent and unbounded faith in the common people. He emphasized this faith in a private letter of 1912 to Bernard Shaw:

> I refuse to admit that there is any distinction whatever to be drawn either in the matter of brain power, or of intuition, between the different sections or classes into which society is divided. Education does not supply the qualities to which I am now referring, and what is called the Statesman's mind which is occasionally found in individuals in the middle and upper classes, like the late Gladstone and Salisbury, is just as common among individuals of the working class as any other.

Hardie's unique standing was much helped by his bearded patriarchal appearance, which made him seem much older than his years. He was not sixty when he died, yet for long he had been known as the 'grand old man of Labour'. Implicit in this role, however, was an admission that by Edwardian times he no longer stood quite at the heart of Labour politics. Labour in Parliament now needed the guidance of an administrator: Hardie was always in spirit a pioneer. 'He is the only man who could have created the Labour Party', explained one acute Liberal journalist in 1908, 'for concentration and intensity are the creative impulses. But he is almost the only man in the party who is not fitted to lead it.' Hardie did act as leader during 1906–8, but he himself realized his disqualifications. 'Nature never intended me to occupy an official position.' He had stood on his own in the Commons in the nineties, and though surrounded by thirty or more colleagues after 1906 he remained a 'loner' by temperament. At times of despondency, indeed, he tended to dismiss all Parliamentary activity and leadership as irrelevant, a temptation to which leaders of earlier extra-Parliamentary working-class movements (such as Chartism) had tended futilely to succumb. As late as 1912 Hardie's attitude towards Parliament was still that of a movement politician, as he revealed to Shaw:

> You seem to assume that the Statesman, like the poet and especially the Dramatist, possesses some special faculty which the working class cannot develop. That I dispute altogether. When did you ever know of a Statesman who ever originated any great law . . . You know as well as I do that it is the invariable rule in politics to wait until agitation has ripened some particular question and the task of the Statesman then consists in getting the Government draftsmen to embody the proposed reform in a Bill.

When asked in 1914 what he would do if appointed dictator Hardie replied half-seriously that he would begin by abolishing the House of Commons; and 'having disposed of these obstructives, I would appoint a commission of three—two of them deaf and dumb—with imperative instructions to convert our native land into the paradise Nature intended it to be'.[15]

Another Scotsman, also of illegitimate birth, came to provide the Edwardian Labour Party with the type of leadership which Hardie could not offer. This was James Ramsay MacDonald (1866–1937). Springing from Highland farming stock, MacDonald first earned his living by journalism. Then in 1896 he married an upper-middle class wife, whose means gave him financial independence and whose strong social conscience and personality reinforced his own. MacDonald developed an evolutionary version of socialism, which he expounded at length in speech and writing during the Edwardian years. Yet it always ran near to vagueness. By 1912, indeed, Beatrice Webb was claiming that MacDonald had 'ceased to be a socialist'. From an organizational standpoint, however, he was making an invaluable contribution to Labour progress. Entering Parliament in 1900, he served as Secretary of the Labour Representation Committee until 1912, Chairman of the ILP

1906–9, and Chairman of the Parliamentary Labour Party 1911–14. Beatrice Webb observed how 'his romantic figure, charming voice and clever dialectic' were 'more than a match for all those underbred and under-trained workmen who surround him on the platform and face him in the audience . . . So far as he has any politics he still believes in the right of the middle and professional class to do the work of government. He does not believe his own mates are capable of it.' We may contrast this description of MacDonald's attitude to the working class with the attitude of Keir Hardie. Lytton Strachey's verdict after meeting MacDonald in 1916 was characteristically incisive—'one of Nature's darlings, whom at the last moment she'd suddenly turned against, dashing a little fatuity into all her gifts.' MacDonald was to become Labour Prime Minister in 1924 and again 1929–31, before 'betraying' his party during the 1931 economic crisis. His shortcomings in these later years can be related back to his insecure social origins and to the elusiveness of his socialist faith.[16]

After Labour's 1906 election success A. J. Balfour (1848–1930), the Conservative leader, wondered with characteristic literary flourish 'what perturbations this new planet, suddenly introduced into our political heavens, will cause in existing orbits'. Balfour had succeeded his uncle, Lord Salisbury, as Premier in 1902. He was brilliant as well as high-born, but he proved unable to use his ability to strengthen his party leadership. He was a keen amateur philosopher, the author of *A Defence of Philosophic Doubt* (1879). When convinced about a course of action he could be tenacious, as in his advocacy of the 1902 Education Act. But where his refined intellect left him partly sympathetic to both sides of an argument, as in the tariff reform controversy which engulfed his Ministry in 1903, he was unable to give a lead:

I'm not for Free Trade, and I'm not for Protection.
I approve of them both, and to both have objection.

He was similarly uncertain in his attitude towards social reform. Beatrice Webb found him in 1904 'honestly concerned about the alleged degeneracy of the race', inclined to 'flirt with new proposals'. But where, he asked, could Conservatives find

Bleriot crossing the channel.

VIII

IX   *Public-house arrests during the 1912 London Dock Strike.*
       Pubs were the clubrooms of the workers.

Railway Strike 1911. Soldiers escorting a traction-engine.

the money to finance large schemes? 'They could not raise revenue out of the kind of taxes put on by Lloyd George.' Mrs Webb decided that Balfour carried the virtue of open-mindedness to excess. 'His opinions shift uneasily from side to side; the one permanent bias being in favour of personal refinement of thought and feeling.' Lloyd George dismissed him as 'just like the scent on a pocket handkerchief'. Balfour was certainly a wit ('history never repeats itself: historians repeat each other'), knowledgeable about music, and enthusiastic about tennis even in old age. His personal attractions made him a leading figure in Edwardian country-house life, an engaging host, 'an incomparable guest'. But to the public at large he seemed less attractive. 'He has no comprehension of the habits or thoughts of his countrymen', remarked a colleague, 'and no idea of how things strike them.' He showed little understanding even of the new businessmen who were gradually taking control of the Conservative Party in the constituencies from the aristocracy and gentry. In 1891 he condescendingly described his successor as Irish Chief Secretary, a worsted manufacturer, as 'that *rara avis*, a successful manufacturer who is fit for something besides manufacturing'. This lack of sympathy with the business middle class contributed to his fall as party leader in 1911.[17]

Balfour's successor, Andrew Bonar Law (1858–1923), a Glasgow iron merchant, was a man of very different origins and temperament. 'I hate big houses, and the rich food, and the chatter', he exclaimed soon after his appointment. But this dislike did not mean that he felt any closer than Balfour to the people. He was tepid towards social reform, feeling that it was an unprofitable line for his party; if the electors wanted it they would not vote Conservative. Law always put such party considerations in first place. As leader he deliberately developed a vituperative 'new style' (in Asquith's phrase) of speaking in Parliament, accusing the Liberals among other things of selling their convictions. 'Revolutionary Governments are always corrupt Governments.' Law's purpose in thus lowering the tone of debate was simply to rouse party loyalty. This he achieved, but at the price of adding to the inflammatory political atmosphere of the time. He had long been an advocate of tariff reform, yet in 1913 he modified his position, not because of any change of conviction but because he found this necessary to maintain party unity. On the death of Joseph Chamberlain in the next year he still claimed to be a 'hero-worshipper' of the tariff reform leader. But Chamberlain himself seems to have detected Law's limitations beneath his protestations of support, once remarking that 'he is no Tariff Reformer'. Chamberlain meant by this that Law was merely interested in trade figures rather than in 'a national and imperial policy'. Law, in short, lacked vision, and lacking vision he could not mould events. 'He is always waiting', noted Lloyd George penetratingly, 'for a course which was inevitable.' Merely to meet the calls of party leadership stretched Law to his limit in the troubled period from 1911–14, when the interest and even the safety of the nation would have greatly benefited from a true statesman as leader of the Conservative Opposition.[18]

Joseph Chamberlain (1836–1914) had been the most forceful personality in government at the opening of the Edwardian era. A radical turned Liberal Unionist, he believed (as we have seen) in 'strong government'. Since his appointment as Colonial Secretary in 1895 he had also become the leading exponent of the 'Imperial idea'. By 1903 he had decided that both Imperial unity and democratic progress at home required a return to some degree of protection. Failing to carry Balfour's Cabinet with him, he resigned office to embark upon a campaign of speech-making in favour of 'tariff reform'. He had begun his political career as a maker of opinion in the country, and he now deliberately chose to revert to this role. He centred his campaign in Birmingham, which he had represented in Parliament since 1876, and where his Unitarian family had become politically predominant. After making a fortune as a screw manufacturer, Chamberlain had retired from business to serve as Mayor of the city 1873–6. He was probably the most successful civic head ever seen in Britain. Birmingham was, in his own words, 'parked, paved, assized, marketed, gas-and-watered and *improved*—all as the result of three years' active work.' After 1876 he set out as a Liberal Member of Parliament to apply Birmingham methods in national politics. In 1880 he became President of the Board of Trade under Gladstone. Five years later he propounded an 'unauthorized programme' for the Liberal Party. This included manhood suffrage, payment of

Members of Parliament, and moderate graduated taxation through death and house duties, plus taxation of unearned increment. But Gladstone preferred Home Rule. Chamberlain refused to go further than a form of federalism, 'Home-Rule-all-round'. He helped to lead the Liberal Unionist Party, and finally in 1895 he entered into coalition with the Conservatives. The epithet 'Judas' was hurled at him from the Gladstonian ranks, even though it was Gladstone, not Chamberlain, who had repudiated established party policy. In refusing to follow Gladstone, Chamberlain consciously sacrificed the almost certain succession to the Liberal leadership. Not surprisingly, he developed an increasingly hard exterior, an eyeglass glinting in his right eye, an orchid nearly always in his buttonhole. Private as well as public adversity had moulded him, two of his wives dying in childbirth. One was the mother of Austen Chamberlain (1863–1937), destined to narrowly miss becoming Prime Minister, the other the mother of Neville Chamberlain (1869–1940), the Prime Minister of 'Munich'. Time always seemed to be working against Chamberlain. He was almost sixty before he gained a clear field for his talents. There may have been a touch of envy in his congratulations to Winston Churchill's mother on her son's first entry into Parliament: 'He has so much ability that he must succeed—and he is so young that he can afford not to hurry too much.' Balfour was said to have remarked that 'wanting to go too fast is Chamberlain's peculiarity'. Certainly, it was Chamberlain, in and out of office, at least as much as Balfour, the Prime Minister, who set the pace of British politics during the very first years of the twentieth century.[19]

CHAPTER FOUR

The Attack upon Free Trade

Background

Chamberlain's campaign for 'tariff reform' rested upon a pessimistic interpretation of Britain's existing and future position inside the international economy of the early twentieth century. Within this international system Britain was the only major power still committed to full free trade, to a policy of imposing tariffs only for revenue purposes, never for economic protection or preference. Some sixty years earlier free trade had become the great article of Victorian commercial faith. Between the eighteen twenties and eighteen sixties all protective duties had been steadily reduced and removed. The most dramatic abolition had been repeal of the Corn Laws in 1846, after over seven years of agitation conducted by the Anti-Corn Law League under Richard Cobden (1804–65), the great 'apostle of free trade'. Victorian (and Edwardian) public opinion believed that repeal of the Corn Laws had produced 'cheap bread' after 1846, but this was an exaggeration. Because of a huge expansion of trade many mid-Victorians enjoyed greater prosperity, and this prosperity gave them the impression that bread was cheaper than before. The great increase in trade was a product of the many other tariff abolitions enacted about the time of Corn Law repeal. For right reasons and wrong, the Victorians came to support free trade with an almost religious intensity of belief. 'Free Trade is a good, like virtue, holiness and righteousness, to be loved, admired, honoured and stead-fastly adopted, for its own sake, though all the rest of the world should love restrictions and prohibitions, which are of themselves evils.' Into Edwardian times this deep conviction continued to be widely accepted as beyond question, until in 1903 Chamberlain boldly publicized his doubts.[1]

In Cobden's day Britain had been 'the workshop of the world', but by the turn of the century she was being rivalled and overtaken by the United States and by Germany. The annual American growth rate from 1870 to 1913 was 4.3 per cent, the German rate was 2.9 per cent, the British 2.2 per cent. During the eighteen nineties both the United States and Germany passed Britain in steel production. By 1910–13

THE UNCOMMERCIAL TRAVELLER

MR. PUNCH: 'Now, Mr. Bull, wake up! You'll have to keep your eye on that chap. He's always at it, speaks their languages, and knows their money.'
JOHN BULL: 'Pooh! My goods are better than his!'
MR. PUNCH: 'I daresay—but you've got to make them understand it!'

Britain was making only just over 10 per cent of world steel, whereas Germany was producing twice and the United States four times as much. As the twentieth century opened, American competition, present and prospective, power political as well as economic, was a recurrent theme in the Edwardian press. Many American innovations in everyday notice, such as the typewriter and the gramophone, had invaded the British market, heralded by strident advertising. More seriously, much of the new machinery used or (even worse) not used by British industry was foreign-made in America or Europe. German progress was regarded as still more alarming than American, for the 'Yankees' could always be consolingly accepted as 'cousins' whereas the Germans were undoubted 'foreigners'. A book called *Made in Germany* (1896) sounded the alarm about the threat to British markets presented by a more thrustful and technically progressive rival. A 1901 *Punch* cartoon entitled 'The Uncommercial Traveller' appreciated the threat posed by German pushfulness, but was apparently still certain of Britain's technical superiority.

Germany now led in metals technology, in mining techno-logy, in the important new field of electrical engineering, and in many parts of the rapidly expanding chemical industry. The British Government was to find in 1914 that all the khaki dye used for British army uniforms came from Stuttgart. Admittedly, accounts of foreign advance were at times exaggerated, as the *Daily Telegraph* emphasized in 1901. 'Every incident of Ameri-can or German progress is shown in the limelight, while the whole vast and steady progress of British trade is left in the shade . . . What is gone is our monopoly. What is not gone is our supremacy.' Britain was still the world's leading trading nation, with twice the commerce of the Americans and one-and-a-half times that of the Germans. Britain, moreover, was successfully shifting some of her effort from manufacturing to profitable 'invisible' services such as shipping, banking and insurance. London in Edwardian times was more than ever the capital of world finance, 'the conductor of the orchestra' of world payments, that pattern of investment, borrowing and lending essential to the international economy. British overseas investment, and the income therefrom, reached unprecedented levels. Between 1870 and 1914 capital exports totalled some

£3.5 million. Nothing comparable in terms of proportion of resources invested has been undertaken by any power since. Between 1905 and 1914 an average of over 7.5 per cent of net national income was being placed abroad. By 1907 net annual investment income from overseas was estimated at some £120 million.[3]

But some of this investment should have stayed at home. Britain's manufacturing competitiveness was declining in important part because of a failure to invest more capital in modernization and development. *The Times*, for example, published in 1912 a long article criticizing 'obsolete engineering works' which still used Victorian methods and machinery. 'Such people often complain about unfair competition, but if any suggestion is made to them about improvements they excuse themselves in busy times by saying that they cannot afford to stop any part of their works for alterations, and in slack times they say they have no money to spend on new ideas.' Another *Times* article in the same year on 'The Coming of the Cheap Car' warned of British failure to match foreign efforts in this economically and socially important field: 'much less would be heard of Juggernauts and road-hogs in the Press and elsewhere if motoring became more democratic . . . If a valuable market is not to a large extent to be lost at the outset, the British manufacturer will have to set himself seriously to work to produce small cars as good and as cheap as those now imported from abroad.' Fortunately, this challenge was to be accepted by William Morris (1877–1963), later Lord Nuffield. His Morris Oxford car was announced at the 1912 motor show though it had hardly gone into mass production when the 1914 war broke out.[4]

Morris was a self-made engineer on the Victorian model, but too many Edwardian industrialists were the sons and grandsons of enterprising Victorians who preferred enjoyment to employment. Operatives, too, now had other interests which could be blamed for diminishing their interest in work:

The once enterprising manufacturer has grown slack, he has let the business take care of itself, while he is shooting grouse or yachting in the Mediterranean. That is *his* business. The once unequalled workman has adopted the motto: 'Get as much and do as little as possible'; *his* business is football or betting. Each blames the other.

Such was the gloomy conclusion of a book on *Industrial Effi-ciency, a Comparative Study of Industrial Life in England, Germany and America* (1909). The 1907 census of production revealed that the value added to the cost of materials by a British worker in specified industries averaged £100: the American average was nearly £500, a measure of the comparative levels of productivity in the two economies. Yet this malaise in parts of Edwardian industry was peculiarly of its time. Renewed industrial progress made under the stimulus of wartime and post-war pressures after 1914 was to show how there was nothing inevitable or irreversible about the pre-war slackening of enterprise.[5]

Some Edwardian industries and groups of industries con-tinued to prosper, but too few of these were new activities with great fresh export potential. Edwardian Britain was over-committed to coal mining, iron and steel manufacture and textile production. In 1907 these accounted for 46 per cent of net industrial output and 70 per cent of all exports. These industries were unenterprising both in their products and in their choice of markets. By 1913 two-thirds of British exports were going to primary-producing countries. Cotton exports boomed (5,365 million yards of piece goods in 1901, 7,075 million yards in 1913), but Lancashire had not responded to increasing foreign competition and tariffs by improving its goods or by cutting costs. Instead it had continued its old methods and simply switched to easier markets in India, the Far East and the Empire. In 1913 less than one-third of British steel output was made by the most modern process, and iron and steel exports relied heavily upon the Empire and the undeveloped world. Coal exports rose from under 42 million tons in 1901 to well over 73 million tons in 1913. But coal was a wasting asset, and already beginning to feel the competition of electricity and oil. Moreover, productivity in the pits was de-clining as the easier seams were worked out. Yet Britain lagged behind Germany and the United States in the introduction of cutting machinery. British coal did still power much of the world's carrying trade. Over one-third of world tonnage sailed under the British flag in 1911, four times the German figure and fourteen times the American.[6]

It was inevitable that Britain should lose some of the great lead gained as the pioneering industrial country. Had she lost more than was inevitable? Tariff reformers said that she had, and that the fault lay with free trade. Chamberlain and his followers, believing in 'strong government', wanted British Government intervention to counter the effects of foreign government intervention in trade. 'The swing of the pendulum from individualism and a "let alone" policy to governmental interference in matters of trade and industry, and involving a change of colonial policy, is an accomplished fact . . . How can the Government interpose to secure fuller employment for the people except by assuming a protective and national policy?' So argued a book on *Perils to British Trade, How to Avert Them* (1895). Yet tariff reform never won the support of leading Edwardian socialists, keen though they were for state intervention in other spheres. Ramsay MacDonald dismissed Chamberlain's campaign as a capitalist diversion. 'We stand for Free Trade not because we think Free Trade will solve any questions, but because we are not going to allow gentlemen interested in the land and in monopoly of capital to mislead us from the cures we intend to apply to the unemployed problem.' The Fabians characteristically recommended national efficiency rather than protection. 'All we have to do is to meet foreign competition by improving our methods . . . if we are then surpassed in economy of production for any reason whatever, we can surrender the industry without regret . . . at the same time entering on a higher industry to get the wherewithal to pay for our imports.'[7]

Edwardian businessmen remained divided as to whether Government should intervene to control the course of trade through tariffs. But they were increasingly sure of the need to control trade through private arrangements. Amalgamations, associations, 'understandings' and price fixing were spreading through many branches of Edwardian industry and distribution. Supporters of these moves usually claimed that unlimited competition had so reduced profits and discouraged investment and rationalization as to work ultimately even against the interests of consumers. The *Daily Mail* attacked the 'soap trust' in 1906 as a would-be profiteering monopoly (selling 1 lb bars

of soap at 15 oz); but Lever Brothers, the leading soap manufacturers, successfully sued for heavy damages. Expert Edwardian economic opinion agreed that (whatever might be the
case in the United States or on the Continent within tariff
barriers) in Britain combinations and arrangements might
improve efficiency without greatly raising charges, so long as
free trade conditions operated. Any attempt at violent price
increases would, under free trade, always be likely to be met by
fresh competition. 'To compete efficiently and combine ade-
quately is the mark of industrialism in nations that are both
progressive and sympathetic. Of the two forces in Western
civilization, it is combination which tends to come too late, and
competition which tends to last too long.'[8]

The Campaign

Nevertheless, some Edwardian industrialists did support
tariff reform in the hope that tariffs plus trade combinations
would afford an easy way of increasing prices and profits. Theirs
was not support which Chamberlain cared to publicize. He
launched his campaign on a lofty note, seeking'Imperial and
economic progress for the benefit not merely of a handful of
industrialists but of all citizens of the Empire. His was the first
full-scale challenge to the supremacy of free trade, but his
arguments were not in themselves entirely new. Gladstone had
removed the last fiscal barriers in the fifties and sixties, but by
the late seventies calls for protection, or at least Imperial
preference, were being made, stimulated by the 'great depression' in trade and by the steady extension of European and
American tariff walls. Cobden had fervently hoped that other
states would gradually follow Britain's free trade example. As
they had refused to do so, some British businessmen and politicians began to argue that the whole case for free trade had
collapsed since unilateral free trade was not Cobden's policy.
'Fair trade', a policy of retaliation against foreigners who insisted on imposing tariffs, became a cry of the eighties. The
National Fair Trade League was formed in 1881 and lasted ten
years. Yet it always lacked a leader of the calibre of a Cobden or
a Chamberlain. It achieved some impact upon public opinion
and some influence within the Conservative ranks, but it failed

to develop further. Chamberlain himself vigorously opposed the fair traders at this time, refusing in 1887 to accept the chairmanship of the Birmingham Chamber of Commerce because of its protectionist leanings.[9]

Nevertheless, the growing feeling in Birmingham in favour of some fiscal defence for its metal trades had begun to impress him. Even more, the idea of closer Imperial union had begun to fire his imagination, and in 1895 he became Colonial Secretary. A year later he called for a zollverein, or system of Empire free trade. The self-governing colonies were not willing, however, to expose their infant industries to British competition and to act purely as suppliers of primary products for the mother country. Chamberlain therefore shifted his ground towards some form of Imperial preference, encouraging trade within the Empire through each member-state taxing foreign products more heavily than their Empire-produced equivalents. This policy was attractive to the self-governing colonies. In 1897 Canada announced a grant of unilateral preference on imports from the United Kingdom. All the other self-governing colonies were eager to grant preferences if Britain would abandon free trade and give them preferences in return. The Boer War delayed Chamberlain's plans, but foreign hostility during its course made him still more anxious to foster Imperial unity. To his deep regret a corn registration duty, imposed in 1902 to meet the cost of the war, was abandoned in the 1903 budget. He had hoped that through its remission to Empire countries a beginning might have been made towards a system of Imperial preference:

We expect the Colonies to do more for us . . . what can we do for them? They are protectionist; we cannot help that; and while we stick rigidly to Free Trade, we have nothing to give them. Now I believe in Free Trade—just as I believe in peace. We believe in the blessings of peace just as much, and for the same reasons, as the Little-Englanders. The difference is that we say sometimes we must go to war, or else our enemies would take away all we have. I should not pretend that a protective tariff would do us any good; only I do say that by Free Trade we are giving up a weapon that we want in order to hit back at our enemies.

In this still tentative language Chamberlain discussed his emerging ideas with his election agent in April 1903. 'For myself I have never been able to get over the difficulty that in fact the protectionist countries like America have prospered under protection. They ought not—but they do.'

DON'T WORRY YOURSELF
Over the puzzle whether
Mr. Balfour is a Chamberlainite
or
Mr. Chamberlain a Balfourite,

It's enough for you that they are both Linked Together

AGAINST FREE TRADE.

Don't forget that whether the Tory candidate calls himself a Balfourite or a Chamberlainite

THE ONLY WAY
to support Free Trade and no Protective Taxes on Food is to

VOTE LIBERAL.

A liberal poster 1906.

On 15th May 1903 in Birmingham Town Hall Chamberlain duly published his opinions. His ringing language was now much less tentative though still generalized:

> The Empire is in its infancy. Now is the time when we can mould that Empire . . . I hear it stated again and again by . . . Little Englanders . . . that our trade with our colonies is less than our trade with foreign countries, and therefore it appears to be their opinion that we should do everything in our power to cultivate that trade with foreigners, and that we can safely disregard the trade with our children . . . I say it is the business of British statesmen to do everything they can, even at some present sacrifice, to keep the trade of the colonies with Great Britian; to increase that trade, to promote it, even if in doing so we lessen somewhat the trade with our foreign competitors. Are we doing everything at the present time to direct the patriotic movement not only here, but through all the colonies, in the right channel? Are we, in fact, by our legislation, by our action, making for union, or are we drifting to separation? That is a critical issue. In my opinion, the germs of a Federal Union that will make the British Empire powerful and influential for good beyond the dreams of any one now living are in the soil; but it is a tender and delicate plant, and requires careful handling.

The Canadians, continued Chamberlain, had offered further tariff preference in return for the imposition of preference in their favour. Adherence to rigid free trade dogma had compelled the British Government to refuse to respond. 'We cannot make any difference between those who treat us well and those who treat us badly.' Chamberlain asked the British people to consider whether free trade was now the right policy. 'You have an opportunity; you will never have it again.'

The response to Chamberlain's speech was immediate and intense, much stronger than Chamberlain himself had expected. His aim had been only to open public discussion with the hope that this would ultimately lead the Government to adopt tariff reform as its official policy at the next general election in one or two years' time. Instead, the tariff question suddenly became the question of the moment, with the Cabinet under strong pressure to commit itself at once either for or against free trade. Free traders were outraged at Chamberlain's move, Imperialists enthusiastic. Throughout the summer it remained uncertain whether tariff reform would or would not be adopted as official Conservative Government policy. The Cabinet was split between Chamberlainites, free traders, and followers of Balfour, the Prime Minister, who strove hard to hold his Government and party together by not clearly committing himself. At heart he seems to have genuinely favoured a middle position, agreeing with the free traders' dislike of food taxes but wanting some power of fiscal 'retaliation' against foreigners. Despite prolonged manoeuvring Balfour ultimately failed to keep his Cabinet together, Chamberlain resigning on 14th September. He emphasized, however, that he was not going into opposition; he was simply taking the issue to the country, preferably as a national cause above party politics. From October to December in launching this campaign of fiscal education he delivered a succession of major speeches in big industrial centres. 'I do not regard this as a party meeting', he exclaimed in his first speech at Glasgow on 6th October, 'I am no longer a party leader.' He regretted that the question could not be decided on its merits rather than as one issue among many party cries at a general election.

Chamberlain's May speech had emphasized the need for tariff reform to unite the Empire, and this was his high theme. But he was well aware of the need to appeal to the pockets and stomachs of the middle and working classes at least as much as to their hearts. His autumn speeches were therefore full of deliberate appeals *ad hominem* and *ad locum*. All major British industries, argued Chamberlain, were suffering severely or were likely eventually to suffer severely from foreign competition. 'Agriculture, the greatest of all trades and industries, has been practically destroyed . . . Sugar has gone, silk has gone, iron is threatened, wool is threatened, the turn of cotton will come . . . At the present moment these industries and the working men who depend on them are like sheep in the field.' 'What I have endeavoured to do', he told a Birmingham meeting in November, 'is to deal in each place I have visited with some of the industries with which the people are familiar.' He then proceeded to do this for Birmingham industry, demonstrating its need for preference in Empire markets. He mentioned particularly the jewellery trade. £170,000 worth more of foreign jewellery had been imported into the country in 1902 than British jewellers had sold over tariff barriers to foreigners. The colonies were still buying twice as much British as foreign jewellery, but outsiders would soon invade the Empire market if it was not defended. And what applied to jewellery also applied to nut-and-bolt making, needle manufacture, pearl button making, the gun trade, the cycle trade, and to other Midland occupations.

At Glasgow Chamberlain admitted plainly that it would be impossible to give colonial preferences without imposing some food taxes. To grant preferences on colonial raw materials would raise British manufacturing costs. 'Therefore, if you wish to have preference, if you desire to gain this increase, if you wish to prevent separation, you must put a tax on food.' But, continued Chamberlain, this could be so contrived as not to add anything to the cost of living. He proposed a duty of not more than 2s. a quarter on foreign corn, a similar duty on foreign flour, a 5 per cent duty on foreign meat and dairy produce (except bacon), and an average duty of 10 per cent on foreign manufactured goods. Colonial products were to be exempt from all these duties. To compensate for the effects of these impositions on the cost of living he proposed to reduce the existing revenue duty on tea by three-quarters, the sugar duty by half, with reductions also in the coffee and cocoa duties. The consequence for the average working-class weekly budget would be that 'the agricultural labourer would be half a farthing per week to the better, and the artisan would be exactly in the same position as at present.' In return for these preferences the colonies would lower their tariffs in favour of British manufactured goods. This, concluded Chamberlain, would increase Empire trade by £26 million and give new employment to 166,000 workers. He promised also that the revenue collected from the tariffs imposed on foreign products would be enough to finance old-age pensions and other social reforms.[10]

To publicize his ideas and to organize support Chamberlain formed in June 1903 a Birmingham Tariff Committee, financed by local businessmen. This was followed in July by the creation of the Tariff Reform League, a national body with headquarters in London but soon with hundreds of branches throughout the country. Its aim was to conduct a campaign of agitation and publicity for fiscal preference just as sixty years earlier the Anti-Corn Law League had campaigned for free trade. It received large financial backing from leaders of the iron and steel, engineering and electrical industries which were all facing strong foreign competition. The nature of this support did, indeed, soon begin to give Tariff Reform League propaganda more of a purely protectionist emphasis than Chamberlain desired, overshadowing his Imperial vision. Both the Birmingham committee and the League began to pour out leaflets and pamphlets by the million, organizing meetings, publishing verses and songs, and even producing pageants and plays.

> Our Joe is straight and square, and he's always played us fair
>   When we've trusted him with jobs before,
> So we'll help him all we can, and we'll find that Joey's plan
>   Is the saving of the John Bull Store.

So ran one music-hall jingle.

Press support was secured from *The Times* and the *Daily Telegraph* among the serious dailies, and from the *Daily Express* and (after some early criticism of 'stomach taxes') from the *Daily Mail* among the popular papers. Arthur Pearson (1866–1921), the proprietor of the *Daily Express*, became chairman of the executive committee of the Tariff Reform League. Day after day the *Express* repeated the slogan 'tariff reform means work for all'. Chamberlain's autumn speeches were widely noticed in all newspapers, and much noise was made by his supporters. Yet by the end of 1903 it was becoming clear that, though converts had been won, tariff reform was not going to win a quick victory. It was also clear that it could not escape becoming a party political question. The Liberals had remained firmly attached to free trade, enthusiastic indeed at the chance which Chamberlain's proposals had given them to restore party unity. Asquith rushed into his wife's room with a newspaper report of Chamberlain's May speech exclaiming 'Now we've got them on the run.' Chamberlain secured the support of his own Liberal Unionist Party; but the Conservatives remained divided, their free trade wing sharply hostile to him. 'This reckless criminal escapade of Joe's', exclaimed Campbell-Bannerman, the Liberal leader, delightedly, 'is the great event of our time. It is playing old Harry with all party relations . . . We are in for a great time.'

By the end of the year Chamberlain realized that he would have to plan for a long campaign, as indeed he had intended before the excited reaction to his May speech had forced the pace. To support these continuing efforts he therefore formed at the end of 1903 a Tariff Commission, a body of experts and representatives of business assembled to collect the detailed information upon which a full tariff programme must be based. Between 1904 and 1909 it issued reports on the iron and steel, cotton, wool, hosiery, lace, carpet, silk, flax, engineering, pottery, glass, and sugar and confectionary trades, and upon agriculture. Free traders derided 'King Joseph's' copying of the form of a Royal Commission. Indeed, they derided his whole policy, foremost in derision being Asquith who in 1903 answered Chamberlain in a series of powerful speeches which helped to mark him out as a future Prime Minister. If Chamberlain's gloomy economic assertions were correct, argued Asquith, then his remedies were inadequate. Either the Empire was not in danger and there was no need for preference; or if it was under threat then much higher duties would be needed to save it. 'There is no ground whatever for saying either that British trade, as a whole, is stagnant or decaying, or that the Empire can only be maintained by reverting to fiscal devices which were tried and found wanting in the old days of Protection.' There was no danger to economic prosperity which could not be overcome by greater business efficiency and more technical education. 'Instead of raising the price of bread let us try to raise the standard of life.'

Expert guidance offered to the Edwardian public by contemporary economists was predictably contradictory. Fourteen university professors and lecturers sent a letter to *The Times* in August 1903 explaining why tariff reform might raise food prices. But tariff reformers found other friendly academics, notably W. J. Ashley (1860–1927), Professor of Commerce at Birmingham University, whose book on *The Tariff Problem* (1903) was widely read. 'The struggle to create an effective British Empire', concluded Ashley rather grimly, 'is, at bottom,

an attempt to counteract, by human foresight, the working of
forces, which, left to themselves, involve the decadence of this
country.' 'That Britain is no longer the workshop of the world',
answered J. A. Hobson, 'is true, and it would be folly to expect
it to be so . . . the world exists for some other purpose than the
exploitation of foreign nations by British factory-owners and
landlords employing armies of people in monotonous occupations.' The Cobdenite faith was reiterated for Edwardians by
the secretary of the Cobden Club. 'The main principle, so far as
the present controversy is concerned, is this: *That it is impossible
to add to the wealth of a nation by preventing the free importation of
foreign goods.*'

Most arguments on both sides certainly passed over the heads
of the Edwardian electors. But the free traders could make
effective play with the simple contrast between the 'little loaf',
which they claimed would be a consequence of tariff reform,
and the 'big loaf' of free trade. Chamberlain, they asserted,
wanted to return to the 'hungry forties' before the repeal of the
Corn Laws. This phrase seems to have been coined in 1903 by
Cobden's daughter, Jane (1851–1949). Chamberlain's answer
to the 'little loaf' charge—that the cost of living could be kept
steady by revenue reductions—was not easy to understand.
Chamberlain himself admitted in one public speech that there
were 'many matters which are scientific questions, and which
it is impossible for me to speak of to a great popular audience'.
Economic sophistication was beyond the comprehension alike
of ordinary supporters and ordinary opponents of tariff reform,
as a *Punch* cartoon on 'Politics for the Masses' suggested during
the first 1910 election campaign:

Orator:	'Take the figures forty-three million seven hundred and fifty-three thousand eight hundred and sixty-two in 1906, and subtract thirty-nine million four hundred thousand six hundred and eighty-seven in 1907, allowing 1.27 per cent for increase of population. Gentlemen, you can draw your own conclusions.'
Enlightened Audience:	''Ear, 'ear.'

Chamberlain never overcame this problem of popular incomprehension.[11]

Many electors, moreover, simply did not feel the shoe pinch-
ing hard or long enough. 1903 had been a year of trade depression, but an international boom had begun by 1905. In December of that year Balfour finally resigned, and the new Liberal
Government called an immediate general election. Chamberlain
had long since abandoned hope of a tariff reform victory at this
first contest. 'We shall be beaten on other issues—education,
Chinese labour, and so on, but when the reaction comes and
we return with a big majority we shall be pledged up to the
eyes to carry out the policy that I have advocated.' But Balfour's
prolonged postponement of the election because of the divisions
among his followers greatly increased the size of the ultimate
defeat. In the jingoistic wartime election of 1900 the Conserva-
tive/Liberal Unionist coalition had won 402 seats and an
overall majority of 134: now the Liberals won 400 seats, giving
them a clear majority of 130, even counting the 83 Irish
Nationalists and 30 Labour members against them. Here was
a famous Liberal victory. At the two elections, however,
numbers of votes cast per party had not differed nearly so much
as numbers of seats won:

	Cons./Lib. U.	Liberal	Labour
1900	1,797,444	1,568,141	63,304
1906	2,451,454	2,757,883	329,748

Changes of voting allegiance cannot entirely explain the
Liberals' 1906 success. They benefited from a new electoral
register, from the greater willingness of agricultural labourers
to vote in a winter election (an 82.6 per cent poll in 1906 against
74.6 per cent in 1900), and from improved party organization.
310 new members entered the Commons, 220 of them Liberals.
With the agricultural labourers voting strongly Liberal
(Chamberlain's appeal for agricultural support had been muted
because he could not expound tariff reform to rural audiences
without emphasizing the food tax aspect of his argument), and
with farmers disgruntled by the 1902 Education Act (which had
increased their rates), the Conservatives did especially badly in
the countryside. Their surviving areas of strength were mainly

urban and suburban. According to one contemporary analysis, 102 tariff reformers (Conservative or Liberal Unionist) were elected; 43 of these came from prosperous suburban London and the South-East (where the bogey of food taxation was less alarming to householders), 20 from Birmingham and the Midlands, 13 from Ireland (mainly Ulster), 5 from Liverpool (but only 1 from the Lancashire cotton district), and 2 from Sheffield (but none from the Yorkshire wool towns). Here was a revealing pattern of support and lack of support. 36 Balfourites, 16 Conservative free traders, and 3 others completed the Opposition muster. The *Manchester Guardian* summed up the election in a cartoon showing a smuggler holding a paper inscribed 'Free Trade wins' and remarking, 'I thought I was going to get a chance again. But this looks as if the days when I was called a free trader are gone for good.'[12]

Tariff reform, however, was down but not out. Though surprised by the size of the Liberal victory, Chamberlain was right in his anticipation that defeat would help to make his proposals into official Opposition policy. In the 1906 Parliament tariff reformers were the largest group within Balfour's depleted following. In July 1906 Chamberlain himself suffered a severe stroke, and though he survived until 1914 he was never able again to take an active part in politics. But Austen Chamberlain and the Tariff Reform League continued the campaign, and in reply to Lloyd George's radical 1909 budget, tariff reform began to gain acceptance by most of Balfour's supporters as a more constructive alternative than simple negation. Balfour now announced that the country must choose between 'the hopeful movement of tariff reform' and the 'downward track . . . to the bottomless confusion of socialist legislation'. He advised the Conservative majority in the Lords to reject the budget, so precipitating a general election in January 1910. The Opposition tried to make tariff reform the big election theme; but the Liberal cry 'the peers versus the people' rang louder. Though the Liberals lost their overall majority (and their majority of English seats), they remained comfortably in power with Labour and Irish support (L. 275, C./L.U. 273, Lab. 40, Irish Nat. 82). After a year of crisis the Liberals were confirmed in office at the general election of December 1910 (L. 272, C./L.U. 272, Lab. 42, Irish Nat. 84). During this second election Balfour had unexpectedly suggested that tariff reform might be witheld by a Conservative Government until after approval at a referendum. Some ardent tariff reformers, including Austen Chamberlain, were astonished at this move, and Balfour's leadership came increasingly under question during 1911. Right-wingers within his party were also dissatisfied by his weakening resistance to the Parliament Bill. He resigned in November, but Austen Chamberlain was unable to win the leadership, the party rank and file still regarding him as an outsider. Bonar Law was chosen as a compromise leader. He had been an apparently keen tariff reformer, but in 1913, under pressure especially from Conservatives in Lancashire (where free trade feeling was strong even among Conservatives), he announced that the Opposition would develop Imperial preference upon returning to power but would not adopt food taxes without a further specific election mandate.[13]

After ten years of tariff reform agitation Britain remained a free trade country. The British people's attachment to free trade can now be seen as economically sound, even though most contemporaries were unaware of the best reasons for their attachment. Economic conditions had much changed since the adoption of unilateral free trade by the early Victorians. Yet in the Edwardian period Britain stood at the centre of a developing multilateral system of international payments. The great expansion of world production which had taken place during the later nineteenth century might have caused serious friction if payment for exchange of goods had continued on the old unilateral basis; this would have required serious encroachments by new competitors upon established trade patterns. The new industrial powers, for example, needed to import additional food and raw materials from primary producing countries which were among Britain's best customers. Fortunately, these new powers did not now need to concentrate their exports in direct competition with British exports. Britain did develop an increasingly adverse balance of visible trade (£64 million per annum in 1871-5 to a peak of £177 million in 1901-5); but this was compensated by steadily rising income from 'invisible' services (£139 million in 1871-5, £226 million in 1901-5, £346 million in 1911-13), which were of benefit to the whole world economy. If Britain had attempted to raise tariff barriers and to extend Imperial preference this great new system would have been upset. Industrial Europe and the United States would then have been forced either to further intensify world competition in manufactured goods, or to adjust their internal economies and to seek new sources of supply through the development of colonies and spheres of influence. Though the international economy of the early-twentieth century was a curious mixture of British free trade and foreign protection, it

worked well, ensuring a great expansion of activity with a minimum of difficulty.

Those Edwardians who wanted Britain to concentrate more upon Empire trade failed to understand the Empire's role within this international framework. They did not realize how the sale of Empire goods throughout the world smoothed the flow of British trade, and how the flow of that trade irrigated the entire international system. Perhaps the Edwardians should have given fiscal protection to some of their newer industries in which they were lagging; but this could have been done without abandoning the whole free trade policy, for even John Stuart Mill (1806-73), one of the great formulators of free trade political economy, had admitted the possible need for protection of infant industries. But the Edwardians were right to change nothing rather than to change everything. In May 1914 Lloyd George, as Chancellor of the Exchequer, congratulated the Commons on an exceptionally prosperous financial year just ended. 'The trade of this country reached the highest point it has ever touched . . . all the more gratifying inasmuch as there was hardly any other country in the world which could put forward the same claim.' The Edwardian free trade era, in other words, was ending with trade booming. 'I find a definite belief that there is no serious break in the weather, and that the trade harvest this year will still be a good average crop.' It was to be a political not an economic breakdown which was to confound this forecast, and to mark the beginning of the end of Britain's Victorian/Edwardian attachment to free trade.[14]

CHAPTER FIVE

The Empire—Imperialist or Liberal?

'England without an empire! Can you conceive it? England in that case would not be the England we love.' So exclaimed Joseph Chamberlain in 1906 in what proved to be his last public speech. The Edwardian British Empire was a world-wide spread of colonies bound in common fealty to the British Sovereign, who at the accession of Edward VII took the additional title of King 'of the British Dominions beyond the Seas'. Notwithstanding this allegiance, by 1901 the major white colonies (Canada, Australia and New Zealand) were already internally self-governing; but the other Imperial possessions (headed by India) were still ruled directly or indirectly by Britain. In 1911 the population of the Empire totalled some 416 million, 344 million of these being coloured people, including over 295 million Indians. Canada possessed a white population of 7 million, Australia about 4.5 million, New Zealand 1 million. As well as being the largest empire ever known, the British Empire was also the most dispersed, depending for its communications upon sea routes defended by the Royal Navy. It was truly (in a phrase often used by Edwardians) an 'Empire upon which the sun never sets'.

Most Edwardians were proud of their Empire, but relatively few of them knew much about it. In times of Imperial crisis, as during the Boer War, both middle and working classes were ready enough to lapse into 'jingoism', a noisy and unthinking expression of Imperial and anti-foreign feeling encouraged by the music halls and popular press. Those middle-class families which provided the administrators and soldiers of Empire were much more knowledgeable in their Imperial pride. The late-Victorian public schools had instilled in them a uniform ideal of service based upon the code of the playing field:

The sand of the desert is sodden red,—
Red with the wreck of a square that broke;—
The Gatling's jammed and the Colonel dead,
And the regiment blind with dust and smoke.
The river of death has brimmed his banks,
And England's far, and Honour a name,
But the voice of a schoolboy rallies the ranks:
'Play up! play up! and play the game!'

Men educated in the spirit of Sir Henry Newbolt's (1862–1938) poem made good routine administrators and soldiers, but they rarely showed much insight or foresight. In a book entitled *The Public Schools and the Empire* (1913) one experienced Edwardian schoolmaster argued earnestly against existing public school emphases. The upper classes must no longer be trained to rule inferior peoples but to share in an Imperial partnership; and training for this required encouragement of 'foresight, sagacity, and adaptability' rather than predictability.[2]

Even many politically progressive Edwardians remained patronizing in their attitudes towards the coloured races of the Empire. The influence of social Darwinism was pervasive. 'The gulf between an Englishman and a Polynesian or a Negro', Gilbert Murray (1866–1957), the classical scholar, assured a conference on 'Nationalities and Subject Races' in 1910, 'is enormous . . . Our relations with the ancient civilizations of the East occupy an intermediate position of special difficulty.' Ramsay MacDonald attacked imperialism in 1900 for its 'assumptions of superiority' leading to territorial expansion. 'We shall do more to civilize Africa by civilizing the East End of London than by governing from the Cape to Cairo.' But even MacDonald ended by making a superior assumption, albeit an inverted one: 'our responsibility for the weaker peoples must be that we protect them from our vices and guard them against those exploiting classes which are our own gravest menace'. J. A. Hobson followed a similar line in his widely-read study of *Imperialism* (1902), an analysis which was acclaimed by Edwardian radicals and socialists but which nonetheless accepted the need for continuing white rule of coloured peoples, even though this should preferably be under international auspices.

'Such interference with the government of a lower race must be directed primarily to secure the safety and progress of the civilization of the world, and not the special interest of the interfering nation.' But most Edwardians were satisfied that Britain would carry out her Imperial 'mission' without any need for internationalization:

> What enterprise that an enlightened community may attempt is more noble and more profitable than the reclamation from barbarism of fertile regions and large populations? To give peace to warring tribes, to administer justice where all was violence, to strike the chains off the slave, to draw the richness from the soil, to plant the earliest seeds of commerce and learning, to increase in whole peoples their capacities for pleasure and diminish their chances of pain—what more beautiful ideal or more valuable reward can inspire human effort?

So rhapsodized young Winston Churchill in 1899. The responsibility, however, was awesome, as another writer admitted, for Britain was 'laying the foundations of States unborn, civilizations undreamed till now.' Churchill was uncertain whether the quality of our men matched the elevation of their mission:

> As the mind turns from the wonderful cloudland of aspiration to the ugly scaffolding of attempt and achievement, a succession of opposite ideas arises. Industrious races are displayed stinted and starved for the sake of an expensive Imperialism which they can only enjoy if they are well fed. Wild peoples, ignorant of their barbarism, callous of suffering, careless of life but tenacious of liberty, are seen to resist with fury the philanthropic invaders, and to perish in thousands before they are convinced of their mistake. The inevitable gap between conquest and dominion becomes filled with the figures of the greedy trader, the inopportune missionary, the ambitious soldier, and the lying speculator, who disquiet the minds of the conquered and excite the sordid appetites of the conquerors. And as the eye of thought rests on these sinister features, it hardly seems possible for us to believe that any fair prospect is approached by so foul a path.[3]

The material rewards of colonization in the huge backward areas of Africa were often small, and the gratitude of the natives for the advantages of 'civilization' smaller still. Kipling, the devoted but not uncritical poet of imperialism, first wrote of 'the white man's burden' in 1899:

> Take up the White Man's burden—
> And reap his old reward:
> The blame of those ye better,
> The hate of those ye guard.

The non-white races within the Empire, noted Graham Wallas (1858–1932), the political scientist, showed 'no signs of enthusiastic contentment at the prospect of existing like the English "poor" during the eighteenth century, as the mere material of other men's virtues'. But the American *New Encyclopedia of Social Reform* (1908) accepted the British Empire as 'in many ways the greatest social reform fact in the world'.[4]

Despite their assumptions of white racial superiority, Edwardians were uneasy about the future. 'The desire to preserve racial purity is common to the higher nations', noted G. P. Gooch (1877–1968), a prominent Liberal academic. 'Yet the wisdom of friendly co-operation between the higher and the lower races becomes ever more apparent.' The 'yellow peril' was a powerful Edwardian bogey—fear that the prolific yellow races would swamp first the Eastern and then the Western worlds. But how was such racial alarm to be reconciled with the continuance of a British Empire in which coloured races predominated numerically? The 'white Australia' policy gave specific form to this Edwardian dilemma, about which the article on the Empire in *Everyman's Encyclopedia* (1913) was uncomfortably inconclusive:

> That this attitude threatens without a doubt the imperialistic idea of unity of empire is openly recognized, but on the other hand there is much to be said for the Australian point of view. They are themselves prepared to admit that their exclusion tests are to a great extent a sham and a delusion, but the Yellow Question is a far more realistic problem to Australia than to the average Briton.

The author of a book called *The Conflict of Colour* (1910) saw danger to the white races from every side. His remedy for the 'yellow peril' was for the whites to back China against Japan; for what he called the 'brown peril' of the Near East he urged the creation of a new state to eṣiablish a balance of power; and for the 'black peril' coming from Africa and perhaps America he wanted intensified conversion of the Negroes to Christianity. 'There exists a widespread racial antipathy founded on colour—an animal-like instinct, if you will, but an instinct which must remain in existence until the world becomes Utopia.' Even Ramsay MacDonald accepted that there was 'a repulsion between the white and the coloured races which becomes active when they live together and the conditions of social equality begin to arise'. MacDonald hoped, therefore, that the races would keep apart. Where, regrettably, intermingling had already occurred his hope was that as coloured people pro-gressed in education and responsibility they would be granted the franchise, as had happened in Cape Colony. Unfortunately, we shall see how in the very year when MacDonald was writing (1909) non-white rights in South Africa were being put in serious danger.[5]

Much of the Edwardian Empire had only been acquired during the last quarter of the nineteenth century. From the eighteen eighties 'imperialism'—the division of the world into formal colonies and spheres of influence—had become the policy of the Great Powers. Notwithstanding late-Victorian Imperial glitter, which reached its peak with Queen Victoria's Diamond Jubilee in 1897, the rise of imperialism had involved a significant diminution of power for Britain, the exchange of early-Victorian informal empire over most of the under-developed world for formal empire over only one-quarter of it. Until the eighteen nineties the word 'imperialism', as used in England, had borne two connotations, both morally neutral. Either it described the policy of those who wished to prevent the existing British settlement colonies from seceding; or (increas-ingly) it was employed to indicate an expansionist attitude towards the control of 'uncivilized' areas. But then between 1896 and 1902 'imperialism' was re-defined by left-wing writers and politicians and lost its neutrality. Commercial expansion in South Africa came under bitter attack for producing first

Jameson's Raid (1896) and then the Boer War (1899–1902), fought to support the position of the Uitlanders working in the Transvaal gold mines who were being treated by the Boers as second-class citizens. Radical and socialist critics now fiercely denounced 'stock-jobbing imperialism'. Such imperialism was presented as merely serving the greed of a relative handful of businessmen, notably the South African millionaires. Hobson's *Imperialism* set out to demonstrate how the whole expansionist movement of the preceding generation had been motivated by economic greed. The rapid technological development of the nineteenth century had given the Western states an irresistible power of intrusion into primitive areas ('We have the Maxim gun, and they have not'). Seeking quick profits from this intrusion, argued Hobson, financiers had poured capital into overseas ventures, leaving workers at home in the grip of poverty caused by under-employment:

> Finance manipulates the patriotic forces which politicians, soldiers, philanthropists and traders generate; the enthusiasm for expansion which issues from these sources, though strong and genuine, is irregular and blind; the financial interest has those qualities of concentration and clear-sighted calculation which are needed to set Imperialism to work.

A similar argument was still being voiced by H. N. Brailsford (1873–1958) in another widely-read work, *The War of Steel and Gold*, published in May 1914. The whole dangerous balance of power struggle, argued Brailsford only three months before the outbreak of war, was a contest to map out exclusive areas of financial penetration, to the neglect of the condition of the workers at home. 'The capitalist must rush abroad because he will not fertilize the demand for more commodities at home by the simple expedient of raising wages.'

Hobson's anti-imperialism was not the less influential because historians have since decided that he exaggerated the influence of high finance behind empire-building. The surplus capital theory does not closely fit the facts of late nineteenth century imperial expansion. Interest rates were not much higher for overseas than for domestic investment, except in certain high risk enterprises such as gold and diamond fields, which attracted only a proportionately small amount of capital. Over two-thirds of the £3,500 million British overseas investment between 1870 and 1914 went to traditional and settled areas (the United States, Canada, Argentina, Australia and South Africa), comparatively little to newly acquired regions. This does not entirely rule out the possibility that one motive behind British participation in the 'scramble for Africa' was the dream of discovering new resources and markets, even though in reality the South African gold and diamond discoveries were to prove dazzling exceptions. But a stronger influence behind British expansion was probably geographical and military— the tendency for colonies to expand into contiguous areas to meet supposed defence needs. Perhaps the strongest motive of all was power political. For a generation the Great Powers of Europe transferred their rivalries from their own continent to the continents of Africa and Asia. In these new settings it was possible for all to win some victories in terms of territory acquired. Such acquisition might prove economically beneficial; at least it was found psychologically reassuring by the Powers. Imperial expansion became a mystical necessity for its own sake, reflected in Winston Churchill's description of his *Story of the Malakand Field Force* (1898) as 'an episode in that ceaseless struggle for Empire which seems to be the perpetual inheritance of our race'.[6]

After the Boer War, however, the emphasis upon further expansion was replaced by concern for Imperial unity and defence. Liberals shared such concern with right-wingers, and in this sense were ready to call themselves 'Imperialists', as Campbell-Bannerman emphasized in 1902:

We hear a good deal nowadays . . . of the word Imperialism —a word that seems to be as uncomfortable for those who like it as it is an object of suspicion for those who do not like it—that we should all desire and endeavour to defend and promote the interest of and strengthen in every way our Empire; that we should knit together in close friendship all the peoples and States within its borders; that we should defend our interests in all parts of the world. That is its reasonable meaning. Who among us dissents from it? This, which is put forward as some novel doctrine, is as old as the British Empire itself.

But Liberals refused to accept that Imperial well-being required tariff reform or schemes of formal Imperial federation. At the 1897 Colonial Conference Chamberlain had proposed the creation of some type of Imperial governing body, a proposal which he repeated at the 1902 conference: 'We do require your assistance in the administration of the vast Empire which is yours as well as ours. The weary Titan staggers under the too vast orb of its fate.' But though eager for Imperial preference, the self-governing Dominions were much less interested in establishing Imperial institutions which might restrict their independent development. Their sense of national differentiation was growing rapidly throughout the Edwardian period, unchecked by the introduction of Rhodes scholarships at Oxford (1902) or of Empire Day in 1904. At the 1902 Colonial Conference the white colonies had still accepted treatment as satellites of the mother country; but by the time of the Imperial Conference of 1911 (a significant change of name) the United Kingdom was claiming no more than to be the first (albeit very much the first) among equals. New generations had grown up in Canada and Australia which had never known Britain as 'home'. New Zealand remained the most British of the Dominions, but when at the 1911 conference her Prime Minister, Sir Joseph Ward (1856–1930) unexpectedly echoed Chamberlain's old proposals for formal links, he was opposed both by the other Dominion Premiers and by Asquith, the British Prime Minister. Such a scheme, declared Asquith, would be 'absolutely fatal to our present system of responsible government'.

By 1911 most Edwardian politicians had abandoned old 'imperialist' ideas of a close-knit Empire—what one publicist was already remembering as 'the old, militarist Imperialism, with its schemes of cash contribution, centralized administration, and British ascendancy perpetuated'—in favour of a looser 'liberal' approach. Chamberlain, and others such as Lord Milner (1854–1925), High Commissioner for South Africa 1897–1905, had presented a sharp choice between stronger Empire government and Imperial disintegration. But at the 1911 conference Asquith pointed to a middle way: 'we are, and intend to remain, units indeed, but units in a greater unity'. Balfour, the Conservative leader, was even beginning to reach towards the post-war 'Commonwealth' idea, based on loose but strong 'family' ties. 'Our experiment is new . . . How are you going to carry out what is the ideal and the ambition of all the great self-governing millions in the Empire, which is a new ideal and a new ambition, that of at once combining the self-conscious national life with the consciousness of belonging to a yet larger whole?' The word 'Commonwealth' was already to hand as a successor to 'Empire'. The formation of the Australian Commonwealth in 1901 had not excluded its use in this wider Imperial context, as Campbell-Bannerman had feared in a speech welcoming the Australian experiment:

> Where could they find a word more exactly indicating the intent and purpose of that great aggregated community of which we are all proud to be citizens? . . . In that great creation of the energy of our people in the past and in the present we sought only the welfare and prosperity of all and to make the common weal shared by all for the use of all. That was the ideal of our Australian friends, and how could it be better expressed than by the homely native phrase the British Commonwealth? But we had been too late. These enterprising kinsmen of ours from the other end of the world had appropriated the word.

The Dominions were almost as unwilling to make contributions towards Imperial defence, first requested by Chamberlain, as to support schemes of Imperial federation. Chamberlain wanted colonial support in money and men, especially for the Royal Navy. But the self-governing Dominions were suspicious of 'taxation without representation'. Only New Zealand made a grant in support of the Royal Navy, Australia and Canada preferring to start their own fleets. Haldane, the Liberal War Secretary, did contrive to create an Imperial General Staff, but national particularism was accepted by the 1909 Imperial Defence Conference, and was not reduced even when greater consultation was arranged in the immediate pre-war years through the Committee of Imperial Defence. The self-governing colonies had sent small contingents to the Boer War, and were to send large forces to Europe and the Middle East during the First World War; but they had refused to bind themselves in

Keir Hardie.

Strikers stop a wagon during the 1911 Dock Strike.

X

Mass unionism—banners on Tower Hill. Asserting the right not only to subsistence but to live well.

XI

advance. Their commitment to the mother country was now much more sentimental than constitutional.[7]

Balfour was much less liberal in his view of the future of the coloured peoples of the British Empire than in his 'family' vision of the future of the white races. In a 1904 debate on the employment of Chinese labourers in the Rand gold mines on terms which the Liberals were denouncing (with some exaggeration) as 'slavery', Balfour asserted plainly that science had shown that 'men are not born equal. They cannot be made equal by education extending over generation after generation'. But anthropological research was challenging this assumption of inbuilt white superiority, as radicals were quick to point out. While not pressing for the abandonment of colonization (as Cobden and some mid-Victorian radicals had come near to suggesting), they did emphasize the need for British rule to show care for indigenous native rights and cultures, encouraging ideas of 'trust' and 'indirect rule' in place of the unrestrained imposition of Western values. Such a policy was pursued with notable success by Sir Frederick Lugard (1858–1945) in Nigeria.[8]

'Indirect rule' was for coloured peoples. For the Boers of South Africa the Liberals hurried to grant self-government within four years of the end of the Boer War. In their last months in power in 1905 the Conservatives had drafted a constitution for the Transvaal giving representative but not responsible government, on the assumption that the Boers could not yet be expected to remain loyal to the Empire. But in February 1906, spurred on by a sudden generous intervention from Campbell-Bannerman, the Liberal Cabinet decided to go the whole way and to trust the Boers at once with self-government. Three years later the Asquith Cabinet accepted a South African proposal to form a union of the old British colonies of the Cape and Natal with the two former Boer republics of the Transvaal and the Orange River to form one Union of South Africa. The Liberals hoped that this would produce another strong Dominion within the British Empire in control of the southern tip of Africa, an important centre of Imperial communications if the Suez Canal were threatened. The Boer leaders, Louis Botha (1862–1919) and J. C. Smuts (1870–1950), pledged their loyalty to the Imperial connection. It was assumed in Empire circles in England that the supposedly more vigorous and progressive attitudes of the English-speaking South Africans would gradually erode Boer rigidity. In particular, Liberals hoped that the advancement of non-white South Africans would continue. These numbered over 5 million (African natives over 4.5 million, half-castes nearly 500,000, Asiatics over 100,000) compared with less than 1.25 million whites. In Cape Colony some 22,000 non-white Africans and Indians already possessed the vote, based upon a property qualification. But the Boer territories had not been required by the Conservatives to establish such a franchise under the peace treaty of 1902. 'The question of granting franchises to natives', the treaty agreed, 'will not be decided until after the introduction of self-government.' The Liberals were bound by this clause when they decided to grant Boer self-government in 1906, a clause which effectively left the Boers free never to concede the vote to non-whites. Liberal Ministers were uncomfortably aware that they risked being generous towards the white Boers at the expense of the non-white Africans and Indians. Ministers 'could not be indifferent to the welfare and interests of that great multitude of natives', admitted Churchill as Colonial Under-Secretary in 1906, 'who were after all subjects of the King and looked to the Imperial Government for protection. None the less he did not intend in any degree to impair the general principles of Liberal colonial policy, which was the principle of self-government.' Here was a damaging contradiction within the Liberal approach to the future development of the British Empire. On the one hand was the wish to grant full self-government to all advanced white settlers: on the other were ideas of 'trusteeship' in respect of backward coloured races. By 1909 Liberal Ministers felt still more uncomfortable when the draft Bill sent from South Africa restricted membership of the Union Parliament to whites and excluded the vast majority of non-whites even from the possibility of qualifying for the franchise. Yet Ministers accepted that it was now too late to prevent discrimination by colour. If the British Government had tried to amend the colour-bar provisions, the South Africans would have taken their stand on the principle of colonial self-government, and would probably have been supported on such ground by the Canadians and

Australians. The goodwill of Botha and his friends would have been lost, and the influence of the Boer extremists strengthened. The Liberals had to take refuge in the sincere belief that a united South Africa (including the Cape, where the non-white franchise was precariously preserved) would soon come to see the injustice of a racially-restricted franchise. At the same time Liberals believed that the economic progress made possible through union would benefit the natives more directly than possession of the vote. Asquith differed emphatically from Balfour in proclaiming his belief that the non-whites in South Africa were capable of progress. His summing up of the South Africa Bill in the Commons reflected his sense of satisfaction at the idea of unity, awkwardly qualified by 'reserve of judgment' at the Bill's handling of the colour question; he could merely hope that the South Africans would 'sooner rather than later' liberalize their franchise.

Only a handful of radicals and Labour men had wanted to take a strong line even to a point of risking the failure of the scheme for union. Keir Hardie argued in Parliament that the Boers would give way rather than lose the union. On the other hand, he saw no chance that they would ever concede votes to non-whites once the union had been secured. Indeed, he believed that even the Cape Colony franchise would eventually come under attack as an anomaly:

for the first time we are asked to write over the portals of the British Empire: 'Abandon hope all ye who enter here.' . . . I hope, therefore, that if only for the sake of the traditions of our dealings with natives in the past, this Bill . . . will be so amended as to make it a real unifying Bill in South Africa. At present it is a Bill to unify the white races, to disfranchise the coloured races, and not to promote union between the races in South Africa, but rather to still further embitter the relationships.

Yet for some forty years the Liberals' South African policy was to be widely applauded as a success. If it now seems to have been a failure, the fault lies perhaps not with those Edwardian Ministers who consciously took the gamble of assuming future good judgment and intentions on the part of white South

Africans; but with those South Africans themselves, of British as well as of Boer stock, who have not shown such judgment.[9]

The conciliatory Liberal policy towards the Boers encouraged Indians to hope for some liberalization of the government of India. British rule in India, 'the brightest jewel in the Empire's crown', was a remarkable phenomenon—an Oriental sub-continent of some 300 million people of many races and civilizations, under the control of a mere 300,000 expatriate white soldiers, administrators and traders, five thousand miles from their Northern homeland. Such a system of rule was too artificial to endure for long, as Cobden and Bright had pointed out in mid-Victorian times. But few Edwardians, even radicals, foresaw how the British withdrawal would occur within only some forty years. Viceregal pomp reached a peak under Lord Curzon (1859–1925), the haughty but energetic Viceroy from 1898 to 1905, whose unconciliatory policy provoked the Indian National Congress to lead an upsurge of nationalist feeling. Liberal policy in the hands of John Morley (1838–1923), Secretary of State for India 1905–10, and of Lord Minto (1847–1914), Viceroy 1905–10, was more sensitive to Indian feeling, though still ready to employ repression in the name of law and order.

> We must persevere [wrote Morley to Minto] with liberal and substantial reforms, perhaps wider than those in your original sketch. Very likely they won't satisfy the educated classes, and it is these classes after all who, in spite of their comparatively scanty numbers, must always set the tone and decide the pitch. Reforms may not save the Raj, but if they don't nothing else will.

In this rather resigned spirit the Indian Councils Act was passed after long gestation in 1909. It overhauled the complex network of provincial legislative and executive councils. The former were enlarged to accommodate twice as many Indians, representing class and communal interests. Members of legislative councils were also now permitted to debate budgetary matters. An Indian was appointed to the Viceroy's executive council, and Indian spokesmen were added to the Indian legislative council. The latter was now the only legislative council to retain an official majority, Morley having persuaded Minto that this would prove a sufficient check upon the others. This policy was intended to produce a consultative autocracy analogous to the Prussian and Japanese systems, opening participation in government to 'a class of persons, Indian in blood and colour, but English in taste, in opinion, in morals, and in intellect'. Morley said plainly that Indian self-government was not in his mind; he was 'doing nothing to loosen the bolts', seeking only to recognize and to reconcile 'individual ability'. But in retrospect his concessions can be presented as an early step towards responsible government, and also (for better or worse) towards two separate Hindu and Muslim states, for the 1909 Act introduced separate electorates. A beginning had been made in the sense that representative majority government pointed the way, however distantly, towards responsible majority government. In the long term, whereas Liberal South African policy was to prove less fruitful than was hoped, Liberal Indian policy was to prove more innovating than was realized.[10]

Lord Cromer (1841–1917), who for a generation had virtually ruled Egypt as part of the British Empire, praised the Indian Councils Act in his book on *Ancient and Modern Imperialism* (1910); but he still emphasized that Britain had 'not the smallest intention' of quitting India:

> In this respect something of the clearness of political vision and bluntness of expression which characterized the Imperialists of Ancient Rome might, not without advantage, be imparted to our own Imperialist policy. Nations wax and wane. It may be that at some future and far distant time we shall be justified, to use a metaphor of perhaps the greatest of Latin poets*, in handing over the torch of progress and civilization in India. All that can be said at present is that, until human nature entirely changes, and until racial and religious passions disappear from the face of the earth, the relinquishment of that torch would almost certainly lead to its extinction.

*'One race increases by another's decrease. The generations of living things pass in quick succession and like runners hand on the torch of life.'

Newbolt's poem, quoted earlier in this chapter, had taken its title from the same phrase of Lucretius as that cited by Cromer—'Vitae Lampada', the torch of life, progress, civilization. The fear modified by hope in Cromer's mind, that the British Empire might one day fall like the Roman Empire but in falling might hand on this torch of progress, involved a comparison often made by Edwardians. An anonymous pamphlet called *The Decline and Fall of the British Empire* was published in 1905, in the form of a work supposedly issued in Japan in the year 2005. It listed eight causes of British decline during the twentieth century—the prevalence of town over country life, the weakening of British interest in the sea, the growth of luxury, the decline of taste, the debilitation of the physique and health of the people, the enfeeblement of intellectual and religious life, excessive taxation and municipal extravagance, and the inability of the British to defend themselves and their Empire. Though the British Empire had shown hopeful signs of adaptability during the Edwardian period, H. G. Wells was right still to be asking in 1914 'Will the Empire live? What will hold such an Empire as the British together?'[11]

CHAPTER SIX

The Introduction of
the 'Social Service State'

Conservative Policy and Liberal Opposition

The period of Liberal rule before 1914 is rightly remembered
for its social reforms. Yet such reform was not prominent as a
1906 election issue. Negatives predominated, notably opposition to tariff reform, to 'Chinese Slavery' in South Africa, and
to the 1902 Education Act and the 1904 Licensing Act. Inside
and outside Parliament the Liberals had vociferously resisted
the passing of these two major Conservative contributions to
social improvement, and they persisted in their resistance for
years afterwards. Only slowly did they take the lead as the
party of social reform. The private correspondence of Liberal
Ministers in 1906 after their overwhelming victory showed them
still without any bold sense of social reform purpose. The
Liberal Chief Whip was happy to congratulate his Prime
Minister on the moderate character of his new following, 'the
preponderance of the "centre" Liberals. There is no sign of any
violent forward movement in opinion . . . There are some
excellent young enthusiasts like Masterman.' As late as March
1907 Haldane, the War Secretary, was attempting to slow down
one older enthusiast, Bernard Shaw. 'As soon as I get out of
office I will write something to prove to you all that the
"Neither-Nor" is preferable—as a guide through life—to the
"Either-Or".'[1]

Shaw and Masterman were enthusiasts because they understood the great need for social reform. They had read and contributed to the succession of pioneering social surveys, local and
national, statistical and impressionistic, official and unofficial,
which had appeared during the Edwardian years. We have

already noticed the two most influential statistical accounts, Booth's *Life and Labour of the People in London* (1889-1902) and Rowntree's *Poverty, a Study of Town Life* (1901). They revealed how some 30 per cent of the urban working class, one in every three or four of the Edwardian town population were living in poverty. Booth divided the people into eight groupings. Class A were the 'residuum', alarming in character but mercifully limited in numbers. Class B, on the other hand, the very poor living on casual earnings, comprised over 100,000 of the population of East London. One of Booth's main proposals for the abolition of poverty was the mass removal of this group to industrial or labour colonies. He argued that 'the poverty of the poor is mainly the result of the competition of the very poor', meaning that the distress of his next two categories C and D, labourers in intermittent work and those in regular employment earning up to 21s. per week, was the direct consequence of the existence of class B. If this class could be removed, its work might easily be done by members of classes C and D, giving them a useful addition to earnings. Fortunately, the impracticality of this solution did not affect the validity of the social discoveries which had provoked it.

The social revelations of Booth and Rowntree undermined the Victorian assumption that poverty was more often than not the outcome of individual character failings. Booth still accepted that a substantial proportion of those in distress must be weak or corrupt; but he argued that it was their environment, and especially their constant struggle for work, not inherent weakness, which had degraded them. This was a halfway position Rowntree, however, made the striking discovery that over half the working men of York suffering from primary poverty were 'in regular work but at 'ow wages'; there was no blameworthy idleness in such cases. One household in every six or seven in primary poverty had fallen into this condition through the accident of the death of the chief wage-earner, again not a cause for blame. Rowntree explicitly stated that though many unskilled workers lacked ideas they did not lack good moral qualities. Poverty, he concluded, was in large part 'the result of false social and economic conditions'. Why should honest workmen be expected to struggle against these conditions unsupported except by charity or by the Poor Law, each with their attendant stigma of inadequacy? Here was an approach to the poverty problem conflicting markedly with that of the Charity Organization Society (1869), which into Edwardian times assumed that poverty involved a failing not so much in society as in individual character, and that relief should be dispensed only with the careful purpose of forcing individuals back into self-support. 'The strength of the people lies in its own conscious efforts to face difficulties and overcome them.' So argued Helen Bosanquet (1860–1925), a leading COS figure. The Society was sternly opposed to all 'socialistic' remedies. But Booth, who insisted upon regarding himself as a Conservative, answered that a small degree of State interference had become necessary to preserve a larger measure of individual freedom. 'Our individualism fails because our Socialism is incomplete.'

The main weakness of Booth's description of poverty and unemployment was his failure to take account of the trade cycle. His picture of poverty was largely static. Rowntree's was more dynamic, allowing for variations both in general economic and family circumstances. He showed how an individual born into poverty could expect a period of prosperity when he left school and started work; how this would decline when he married and had children, rise again as his own family began to earn and finally worsen with old age. Here was dynamic poverty, accurately presented not as a snapshot but as a moving picture. Rowntree carefully defined two levels of poverty: 'primary' ('families whose total earnings were insufficient to obtain the minimum necessaries for the maintenance of merely physical efficiency') and 'secondary' ('families whose total earnings would have been sufficient for the maintenance of merely physical efficiency were it not that some portion of it was absorbed by other expenditure, either useful or wasteful'). Nearly 10 per cent of York's population was sunk in primary poverty, nearly 18 per cent in secondary poverty. These proportions closely matched Booth's findings for London. Rowntree's conclusion was expressed with stern Quaker clarity:

> That in this land of abounding wealth, during a time of perhaps unexampled prosperity, probably more than one-fourth of the population are living in poverty, is a fact which

may well cause great searchings of heart. There is surely need for a greater concentration of thought by the nation upon the well-being of its own people, for no civilization can be sound or stable which has at its base this mass of stunted human life. The suffering may be all but voiceless, and we may long remain ignorant of its extent and severity, but when once we realize it we see that social questions of profound importance await solution.

In the years following the publication of Rowntree's survey, official enquiries were made into the cost of living among the working classes (1908), into earnings and hours of work for textile workers (1909), for the building and woodworking trades (1910), in public utility services (1910), in agriculture (1910), in the metal, engineering and shipbuilding industries (1911), on the railways (1912–13), and in various miscellaneous trades (1912–13). These enquiries provided data which could be related to Rowntree's figure of 21s. 8d. as the minimum weekly wage needed to keep a family of two adults and three children in a state of Spartan 'physical efficiency'. By 1914, when inflation had raised this minimum to 24s., nearly òne quarter of all adult male wage earners were earning less than 25s. per week.[2]

The contrast between this problem of poverty and 'the problem of riches' was scathingly drawn in 1909 by one radical Member of Parliament, Arthur Ponsonby (1871–1946). He suggested a companion volume to Booth and Rowntree, to be called *The Life and Leisure of Some People*, or *Riches: a Study of Town Life*. He compared a rich man of 'no occupation' with the case of a poor man also of 'no occupation' (through illness) cited by Rowntree. 'Married. Two children. Four houses. London house —— Street, W. Sixty-two rooms; one of the country houses considerably larger. Thirty-six indoor servants'. Each year on the day after the Lord Mayor's sumptuous banquet the remains of the feast were condescendingly distributed to the 'deserving' London poor. In addition, noted one observer, the less poor of the capital regularly helped the more poor. 'It is peculiar to London, this custom of placing leavings where the first comer who is hungry can see them, and it materially helps to keep the man in the street—the real man, not the imaginery figure of editors and orators—from starving.' The author of this description of 'Charitable and Benevolent London' (1904) was apparently more impressed by the extent of Edwardian charity than by the extent of endemic poverty linked to it. But the evidence of the social surveys was proving conclusively that charity, however well meant, had failed to control (even less to conquer) what was now measured as a major national problem.[3]

Not only Liberals, radicals and socialists but also Conservatives were worried by the social question. If left-wingers were moved more especially by 'social conscience'. many right-wingers thought especially in terms of national and Imperial defence. Rowntree had collected alarming figures showing how nearly one half of would-be army recruits in York, Leeds and Sheffield were rejected on medical grounds between 1897 and 1901. The need for greater 'efficiency' in all aspects of national life—governmental, commercial, military—was a persistent theme at the start of the new century. Fundamental to everything must be the physical efficiency of the British 'race'. Edwardians began alarmedly to ask if it was deteriorating in its new urban environment. 'The certainty of the approaching exhaustion of the street-bred people of Britain', claimed the author of *Efficiency and Empire* (1901), was a general topic of conversation. General J. F. Maurice (1841–1912), a veteran of several African campaigns, asserted in 1902 that sixty per cent of Englishmen were physically unfit for military service, a figure apparently confirmed in the following year by the Director-General of the Army Medical Service. In response to such alarms the Balfour Government set up an Inter-Departmental Committee on Physical Deterioration (1903–4). Its terms of reference were:

(1) To determine, with the aid of such counsel as the medical profession are able to give, the steps that should be taken to furnish the Government and the Nation at large with periodical data for an accurate comparative estimate of the health and physique of the people; (2) to indicate generally the causes of such physical deterioration as does exist in certain classes; and (3) to point out the means by which it can be most effectually diminished.

The committee came to partly reassuring conclusions. It found Maurice's gloomy statistics to be exaggerated; and it did not discover evidence of racial degeneration. But it collected much expert testimony about ill-health and bad conditions among the Edwardian working class. It took evidence on the effects of urban overcrowding, about air pollution, working conditions, the care of infants and schoolchildren, venereal disease, and physical defects. The committee's report was 'emphatic in recommending that a systematised medical inspection of children at school should be imposed on every school authority as a public duty'. It also proposed local authority feeding of hungry schoolchildren. Though the Conservative Government was still reluctant to authorize increased local expenditure on social welfare, in 1905 under pressure from some of its own supporters it finally issued an Order permitting Poor Law Guardians to give relief in the form of meals to underfed schoolchildren.[4] The Balfour Government also promoted the Unemployed Workmen Act of 1905, a last effort to deal with temporary unemployment by means of relief work. The quickly apparent ineffectiveness of this measure finally turned Edwardian social and economic planners— notably Sidney Webb and William Beveridge (1879–1963)— in search of a new approach to the whole problem of unemployment.[5]

Balfour had told one of his junior Ministers that with respect to school meals and medical inspection he 'could be as sympathetic as he liked but there would be no increase in rates'. On school organization, however, Balfour was much more willing to be an innovator. Here he had become convinced that national safety and progress required fresh legislation and increased expenditure. English education was much less efficient than that of our American and Continental rivals, (in Balfour's words) 'utterly behind the age'. By 1902 the elementary education system established by the famous 1870 Education Act had been working for a generation. The Act gave State support to schools run by the religious denominations where these existed (8,281 schools in 1870), adding 'Board Schools' in the many urban areas where denominational schools were too few. In 1880 elementary education had been made compulsory, and in 1891 it became free. Because only Board Schools enjoyed use of the local education rates they had come, in general, to be the best equipped and staffed. By 1900 though Board Schools numbered only 5,758 compared with 14,559 voluntary sectarian schools, they were teaching almost as many children, 2.25 million compared with 2.5 million. Most elementary schools concentrated upon instruction in the three 'rs', but Charles Booth thought that their main influence had been social rather than scholastic:

A whole generation has been through the schools, but in scholarship there is not much to show for it. Almost all can, indeed, read, though with some effort, and write, after a fashion; but those who can do either the one or the other with the facility that comes of constant practice are comparatively few. Nevertheless, popular education has been far from wasted even in the case of those who may seem to have learnt but very little. Obedience to discipline and rules of proper behaviour have been inculcated; habits of order and cleanliness have been acquired; and from these habits self-respect arises.

The report of the Committee on Physical Deterioration included some striking photographs comparing the ragged appearance of children in London Board Schools of the seventies with the much better dressed children in the same schools by 1903.

A major educational problem for the new century was how to raise the standard of the sectarian schools up to the level of the Board Schools. How could public money be provided for them without seeming either to end their independence or to subsidize unfairly the nearly 12,000 Church of England schools, which were much the most numerous. The Nonconformists conducted only some 1500 schools, the Roman Catholics upwards of 1000. The best Board Schools had even begun to extend their activities into secondary education, until in 1901 the Cockerton Judgment ruled that the 1870 Act had not authorized the financing of such teaching from the rates. It was also ruled that children alone could be taught out of such funds; adult evening classes were not permissible.

Clearly, as Balfour recognized, the system of elementary education needed re-organizing. So did the system, or rather lack of system, of secondary education, which was seriously inadequate for the needs of an advanced industrial nation. This had been emphasized by the Bryce Report on Secondary Education in 1895. The English educational tradition had been to try and do as much as possible, and more than was possible, by voluntary effort, with central and local government attempting only to play a supplementary part. This had still been the intention behind the 1870 Act. But it had now become plain that both in primary and secondary education national and local government must lead rather than follow:

> We cannot refuse to strengthen the hold of the State upon our education. Irresistible forces drive us on. We are in the suck of a strong current. Act we must, because other nations with whom we have to compete, not only in the sphere of industry and commerce, but in the more momentous struggle between national ideals, have thrown themselves with all their energy into the work of educational reconstruction.

So explained Michael Sadler (1861–1943), a leading Edwardian educationalist and member of the Bryce Commission.

The Conservatives made a start by creating the Board of Education in 1900. This was a first step towards shaping the English system of public education into a harmonious whole, as recommended by the Bryce Report. Balfour became convinced that this could only be achieved through the abolition of the School Boards and by the transfer of educational control to the local authorities. These changes, plus an improved system of teacher training, were secured by the 1902 Act. But the Nonconformists objected bitterly to proposals to subsidize the sectarian, predominantly Anglican elementary schools out of the rates. In return for providing the buildings the managers of such schools were to continue to appoint the teachers, even though running expenses were to be met, like those of the former Board Schools (now renamed 'provided' schools), out of the local rates. In the 'provided' schools undenominational religious instruction was permitted to continue. These proposals were drafted by Robert Morant (1863–1920), soon to become the energetic Permanent Secretary to the Board of Education; but they passed only because of the determination of Balfour, the new Prime Minister. 'If we hesitate to do our duty and carry through this great reform, then I say we shall receive the contempt of the parents of the children living and to be born, for the next generation.'

In rural areas Church of England schools were often the only ones available, making it impossible for Nonconformist children to attend elsewhere. Nonconformists had hoped to see this monopoly end for lack of money, and now they feared that it was to be prolonged indefinitely partly at their own expense as rate-payers. They demanded instead a system of entirely undenominational schools. This demand was voiced by the Liberal front bench, but most eloquently by the young Lloyd George from the backbenches. The 1902 Act was passed only after fifty-nine days' debate. Yet in retrospect its elementary education proposals can be seen to have provided a sensible solution to a serious conflict of interests. Balfour was accused of cunningly seeking to extend the influence of Anglicanism, a particularly unfair charge against a man who was much too fastidious to be a religious partisan.

During the passing of the Act, and of a similar measure for London in 1903, and for years thereafter, the Nonconformists campaigned against it under the banner 'The Church on the Rates'. Large protest meetings were held, and a National Passive Resistance Committee was formed to organize a mass refusal to pay education rates. This movement was led by Dr John Clifford (1836–1923), a much respected Baptist minister. Support came from many parts of England, and most of all from rural Wales. By the end of 1903 over 7,000 summonses had been issued, and distraint of goods in lieu of payment had occurred in 300 cases. Such resistance by otherwise respectable citizens continued up to 1914, although never with sufficient effect to endanger the new education system. Clifford was sure that the Church of England was unscrupulously seeking to extend its power. 'It is not the tolerant and inclusive Church of the days of Lord Shaftesbury, but the bigoted and persecuting Church of the times of Laud and Whitgift.'

Balfour described the 1902 Act as 'an organic whole', meaning that its proposals for secondary education linked with its reorganization of primary education. For the first time the provision of secondary education was now recognized as a duty of the State. Secondary education was placed under local authority control alongside elementary school teaching, and a 'ladder' was provided whereon able children could rise from primary to secondary instruction. This 'ladder' concept, originally articulated by T. H. Huxley (1825–95), the famous Victorian scientist, was now put at the centre of English State education. It implied, of course, rigorous selection for admission to the secondary schools. 'An important though subsidiary object' of elementary education, explained the Elementary Education Code issued by the Board of Education in 1904, was 'to discover individual children who show promise of exceptional capacity' and to prepare them for entry into the secondary schools. For the majority, however, the code laid down a programme of education which has been characterized by one historian as 'training in followership rather than leadership training'. It gave as much emphasis to character formation as to academic instruction, emphasizing particularly the virtues of hard work, respect and reverence.

In 1907 the Liberals introduced the 'free place' system. Secondary schools which did not reserve one-quarter of their places, free of fees, for children educated in public elementary schools were to receive a lower State grant. Here was a limited but significant easing of the selective principle, in that not merely outstandingly brilliant working-class children but boys and girls of simply good ability might now win secondary school places. After 1902 a rapid expansion in secondary school provision took place. In 1901–2 there had been 341 establishments in England providing education above the elementary standard, attended by almost 28,000 pupils and in receipt under the complicated system then operating of government grants totalling £140,888. Within five years the number of these establishments had risen to 689, the number of pupils to 66,000, and the grants to £246,220. *Regulations for Secondary Schools* (1904) provided guidelines for the spirit and content of State secondary education. The emphasis was to be upon a good general course, and arts subjects (including compulsory Latin) were favoured; but teaching in science and mathematics was made compulsory. Though not an adventurous syllabus, it was a coherent one.

Most Edwardian women were not suffragettes—they preferred shop-window gazing to shop-window smashing.

Mrs. Pankhurst and Christabel Pankhurst in prison clothes.

XII

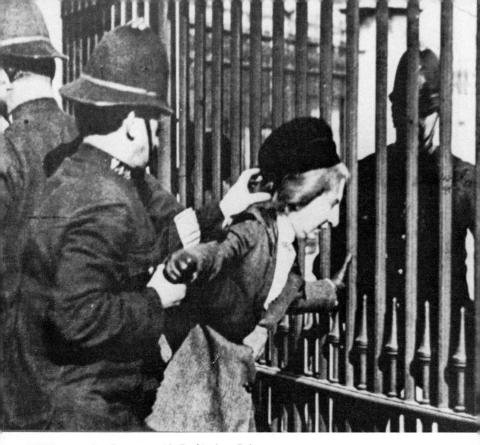

XIII   *A suffragette outside Buckingham Palace.*

*Mrs. Pethick-Lawrence and Mrs. Pankhurst leaving Bow Street
Station after being released, April 3, 1912.*

'Equality of educational opportunity' was now much written and spoken about, not so much by the working classes themselves as on their behalf. We have already noticed, and shall remark further, how this tended also to be the case with the impetus behind other Edwardian social reforms. A writer of 1899 on *What is Secondary Education?* was explicit on this point: 'the nation is stirred by an increasing desire for greater equality of educational opportunity. This feeling is at present less noticeable among the labouring classes themselves than among those who are touched by the feeling that others unfairly lack opportunities which they themselves have enjoyed.' Another writer in the same volume made it plain, however, that equality of opportunity meant selection on Darwinian lines. 'There must be the means of sound and efficient Secondary Education within the reach of every lad of unusual ability whom Dame Nature may throw up, as it were in sport, from even the most unlikely and unpromising surroundings.' In the event, only relatively small numbers from the humblest origins were to win their way into the new Edwardian system of secondary schools. The main beneficiaries of the new opportunities were children of the lower middle class. Of boys born in the years 1910–29 still only one-fifth reached secondary school, and middle-class children were four times more likely than working-class children to figure among this number. 40 per cent of middle-class boys attended secondary school, only 10 per cent of working-class boys. 'Equality of opportunity' even within the Edwardian definition was far from fully achieved. Yet the securing of an approach to equality of opportunity for middle-class children was itself of great national benefit. Writing as early as the mid-nineteen twenties, Halévy, the French historian, recognized that 'a social revolution of the first magnitude' had occurred via the new secondary education system:

> Throughout the whole of the nineteenth century the sole means by which members of the lower middle class in the towns and country districts could rise in the social scale was by becoming wealthy. It was only for his sons that the successful manufacturer or merchant could hope for an education not picked up at random, that genuinely liberal education which would admit them to the Universities and

through the Universities to the polish and refinement which distinguished the upper classes. In future there was no county or town in which the lower middle class was unprovided with secondary schools where for a low fee, or even without payment, their children could receive an education as good as that given to the children of the gentry or upper middle class.[6]

Facilities for scientific and technological higher education remained limited in Edwardian England, though increasing. The Imperial College of Science and Technology was formed in 1907; Birmingham University, keenly supported by Joseph Chamberlain, was given its charter in 1900, and the federal Victoria University was divided into the Universities of Manchester (1903), Liverpool (1903), Leeds (1904) and Sheffield (1905). These new universities were each strong in various fields of science and technology. Ernest Rutherford (1871–1937), the great atomic physicist, conducted some of his most important research at Manchester between 1907 and 1919. Numbers of university students grew from upwards of 20,000 in 1900–1 to over 33,000 in 1910–11. But the amount of State and municipal financial support for universities, about £250,000 in 1914, was still only one-third of the Prussian figure. Moreover, at the school level the Board of Education under Morant was slow to recognize technical and commercial education as a vital need within an industrial society. Only gradually did Morant begin to abandon his 1904 emphasis upon a highly generalized grammar school course as the only worthwhile secondary education. H. G. Wells, himself the holder of a science degree, campaigned persistently for greater recognition of the claims of science, technology and technical and commercial subjects. He thought it particularly disturbing that few of the ruling class had received much practical education. 'Scientific education—and more particularly the scientific education of our owning and responsible classes—has been crippled by the bitter jealousy of the classical teachers who dominate our universities, by the fear and hatred of the Established Church, which still so largely controls our upper class schools, and by the entire lack of understanding and support on the part of those able barristers and financiers who rule our political life.'

Too often science at public school remained 'stinks', mere comic relief: 'there was no prestige or scholarships in science'.[7]

For the many whose schooling had been deficient adult education made rapid progress in the new century. The Workers' Education Association was formed in 1903, and began to conduct tutorial classes five years later. University extra-mural classes also greatly increased in number until about 50,000 students were attending each year. Unfortunately, scientific and technological subjects could hardly be taught by such methods. Economics and economic history were favourite WEA courses. In step with this movement 400 public libraries were opened between 1897 and 1910, and public library book loans doubled in the same period. As with the secondary schools, however, these new libraries and adult groups tended to serve the lower-middle and artisan classes much more than the solid working class, attracting men and women already sufficiently educated to feel the need for more education and sufficiently well dressed to dare to venture forth in public.[8]

Between 1902 and 1913 local authority spending upon education in England and Wales grew from £9.5 million to £30.6 million. Central government expenditure increased from £12.5 million to £19.5 million. Education was being given much higher national priority, even if sectors of serious neglect remained. But were the Edwardian priorities right even in those sectors given most attention? Already by 1914 criticism was being heard of the selective principle and of the educational 'ladder'. The WEA called for a 'highway' which would avoid the irrevocable exclusion at set stages of millions of children and adults from further educational opportunities, 'a free and open highway upon which the only tolls are to be mental equipment and high character'. This still assumed that selection would operate within the schools, but with the effects of selection modified through extensive provision of adult education. But the idea of school secondary education for all without selection was already being voiced by Edwardian radicals and socialists. Here was true 'equality of opportunity', as J.A. Hobson argued in 1909:

What is needed is not an educational ladder, narrowing as it rises, to be climbed with difficulty by a chosen energetic few, who as they rise enter a new social stratum, breathe the atmosphere of another class, and are absorbed in official and professional occupations which dissociate them from the common life of the people. It is a broad, easy stair, and not a narrow ladder, that is wanted, one which will entice everyone to rise, will make for general and not for selected culture.

Margaret McMillan (1860–1931), the pioneer socialist educationist, asserted firmly that 'University or Higher Education is the right not of a few, but of all'. At the least, the school leaving age ought to be raised to sixteen:

> There can be no serious opposition to this reform except the opposition of the working-class parent himself. He is opposing it today, and we are arguing with him. He fights against the raising of the school age, in some cases because he is poor, but not always. Often he does it because he cannot imagine a good which he has never experienced. The *real* cause of his strange indifference shows behind all his 'independence', his 'shrewdness', etc. He is stunted, and cannot know it.

Here was another instance of social reform being demanded in the interests of the working classes but almost in spite of themselves.[9]

Liberal Policy and Conservative Opposition

The Liberal Government was committed to modifying the 1902 Education Act to meet Nonconformist complaints. In its 1906 Education Bill, therefore, the new Government proposed to replace the dual system of English elementary education by a single system. This was to be under complete public control, but with 'facilities' for religious instruction by clergymen. The special purpose of this scheme was to eliminate Anglican influence in single school rural areas. It was now the turn of Anglicans and Roman Catholics to protest loudly, faced with the prospect of losing their separate schools. Liberal Ministers found themselves opposed in Parliament not only by the Conservatives but also by the Catholic Irish Nationalists and by Labour members. The Bill eventually passed the Commons, but was so drastically amended by the Conservative majority in the Lords that Ministers refused to proceed with it. Further Bills in 1908 proved unsatisfactory even to the Nonconformists, and thereafter the Liberal Government tacitly accepted the 1902 reorganization. They were the more easily able to do this because religious feeling was now noticeably declining in social and political influence.[10]

By contrast, on other social questions Liberal Ministers were to move in quite the opposite direction, starting hesitantly in 1906, then becoming bolder from 1908. The Poor Law Guardians had soon proved themselves unable to feed poor school-children as permitted under the 1905 Order; and when the Liberals took office an Act was passed allowing local authorities to arrange school meals. This was followed in 1907 by legislation authorizing school medical inspection. Though only permissive, these two Acts can be seen in retrospect as marking a new beginning in British social legislation. The State was now intervening in family matters which the Victorians had assumed to stand outside its range, except under the stigma of the Poor Law. The authorities were offering *services* to the poor, no longer only harshly correcting the poor's failings. Intervention for the benefit of the young was soon logically extended to care for the old, in the form not of relief but of pensions (1908); and finally in 1911 the enactment of health and unemployment insurance recognized that the welfare of individuals of working age could also concern the State.

But the Liberals did not realize in 1906 just how far and how fast they were destined to go. The School Meals Act was introduced on Labour initiative with the Government merely lending support. C. S. Loch (1849–1923), secretary of the Charity Organization Society, had opposed free meal provision in evidence before the Committee on Physical Deterioration on the ground that it might undermine family effort and unity. Meals, argued Loch, did not 'educate the child and make it think how to obtain the meal . . . The whole movement it seems to me is purely a movement against destitution without regard to education, and that in itself is a strong criticism of it.' Labour supporters of the 1906 Act admitted that unlimited charity might undermine personal responsibility, and they agreed that parents who could afford to pay for the food should be made to do so. But they urged the need for the free feeding of children from that large class of workers, discovered by Rowntree, whose 'economic condition when they were in work was of such a nature as almost to exclude any possibility of making that provision for their children which they might so much desire'. The Act was not mandatory, and by 1913–14 over half the education authorities in England and Wales had not begun the service. Nevertheless, at this date some 310,000 schoolchildren were receiving meals, and in 1914 the Board of Education was given power to compel local authorities to undertake the feeding of necessitous children. Section 4 of the 1906 Act had reflected the contrast between old Victorian and new Edwardian attitudes. Poor Law stigmatization was specifically rejected, the statute stipulating that notwithstanding any failure by a parent to pay for meals provided, he should not suffer any loss of civil rights or privileges. In other words, the meals were to be given free if this could not be avoided, as a State service not as a State charity. Writing in 1914 Dicey, the Conservative jurist, gloomily but rightly traced the whole movement towards the social service State from this measure. 'Why a man who first neglects his duty as a father and then defrauds the State should retain his full political rights is a question easier to ask than to answer.'

The gradual establishment of a school medical service under one clause of the 1907 Education (Administrative Provisions) Act excited less controversy than the introduction of school meals. Yet here again the Liberal Government had been hesitant, only sponsoring the proposals under back-bench pressure. The Act required medical inspections, and permitted (though not explicitly) the provision of medical treatment. By 1914 three out of four education authorities were giving some treatment under their own auspices; and 53 local authorities were contributing for treatment of schoolchildren in about a hundred voluntary hospitals.[11]

The young were beginning to be served by the emerging social service State. It was next the turn of the old. With a longer-living population the problem of the aged poor was assuming increasing significance. At least ten countries (notably Germany) were already providing State pensions for the aged, and in Britain discussion about both principles and alternative schemes had been continuous for some thirty years. In the mid-eighties a Commons Select Committee considered the question, and heard evidence from the friendly societies in opposition to any universal compulsory contributory scheme. In 1891 Charles Booth published his first old-age pension proposals, and thereafter Booth's ideas were often under discussion. In 1899 he published *Old Age Pensions and the Aged Poor*, again revising his plan three years later in the last volume of his *Life and Labour*. His final thoughts came in a pamphlet published in 1907. Booth was always anxious to emphasize how his suggestions—pensions of 7s. (originally 5s.) at seventy for men, of 5s. for women—would supplement rather than undermine the efforts of private charity and of the Poor Law. Critics always claimed that the prospect of a pension would undermine thrift. The foremost agencies of such thrift were the friendly societies, with no fewer than 24,000 branches and 4.25 million members. Booth contended that the prospect of a pension would 'stimulate individual effort to hold out till it comes' and to add something through saving to its 'meagre provision'. 'Thrift tests are unnecessary and delusive. To adopt them is to drop the reality in catching at the apparent, like the dog in the fable.' But the friendly societies remained suspicious of any government intervention in their field, and only slowly came to appreciate the benefits to them of tax-supported pensions payable to their members. Other critics complained of the 'huge cost' of Booth's scheme, perhaps £20 million per annum. Cost discouraged leading politicians of both main parties from committing themselves. Joseph Chamberlain came nearest to firm commitment among the party leaders when in 1891 he voiced general support for a voluntary state-backed scheme of 5s. pensions, payable only to persons who had already made the effort to partly provide for themselves in old age. Chamberlain and Booth played a prominent part in the proceedings of the Royal Commission on the Aged Poor (1893-5) in opposition to Loch of the COS who tried to show that more rigorous Poor Law administration, together with pensions financed from endowments and donations, would produce sufficient support for the aged. A National Committee of Organized Labour on Old Age Pensions formed in 1899 to support Booth, was matched by a COS inspired Committee on Old Age Pensions, started in 1900. Each body conducted propaganda campaigns seeking to influence both the public and the politicians. After 1895 Chamberlain had shifted his main attention from social to Imperial questions, and though he continued to express interest in the idea of pensions for the poor he was no longer ready to take the lead. From the turn of the century the high cost of the Boer War reinforced the reluctance of his Conservative allies to spend money on pensions. 'Joe's war', recollected Balfour self-excusingly years later, 'had stopped Joe's pensions.' Chamberlain did at first propose that pensions should follow the adoption of tariff reform, financed by tariffs levied on foreigners, but this proposal soon fell from prominence in his campaign.

The Liberals therefore had a clear opportunity when they took office at the end of 1905. Even so, the bolder members of the Cabinet could only slowly win over the Gladstonians, who were as fearful as Balfour of increased expenditure. Not until 1907 could Asquith promise action, and then only after a further year when a budget surplus was anticipated. A Cabinet paper of December 1906 had contrived to link demonstration of the great social need for old-age pensions with persuasive indication of likely large savings in Poor Law costs if pensions were introduced. 18.3 per cent of the English population over sixty-five were paupers, already maintained at public expense. The paper also emphasized the psychological uplift which would be given to nearly one-third of Britain's old people, at present spending some period of their retirement under the stigma of parochial relief, if they could be given pensions instead. Most shades of opinion now agreed that it was harsh to mark citizens as paupers simply because they had lived past working age. The practicality of all forms of contributory pension schemes was also increasingly doubted. The poor themselves heartily rejected the idea of paying for benefits which they might not live to enjoy. Moreover, it could be claimed that non-contributory pensions would avoid the diversion of funds from investment in the friendly societies. Asquith told the Commons in 1907 that he rejected 'as altogether inadmissible and unworkable the so-called contributory schemes':

I do not believe it is possible to adjust contributing schemes in such a way that the burden will fall equitably on the shoulders of those who ought to bear it, and the result you want to attain—a really genuine system of pensions for old age—be really secured. The second condition to which we attach equal importance is that both in the working and in the administration of any such scheme it should be dissociated from what I may call the ordinary machinery of the Poor Law. It ought not to be regarded as a substitute for any of those doles or pauperizing subventions which at the present time, and under our present system, inflict disabilities and carry with them a certain amount of public discredit.

Yet the Liberal plan finally proposed by Asquith in 1908—pensions of 5s. for individuals and 7s. 6d. for married couples—was not 'universal', as Booth had desired. Pensions became payable only at seventy (not sixty-five) and only persons with incomes not exceeding £21 per annum were to receive the full pension. A sliding scale operated above this figure, with no pensions payable on incomes over £31 10s. Only British subjects resident in the United Kingdom for twenty years and not in receipt of poor relief (other than medical relief) since 1st January 1908 were eligible, nor must they have been in prison within the previous ten years. Finally, a pensioner must not have 'habitually failed to work according to his ability, opportunity, and need'. Asquith's system, in short, represented a compromise between the demand for a simple universal scheme and the attachment of Gladstonian Liberals, the COS and many friendly societies to the Victorian gospel of thrift. The several restrictions upon payment, however, did not affect the underlying new intention: the State was now offering the poor a benefit as of right without stigma. 'The receipt of an old-age pension under this Act', affirmed the statute plainly, 'shall not deprive the pensioner of any right, franchise or privilege.' The Poor Law disqualification applied only for two years, and the test of industry proved unworkable, being formally abandoned in 1919.

In the Commons' debates the Conservative leaders were embarrassed by their own failure to act on pensions. Their tactic was to try to expand the Bill beyond the limits of prudent finance. 'To overballast the ship so that it would sink', as Lloyd

George remarked. Back-bench Conservatives such as Lord Robert Cecil (1864–1958) still feared to undermine individual independence: 'if they had to enter upon a great life and death struggle, as might well happen, and they had weakened the fibre of their people by a system and by a policy of which this was only the beginning, then the Statesmen in the House of Commons who had sanctioned that miserable backsliding from the true statesmanship of Empire would have much to answer for.' The Lords were highly critical; but Asquith had adroitly designated the pensions measure a money Bill, and by tradition the peers could not insist upon their amendments.

'God bless that Lord George' was the cry at backwoods post offices when the first pensions were paid at the start of 1909. Old-age pensions were one social reform generally and immediately popular among the Edwardian working class. Over 400,000 pensions were soon being distributed in England and Wales to nearly 45 per cent of the population aged over 70. Outdoor poor relief for this age group became almost unnecessary, a sign that the new payments were successfully serving a major social need.[12]

Lloyd George had inherited Parliamentary supervision of the old-age pensions Bill from Asquith on becoming Chancellor of the Exchequer. Churchill took his place at the Board of Trade. Asquith's advocacy of pensions had been characteristically lawyer-like, severly practical, with frequent reference to the limits of available funds. 'He made no electoral capital out of them', commented one journalist, 'seemed indeed to be unsympathetic. He had won the victory for you almost before you realized that he was on your side.' But Lloyd George and Churchill now decided upon further much more ostentatious action. The grant of pensions, explained Lloyd George, marked 'a real beginning' but only a beginning:

We do not say that it deals with all the problem of unmerited destitution in this country. We do not even contend that it deals with the worst part of that problem. It might be held that many an old man dependent on the charity of the parish was better off than many a young man, broken down in health, or who cannot find a market for his labour.

Lloyd George and Churchill agreed that the next beneficiaries must be the sick and the unemployed:

> The provision which is made for the sick and unemployment
> is grossly inadequate in this country, and yet the working
> classes have done their best during fifty years to make
> provision without the aid of the State. But it is insufficient
> . . . These problems of the sick, of the infirm, of the men who
> cannot find means of earning a livelihood, though they
> seek it as if they were seeking for alms, who are out of work
> through no fault of their own, and who cannot even guess the
> reason why, are problems with which it is the business of the
> State to deal; they are problems which the State has neglect-
> ed too long.

Accepting the existence of the capitalist system with its
fluctuating demand for labour, the State must intervene both to
provide labour exchanges and unemployment insurance. Here,
said Lloyd George and Churchill, was the 'new Liberalism',
more radical than Gladstonian Liberalism but less disruptive
than socialism. 'Socialism', declared Churchill, 'seeks to pull
down wealth; Liberalism seeks to raise up poverty. Socialism
would destroy private interests; Liberalism would preserve
private interests in the only way in which they can be safely and
justly preserved, namely reconciling them with public right.'
Germany, which Lloyd George specially visited in the summer
of 1908, had begun social insurance as far back as the eighteen
eighties. 'She is organized', Churchill warned Asquith, 'not
only for war, but for peace. We are organized for nothing
except party politics.'

Not that Churchill was indifferent to such politics. He emphasized to Asquith how social legislation might 'not only
benefit the State but fortify the party'. Seven seats were lost to
the Conservatives at by-elections between January and September 1908, including Churchill's own Manchester seat when
he stood for re-election on changing office. The 1906 Liberal
programme had been too negative to retain much enduring
appeal, and even in pursuit of these negatives it had been
seriously impeded by the House of Lords. 'There is a tremendous policy in Social Organization', Churchill told Asquith;

'. . . the very class of legislation which is required is just the kind the House of Lords will not dare to oppose.' Churchill and Lloyd George were well aware that social reform was viewed with apathy or even suspicion by many working men. The Liberal hope was that the masses might show election gratitude after its enactment, though Churchill conceded that even this was not certain. 'The Minister who will apply to this country the successful experiences of Germany in social organization may or may not be supported at the polls, but he will at least have left a memorial which time will not deface of his administration.'[13]

Churchill believed in 1908 that unemployment was especially 'the problem of the hour'. Trade was again widely depressed, making it 'a paramount necessity for us to make scientific provision against the fluctuations and setbacks of industry'. Revealingly, the very word 'unemployment' had only come into general use during the last twenty years of the nineteenth century, still described by the *Encyclopedia Britannica* in 1911 as 'a modern term'. It was 'more particularly within the 20th century', continued the same article, 'that the problem of unemployment has become specially insistent, not by reason of its greater intensity', which was doubtful, 'but because the greater facilities for publicity, the growth of industrial democracy, the more scientific methods applied to the solution of economic questions, the larger humanitarian spirit of the times all demand that remedies differing considerably from those of the past should at least be tried.' Acceptance of the concept of 'unemployment' implied recognition that a man out of work was not necessarily a blameworthy idler. His idleness might be a consequence not of his own failings but of failings in the economic system. This had been made apparent during the 'great depression' of the last quarter of the nineteenth century. Socialists pushed this new acceptance to its logical conclusion by asserting 'the right to work', emphasizing the responsibility of the State to ensure employment. During 1908, backed by a nationwide campaign, the Labour Party tried unsuccessfully to force a Right to Work Bill through Parliament. Comprehensive unemployment statistics were not available to the Edwardians, and are not now calculable. But unemployment percentages among members of certain trade unions crudely reflected the overall trend—rising gradually to a peak 6 per cent in 1904, falling to 3.6 and 3.7 per cent in 1906 and 1907, jumping to 7.8 and 7.7 in 1908 and 1909, and falling again to 4.7 per cent in 1910 and to as low as 2.1 per cent in 1913. Rowntree estimated the numbers of Edwardian unemployed as about 330,000 in the best times, 1,425,000 in the worst.

The depression of 1904–5 had stimulated the Balfour Government to appoint a Royal Commission on the Poor Laws and Relief of Distress. Its majority report appeared in February 1909, also a minority report signed by four socialist members headed by Beatrice Webb. (Their report was largely written by Sidney Webb). The majority wished to reform and retain (even though to rename) the Poor Law; the Webbs wanted to abolish it. Both reports agreed on the need for thorough reform of the Edwardian machinery for controlling poverty and unemployment. 'Something in our social organization is seriously wrong', asserted the majority report plainly. Expenditure of £60 million on poor relief, education and health in 1905–6 still seemed unable to contain the problem of poverty. England was supposedly the 'land of hope and glory'; yet 'to certain classes of the community into whose moral and material condition it has been our duty to inquire, those words are a mockery and a falsehood'. The majority signatories still believed that State aid should be geared to stimulating individual self-help; but during the Commission's investigations they had come to accept that this required an extension of State machinery and State involvement far beyond what voluntary bodies such as the COS had previously admitted to be necessary. 'Great Britain is the home of voluntary effort, and its triumphs and successes constitute in themselves much of the history of the country. But voluntary effort when attacking a common and unbiquitous problem must be disciplined and led.' The COS members of the Commission, led by Loch, all signed the majority report. It recommended the transfer of Poor Law administration (to be renamed Public Assistance) to the county and county borough councils. It advised more specialized provision for old people, children and able-bodied unemployed. Unemployment should be checked through decasualization, through the discouragement of blind-alley jobs, the raising of the school leaving age to fifteen, the opening of labour exchanges, and the postponement of public works to slack times. Relief of the unemployed should remain a Poor Law responsibility, but should be restorative and discriminating. For decent working men (if not helped by voluntary aid committees) support should be given in industrial institutions or in agricultural colonies; loafers should be sent to detention colonies. Unemployment insurance and invalidity insurance (for early superannuation) were recommended. Insurance should be aided from public funds, but a general scheme was rejected in favour of one based on separate industries, neither compulsory nor universal. Medical care should be provided through provident dispensaries; but a 'gratuitous medical service' was rejected except for paupers. Disfranchisement should not apply to recipients of medical relief, nor to anyone receiving other relief for less than three months per year. Victorian ideas of deterrence, deliberately making poor relief uncongenial, were to be replaced by 'preventive, curative and restorative' help.

The Webb-inspired minority advocated what has been called 'administrative functionalism'. This meant that government services should be organized for specific purposes, not for special groups (such as 'the poor'). The poor were not a separate race with common failings, but ordinary human beings suffering from identifiable difficulties, often undeserved. Recognition of this truth, argued the minority, meant abolition of the Poor Law and the distribution of its functions among other official bodies, local and national, including a new Ministry of Labour with the duty of 'so organizing the National Labour Market as to prevent or minimize Unemployment'. The Webbs were looking beyond the surface facts of poverty to the causes of destitution, and were seeking to ensure the 'national minimum'. They found 'certain roads down which people are continually slipping into this morass'—neglect in infancy, neglect as schoolchildren, neglect in sickness. 'Then there is the broad road of unemployment, and we hear the tramp, tramp of the men thrown out of work through no fault of their own, marching with a sort of fatal inevitableness down that broad road into the morass of destitution.' Preventive action must be taken. The Webbs agreed with the majority about the importance of encouraging individual responsibility. 'You can never bring home to any citizen his responsibility . . . unless you at the same time secure to every man the opportunity of fulfilling his responsibility. That can never be done by any Poor Law.' 'Altering the environment' was a pre-condition for 'bringing home to the individual his responsibility for maintaining himself.'

To disseminate their ideas the Webbs moved from their usual place behind the scenes into organizing a mass agitation. In June 1909 they formed the National Committee for the Break-up of the Poor Law, afterwards more positively renamed the National Committee for the Prevention of Destitution. This body attracted 25,000 members and 400 volunteer lecturers, and published hundreds of thousands of leaflets and pamphlets. But the Liberal Government had its own ideas, and refused to be deflected. The main proposals of both the majority and minority Poor Law reports were ignored by Lloyd George and Churchill. A unanimous report might have exerted more immediate influence. Nevertheless, in publicizing their wide-ranging proposals the Webbs were contributing notably to forward thinking along lines which were eventually to produce the welfare state.[14]

Just as the late Victorians had faced 'unemployment' so the Edwardians discovered 'under-employment', which was discussed in both Poor Law reports. William Smart (1853–1915), Professor of Political Economy at Glasgow University, had defined the new term in 1906:

As regards employment, a new problem, touching the most vital interests of the community, has been gradually evolving itself, and is now becoming acute. To put it in a word, the partial employment of great numbers—a phenomenon so striking as to have induced the coining of a new word. An unemployment which contracts in good years, but never disappears even in the best, is a concomitant, if not a consequence of high industrial organization. I make no scruple of saying that this connexion of unemployment with the perfecting of our industrial system presents the greatest problem of modern economic life, raising, indeed, a very grave doubt whether, even at this late stage, we may not have to retrace some of the steps of our industrial progress.

The fullest discussion of under-employment came in Beveridge's pioneering survey, *Unemployment, a Problem of Industry* (1909). Beveridge explained how under-employment was especially a problem for members of Booth's social groups B and C. Some occupations, such as dock labour, were entirely organized round a permanent pool of casual labour. Workmen in such circumstances were always the most likely to fall into unemployment; they were also the nearest to demoralization and collapse into category A, the unemployables. Temporary relief work, as provided under the 1905 Unemployed Workmen Act, could not solve such a problem. 'To give them temporary work in times of exceptional depression', remarked Beveridge, 'is to throw them back upon chronic poverty at its close; it is like saving men from drowning in order to leave them on a quicksand.' Beveridge's solution to under-employment was decasualization of labour through the establishment of labour exchanges. 'The larger and more varied the area of employment covered by an Exchange, the more completely will it be able to regularize the work of this reserve, because the more nearly will the independent fluctuations of many businesses neutralize one another to yield a steady average.' The sharp mind of young Winston Churchill soon grasped the nature of the under-employment problem:

that the casual labourer who is habitually under-employed, who is lucky to get three, or at the outside four, days' work in the week, who may often be out of a job for three or four weeks at a time, who in bad times goes under altogether, and who in good times has no hope of security and no incentive to thrift, whose whole life and the lives of his wife and children are embarked in a sort of blind, desperate, fatalistic gamble with circumstances beyond his comprehension or control, that this poor man, this terrible and pathetic figure, is not as a class the result of accident or chance, is not casual as the consequence of some temporary disturbance soon put right . . . He is here as the result of economic causes which have been too long unregulated. He is not the natural product, he is an article manufactured, called into being, to suit the requirements, in the Prime Minister's telling phrase, of all industries at particular times and of particular industries at all times.

Churchill invited Beveridge, behind whom stood the Webbs, to become a civil servant at the Board of Trade. But this did not mean that Churchill had become a Webb convert, eagerly though at this time he read their writings and attended their dinner parties. 'You never quite know what he's going to hand back to you afterwards as his version of your idea', admitted Beatrice Webb ruefully. A fundamental difference of attitude soon emerged between Churchill, Lloyd George and the 'new' Liberals on the one hand, and the Webbs on the other. The Webbs wanted to attack root causes; Churchill and Lloyd George, being practising politicians aware of the need to retain some contact with party and public opinion, aspired no further than to attack effects. The Webbs argued that labour exchanges should be made compulsory. If an employer could hire workers only through exchanges, and workmen could find work nowhere else, the government would be able to organize the labour market. Unemployment insurance on a voluntary basis would then be sufficient. Instead, Churchill and Lloyd George preferred to make labour exchanges voluntary but unemployment insurance compulsory in certain trades. In other words, they acted to fight the problem of destitution by relieving the unemployed rather than by attempting to prevent unemployment. The social and political theory underlying such action may have been uncertain, but the new Liberalism soon proved that it could work.

Unemployment, Churchill argued arrestingly, was 'primarily a question for the employers. Their responsibility is undoubted, their co-operation indispensible.' Churchill believed that employers did recognize this responsibility, and that legislation was necessary 'only to give concrete embodiment and scientific expression to a powerful impulse of just and humane endeavour'. A system of compulsory unemployment insurance 'associates directly for the first time the practical interest of the employer and the unemployed workmen. Both contribute to a common fund; both are concerned in its maintenance and its thrifty administration. Such a system will afford a powerful motive for the voluntary support of Labour Exchanges.' In short, compulsory unemployment insurance and labour exchanges represented two sides of the same coin. 'Together they organize in due proportions the mobility and stability of labour.' In the end, however, these innovations were introduced only at a two-year interval, because of the constitutional crisis arising out of the 1909 budget. The Labour Exchanges Act passed through Parliament without much dispute during the early stages of the crisis, Churchill explaining how exchanges would counter 'two main defects in modern industrial conditions', lack of labour mobility and lack of information. The new system began in February 1910, when 61 existing private exchanges were absorbed into an official network. By the end of 1913 430 exchanges were spread over the United Kingdom, plus over a thousand small rural agencies dealing exclusively with unemployment insurance. This rapid spread of labour exchanges was a sign of their success. About 10 per cent of vacancies filled fell outside the region of the exchange of first application. To this important extent, therefore, was the flexibility of the labour market increased. But Churchill's hope that the exchanges might develop as social centres—providing 'facilities for washing, clothes-mending, and for non-alcoholic refreshments'—was destined to be disappointed.[15]

Alongside the Labour Exchanges Act Churchill promoted the Trade Boards Act, creating machinery for fixing minimum wages in designated 'sweated' trades. The problem of such trades had disturbed the public conscience since the eighties, and it now came to be widely agreed that the government must intervene. A National Anti-Sweating League, formed in 1906, had conducted an effective publicity campaign, holding exhibitions to reveal the extent of over-work and under-payment especially in activities employing mostly female labour often on a domestic basis. Such workers had proved unable to organize and to protect themselves through trade union action. 'The widow, the women folk of the poorest type of labourer, the broken, the weak, the struggling, the diseased—those are the people who largely depend upon these trades.' Churchill's Act applied in the first instance to four occupations—tailoring, box making, lace making and chain making, employing about 200,000 workers, 140,000 of them women and girls. Intervention was successful in raising wages, and six more trades were added in 1913, employing 170,000 work-people. In its specific range the Trade Boards Act had been a limited measure; but in its implications it was a much larger innovation than the provision of voluntary labour exchanges, for it assumed (however indirectly) that the State now had an interest in ensuring a minimum wage. The Liberals' biggest innovation, however,—national insurance—was still to come, enacted only after the long fight over Lloyd George's 1909 budget.[16]

Lloyd George deliberately set out to make his first budget a bold one. The Liberals were still losing by-elections, three seats to the Conservatives and two to Labour between March and October 1909. A 'people's budget' might check this erosion of the Liberal majority from both left and right. The Government expected such a budget to be hotly contested in Parliament, but neither Lloyd George nor Asquith seem to have schemed to produce a Finance Bill which they expected the Lords to reject. Lloyd George did remark that repudiation of his budget would advance the Liberal cause still more than acceptance. Some of his proposals were disliked even within the Liberal Cabinet, notably his land taxes. The Chancellor needed to find nearly £16 million to meet the cost of old-age pensions and new battleship building. He also wanted fresh sources of revenue to finance social insurance. *Punch* portrayed Lloyd George as 'the Philanthropic Highwayman', pistol at the ready, waiting as the 'idle rich' came into sight in their motor cars, exclaiming '*I'll* make 'em pity the aged poor'. In his budget speech he put a series of key questions:

> Can the whole subject of further social reform be postponed until the increasing demands made upon the National Exchequer by the growth of armaments have ceased? Not merely *can* it be postponed, but ought it to be postponed? Is there the slightest hope that if we deferred consideration of the matter, we are likely within a generation to find any more favourable moment for attending to it? . . . If we put off dealing with these social sores, are the evils which arise from them not likely to grow and to fester, until finally the loss which the country sustains will be infinitely greater than anything it would have to bear in paying the cost of an immediate remedy?

While leaving rates of earned income tax unchanged up to £3000, Lloyd George raised the tax upon higher earned and all unearned incomes from 1s. to 1s. 2d. in the £. A £10 tax allowance was given to small income tax payers earning under £500, but a maximum of 5d. super tax was introduced upon incomes over £5000. By later twentieth-century standards these rates seem Elysian, but they appeared very heavy in its first decade. Death duties, liquor licensing duties, and tobacco and spirit duties were also increased, while taxes on cars and petrol were introduced. But the most contentious features of the budget were its new revenue taxes on land: 20 per cent on the unearned increment in land values, a capital tax of ½d. in the £ on the value of undeveloped land and minerals, and a 10 per cent reversion duty on any benefit falling to a lessor at the end of a lease. Lloyd George was determined to extract money from those landowners who could make great profits with no effort simply because chance of nature had endowed their land with valuable minerals or because urban development had raised site values. 'It is undoubtedly one of the worst evils of our present system of land tenure that instead of reaping the benefits of the common endeavour of its citizens a community has always to pay a heavy penalty to its ground landlords for putting up the value of their land.' The yield on these land taxes was to prove disappointing, but the Conservatives concentrated their fiercest attacks upon them. They denounced such 'socialism' as 'the beginning of the end of the rights of property'. The taxes were made the more offensive by provision for an inquisitorial preliminary valuation of land. Lloyd George defended his proposals as a 'war budget . . . for raising money to wage implacable war against poverty and squalidness'. But before this war budget could be passed the country had to endure warfare of another type, party political conflict of remarkable bitterness.[17]

By July 1909 it was becoming clear that the Conservatives might reject the budget in the upper house. In the Commons they resorted to delaying tactics, some seventy days of debate being needed to pass the Finance Bill despite the Liberals' large majority. In the country a Budget Protest League was matched by a Liberal Budget League. As president of this latter body Churchill spoke with characteristic pugnacity up and down the

country during the summer and autumn of 1909. He emphasized 'the increasing sense of reality which political affairs have
acquired during the last few months . . . Across and beyond the
complicated details of finance, the thousand amendments and
more which cover the order paper, the absurd obstruction, the
dry discussions in Committee, the interminable repetition of
divisions, the angry scenes which flash up from time to time, the
white-faced members sitting the whole night through and walking home worn out in the full light of morning—across and
beyond all this, can you not discern a people's cause in conflict?'
A new question, claimed Churchill daringly, must now be
asked:

> We do not only ask today, 'How much have you got?' we also
> ask, 'How did you get it? Did you earn it by yourself, or has
> it just been left you by others? Was it gained by processes
> which are in themselves beneficial to the community in
> general, or was it gained by processes which have done no
> good to any one, but only harm? Was it gained by the
> enterprise and capacity necessary to found a business, or
> merely by squeezing and bleeding the owner and founder of
> the business? Was it gained by supplying the capital which
> industry needs, or by denying, except at an extortionate
> price, the land which industry requires? . . . It is a tremen-
> dous question, never previously in this country asked so
> plainly, a new idea, pregnant, formidable, full of life, that
> taxation should not only have regard to the volume of wealth,
> but, so far as possible, to the character of the processes of its
> origin.

Lloyd George himself was more tied to Parliament than
Churchill, but his few outside speeches had great effect. At
Limehouse on 30th July he roused Conservative hostility
perhaps even more than he anticipated, making his speech a
decisive event and the word 'Limehouse' a synonym for extreme
invective. Yet his language now reads as relatively restrained,
offering a reasoned defence of the budget, though peppered
with sharp hits at landlords, brewers and peers. He defined a
landlord's 'sole function, his chief pride' as 'stately consumption
of wealth produced by others'. The impact of such sallies can
only be understood against the Edwardian background of social

hierarchy and deference. To question this hierarchy seemed to Conservatives to be threatening the stability of the whole fabric of society. By October, with Conservative resistance now hardening to the point of rejection of the budget, Lloyd George's tone had become sharp indeed. He claimed in a speech at Newcastle that most of those who worked for a living were Liberals, most of those who did not were Conservatives. He found two selfish groups opposing the budget, tariff reformers who wanted to tax food, and landlords who contrastingly did not want their land taxed. He charged the Lords with forcing a revolution. 'Who talks about altering and meddling with the Constitution? The Constitutional party—the great Constitutional party. As long as the Constitution gave rank and possession and power to the Lords it was not to be interfered with . . . the moment the Constitution begins to discover that there are millions of people outside park gates who need attention, then the Constitution is to be torn to pieces. . . . The Lords may decree a revolution, but the people will direct it.'

The budget finally passed the Commons on 4th November but by this date Balfour had decided to use his majority in the upper house to defeat the Government. On 30th November the Finance Bill was rejected by 350 votes to 75. A general election was now bound to follow. This time the Lords had not simply rejected one measure, they had refused supply, without which no Government can rule. The peers had virtually claimed the right of deciding when a Parliament should end. Balfour did not believe that he was endangering the constitution by this extreme action. On the contrary, he argued that it was Liberal policy, not Conservative resistance to it, which was constitutionally dangerous. The motive of the Government in imposing land taxes, he explained in a private letter, 'was to please the "mass" of the voters, or, as your friend puts it, "the poor".' This is precisely the crime that lies at their door. They have chosen a particular section of the community, and a particular kind of property which they think both unpopular and helpless, and have proceeded to mulct it—demagogism in its worst aspect. As you and I own but little of it, *this* part of the Budget will not make much difference to us. But this only increases my indignation.'

In contrast to these allegedly dangerous budget tendencies the Conservatives and Liberal Unionists emphasized the prospective benefits for all classes of tariff reform, which Balfour was now inclined to support. Lord Lansdowne's rejection motion also attempted a show of democratic virtue: 'That this House is not justified in giving its consent to the [Finance] Bill until it has been submitted to the judgment of the country.' There never was an occasion, claimed Balfour, 'when the power, vested by the constitution in the second chamber, was more absolutely justified'. But the electors did not agree. In the general election of January 1910, as Austen Chamberlain admitted, 'they voted against the Lords, and, above all, against the landlords'. The Conservatives regained many rural seats which they had lost only because of the exceptional swing against them in 1906; but Liberal and Labour candidates still gained 51 per cent of the votes cast, against only 46.9 per cent for the Opposition. Here was a clear majority for the Government, even though the Liberals lost their overall lead in seats. The verdict was strengthened by the highest percentage turnout (86.6) in election history.

The Conservatives had tried to minimize the constitutional aspect of the crisis and had failed. Their call for tariff reform could not outmatch the Liberal cry of 'the peers versus the people'. Asquith announced that if his Government were re-elected acceptance of the budget by the Lords would not now be enough; the Liberals would insist upon a reduction of the powers of the upper house. Experience since 1906 had shown this 'to be necessary for the legislative utility and the honour of the party of progress'. 'Is this nation to be a free nation and to become a freer one', asked Lloyd George, 'or is it for all time to be shackled and tethered by tariffs and trusts and monopolies and privileges? That is the issue.' Lansdowne, the Conservative leader in the Lords, had argued that early acceptance of the budget by the peers against their known inclinations would have 'permanently impaired' their powers; they could never again have resisted, 'however outrageous the financial policy of a radical Government might be'. This was probably true. But either way the Lords were bound to lose, if the electorate remained firm behind the Government. Lansdowne himself foresaw this. He expected to be defeated at a first general election, but (rightly) anticipated the calling of a second one before the Lords question could be settled. Time, he believed, would cool feelings and work in favour of the Conservatives, of the preservation of the powers of the upper house, and of tariff reform. But Lansdowne and Balfour were aristocrats, whose views about the role of the Lords were inappropriate for the twentieth century. They were congenitally unable to attune themselves to the majority of the electorate, and the electors enjoyed the final say.[18]

Nevertheless, the path from the election of January 1910 to the passing of the Parliament Act in August 1911 was to be long and difficult. At first Asquith seemed to be stumbling. The Cabinet wandered from the clear issue of the Lords veto to the much less clear question of reform of the composition of the upper house. Fortunately, the Premier finally asserted himself, announcing on 18th March that the Government intended to proceed both with the budget and with a Bill limiting the powers of the Lords. He introduced the Parliament Bill on 14th April. Its provisions were inspired by a scheme outlined by Campbell–Bannerman in 1907. The upper house was to lose all authority over money bills, but was to be left with power to delay legislation for two years. A measure (such as an Irish Home Rule Bill) sent up by the Commons in three successive sessions could become law on the third occasion regardless of the Lords' opposition. Asquith made it clear that if the peers rejected these proposals he would again appeal to the country, but only if the King were willing, when requested, to create enough peers to muster a favourable majority, the Liberals having won the election. Without such a royal promise the Government would resign forthwith, and let Balfour (if he dared) try to govern against the wishes of a majority of the Commons—with the King by implication condoning the attempt. On 28th April the Lords passed the budget in a few hours, Lansdowne accepting that the January election had settled the issue. The centre of dispute now shifted to the Parliament Bill.[19]

The culmination of the crisis was delayed, however, by the death of Edward VII on 6th May. Asquith felt that it would be unfair to expect the new King, George V, to be ready to honour his father's commitment until he had grown used to his new role and until one last effort had been made at a settlement. A constitutional conference was arranged between Government and Opposition leaders, who met during the summer of 1910 and again during October and November. Much ground was traversed both in relation to limitation of the power and to reform of the membership of the House of Lords. With varying degrees of readiness, the Liberal delegates proved willing to modify the Parliament Bill, Asquith especially so. But the discussions finally foundered over Irish Home Rule, to which the Conservatives were passionately opposed. They wanted such constitutional legislation, if twice rejected by the Lords, to be next submitted to a referendum. The Liberals refused to allow the Lords this new power to force an appeal to the country. On 15th November the Cabinet agreed to ask the King for a dissolution of Parliament on the terms announced by Asquith a year before. With great reluctance the King agreed, on the understanding that his promise would not be made public unless and until the need for creations was apparent.

So a second general election took place in December 1910, dominated by the Lords question, but without public knowledge that Asquith, if he won, would be able in the last resort to secure a massive creation of peers. The elections produced little overall change in the position of the parties, and the contest was said to be dull. Nonetheless, the turnout was still high (82.6 per cent) and 56 seats changed hands. Asquith introduced the Parliament Bill to the new House of Commons on 21st February 1911. Churchill, who shared the Bill's management with the Prime Minister, urged his chief not to be afraid of making '500 peers if necessary'. Asquith and most members of the Cabinet hoped earnestly, however, that such drastic action would not ultimately prove necessary. Everything depended upon the Conservatives in the Lords. Logically, having rejected the 1909 budget for allegedly good reasons they ought to reject a measure designed to prevent them acting in the same manner again. But the first move had proved a blunder, and Balfour now accepted that it would be an even greater blunder to force a dilution of the peerage in futile resistance to the Parliament Bill, 'so profoundly modifying the constitution of the second chamber that it would become with regard to some important measures a mere annexe to the present House of Commons'. If the peers gave way over the Parliament Bill, Balfour realised that they would still be able to delay a Home Rule Bill for two years: whereas if the Liberals acquired a Lords majority, Home Rule would be enacted at the first attempt. Lansdowne was more reluctant to surrender. In May 1911 as an alternative to the Parliament Bill he introduced an abortive scheme for comprehensive reform of the membership of the upper house, which would nevertheless have perpetuated its Conservative majority. When early in July the Lords began drastically to amend the Parliament Bill Asquith asked George V to be ready to make a huge creation of Liberal peers. It now became known to the Opposition that the King was firmly committed to such action. This destroyed the position of those, including Lansdowne, who had kept up resistance in the belief that Asquith was bluffing. 249 candidates for ennoblement were now listed by the Government Chief Whip, including Thomas Hardy, the novelist, J. M. Barrie (1860–1937), the playwright, and Bertrand Russell (1872–1970), the philosopher. On 26th July *Punch* carried a cartoon depicting a conversation between the Chief Whip ('I can raise the coronets all right; but I can't answer for the "Norman blood"') and the Prime Minister ('Never mind the "Norman blood"; it's the "kind hearts" and the "simple faith" that I'm worrying about').

As July moved into August the Conservative peers were convulsed in argument. 'Hedgers' prepared to give way under protest: 'ditchers', led by the pre-Victorian Lord Halsbury (1823–1921), were ready to die in the last ditch. During 9th–10th August, with the temperature well into the nineties, the final Lords' debate took place. The result was in doubt to the end. But Lansdowne and the bulk of his followers were now for 'hedging'. They abstained; while 37 Conservatives, urged by Lord Curzon to avert 'pollution' of their order, actually voted for the Bill. The Liberals mustered 81; 13 bishops supported them. Here were 131 votes in all. The 'ditchers' could total only 114. So the Parliament Bill passed by 17 votes, thanks to substantial Conservative voting for a measure which all Conservatives abhorred. Into such a paradoxical situation had Balfour and Lansdowne led their party. Balfour despondently left the country before the final Lords' debate began. Within three months he had resigned as party leader. The first part of the constitutional struggle was now over. But an even fiercer dispute over Home Rule for Ireland was bound to follow. And in this second clash the Lords intended to use their remaining powers of delay to the full.[20]

The other major piece of legislation in 1911 was the National Insurance Act. 'That is the future—Insurance against dangers from abroad, Insurance against dangers scarcely less grave and much more near and constant which threaten us here at home in our own island.' So argued Churchill in 1909. Social insurance, 'the magic of averages' as he called it, was a much greater innovation in social reform than old-age pensions:

We seek to substitute for the pressure of the forces of nature, operating by chance on individuals, the pressures of the laws of insurance, operating through averages with modifying and mitigating effects in individual cases. In neither case is correspondence with reality lost. In neither case are pressures removed. In neither case is risk eliminated. In neither case can personal effort be dispensed with. In neither case can inferiority be protected. Chance and average spring from the same family, both are inexorable, both are blind, neither is concerned with the character of individuals or with ethics or with sentiment . . . the true economic superiority of the new foundations of averages, over the old foundation of chance, arises from the fact that the processes of waste are so much more swift than those of growth and repair, that the prevention of such catastrophes would be worth purchasing by diminution in the sense of personal responsibility; and, further, that as there is no proportion between personal failings and the penalties extracted, or even between personal qualities and those penalties, there is no reason to suppose that a mitigation of the extreme severities will tend in any way to a diminution of personal responsibility, but that on the contrary more will be gained by an increase of ability to fight than will be lost through an abatement of the extreme consequences of defeat.

Churchill had done most of the preparatory work for un-employment insurance, but in 1910 he left the Board of Trade, and it was Lloyd George alone who pressed forward with national insurance. His 1908 visit to study the German system had deeply impressed him with the need to catch up in this sphere as in others. 'Twenty-seven millions of money raised as a fund—raised as a parapet between the people and the poverty that comes from sickness and unemployment! I worked hard at that parapet . . . I do not say that it will ensure an era of abundance, but it will inaugurate it.' The unemployment provisions of the 1911 Act provoked little Parliamentary debate. It was actuarily sound, being confined to certain trades exposed to cyclical unemployment but not chronically depressed—building, shipbuilding, mechanical engineering, ironfounding, vehicle construction, and sawmilling. Employers and employees were to each pay 2½d. per head per week, the Treasury adding one-third. The Government was feeling its way with deliberate caution, though Lloyd George and the radicals envisaged that this limited scheme would be gradually extended trade by trade until it became universal.[21]

The health insurance scheme was much bolder, and was passed and operated only after a struggle with powerful pressure groups. Both the friendly societies and the insurance companies had to be placated, for Lloyd George knew that their army of door-to-door collectors could exert great influence in the constituencies. They were therefore made 'approved societies' through which much of the scheme functioned. Insurance was made compulsory for all manual workers and voluntary for anyone earning less than £160 a year. The self-employed and non-employed were not covered. Workmen contributed 4d. weekly, employers 3d., and the State not quite 2d., making (in Lloyd George's phrase) 'ninepence for fourpence'. 10s. sickness benefit was provided for twenty-six weeks, backed by medical, maternity and sanatorium care.

Yet health insurance was not popular. The Liberals lost three by-elections towards the end of 1911 while the Act was passing through its final stages. The Northcliffe press, and Conservative extremists, encouraged a short-lived but noisy agitation against payment of contributions especially by means of stamps stuck on insurance cards and above all by mistresses in respect of domestic servants. This agitation produced a mass meeting of mistresses and servants in the Albert Hall, organized by two ladies of title. The playing of 'Men of Harlech' as part of the introductory music, reported *The Times*, provoked a 'tornado of hissing'. Insurance, argued the noble chairwoman, would ruin 'that beautiful intimacy which had hitherto so often existed between mistresses and servants'. More seriously, the scheme was presented to the working classes as an oppressive system of deduction from wages. Finally, after the Act had passed but before medical benefit came into effect in January 1913, extreme opinion tried to exploit the fears of the doctors. Throughout 1912 the medical men grumbled about their prospects under the scheme. The President of the British Medical Association went so far as to describe Lloyd George as a 'national calamity'. But the Association's leaders overplayed their hand, and by making important concessions the Chancellor was able at the last moment to enlist most of the less affluent doctors. He took care not to seem to be creating a salaried state medical service. Nor did he break up (or even rename) the Poor Law. Throughout two years of difficult negotiations he had prudently gone not a step further than necessary to achieve his radical (but not socialist) ends.[22]

Lloyd George was pleased to make the position of the Conservative leaders (on Balfour's own admission) a 'difficult one' in regard to health insurance. They dared not oppose it totally, but they were glad to voice criticisms on behalf of the friendly societies, as they had done over old age pensions, without seeming to oppose the whole principle of a measure of popular welfare. 'Confound Lloyd George', grumbled Austen Chamberlain. 'He has strengthened the Government again.'[23]

A 'social service state', in which certain minimum standards were assured, was now beginning to emerge, although this minimum was far from universally available by 1914. The true 'welfare state', embracing the idea of the optimum, of the best affordable standard for all without distinction of persons or wealth, still lay forty years in the future. But the principle of provision through insurance was already established. This contrasted with the socialist method, advocated by Keir Hardie and Philip Snowden in opposition to the 1911 scheme, of financing benefits entirely through graduated taxation.

Snowden was sure that the demand for non-contributory insurance would grow, 'and that within the next generation we shall do what we have done in regard to national education and other services which have come to be recognized as national in character, and the State will accept entire responsibility.' But Ramsay MacDonald accepted the contributory principle in 1911, and the 1945 Labour Government followed his lead, not Snowden's, when it created the present-day welfare state.[24]

The expression 'the welfare state' had not yet been coined. But Hilaire Belloc feared the emergence of what he named 'the servile state', wherein workmen became slave-bound to the capitalist system. Workers were now forced, complained Belloc, to contribute out of wages to unemployment insurance, even though the funds so collected were entirely beyond their control in the hands of State officials. Yet while this State pressure upon the workers was being intensified, the capitalists remained substantially unaffected: 'the complementary truth that what should be the very essence of Collectivist Reform, to wit, the translation of the means of production from the hands of private owners to the hands of public officials, is nowhere being attempted.' Belloc has of course been proved right to the extent that the welfare state has been created within a still predominantly capitalist 'mixed economy'; but the bureaucratic state has proved in general the servant rather than the master of the people, and the equal if not the master of the capitalists.[25]

We have already seen how the Edwardian masses were suspicious of the emerging social service bureaucracy, albeit for reasons quite different from Belloc's. They were conditioned by their experience of the police and of the Poor Law authorities. We have quoted Lloyd George recognizing in 1908 how the people would have to be lifted out of their 'stupor of despair' not by themselves but by 'others outside', headed by himself. His hope was that though social reform might not prove electorally appealing before or even just after its enactment, it might acquire appeal as measure followed measure and as its cumulative benefits began to be felt. In this spirit after the introduction of national insurance he prepared to lead the Liberals into another major area of social improvement, land reform. This had been a traditional Liberal aspiration since the days of Cobden and Bright, but the public demand for it had never been strong. *Punch* carried a cartoon (24th July, 1912) entitled 'Oliver asks for Less', showing Oliver's bowl of 'social legislation' overflowing but with Lloyd George preparing to add 'land policy' to it. The Chancellor admitted that public opinion was not ready for immediate legislation. The people needed educating, and he persuaded the Cabinet to allow him to mount a 'land campaign' of speech-making in the autumn of 1913 intended to begin the arousal of the electorate. Land reform was being prepared as a major part of the Liberal programme at the next general election, due to be held in 1915. The Liberals had performed relatively poorly in agricultural constituencies in 1910, and they hoped that this new emphasis would win them more rural seats next time.

Lloyd George had been closely acquainted with land problems all his life, well aware of the privileges of landlords in rural Wales and of the poverty of landless agricultural workers. But he recognized the need for firm statistical evidence, and to this end he inspired the formation of a Land Inquiry Committee, a group of Liberals including Seebohm Rowntree. Its reports appeared in two large volumes in 1913 and 1914. Rowntree also published *How the Labourer Lives* (1913), a rural exposure complementary to his first influential book on urban poverty. Round the evidence from these sources Lloyd George built his speeches, beginning at Bedford in October 1913. Once again he castigated the selfish landlords, as he had done in his 1909 speeches. 'The Sovereign of this Empire has no power over his subjects comparable to the power which the landlord has over his subjects.' Labourers' wages, claimed Lloyd George, were now less in real value than in the reign of Henry VII. 'That is what we have done with him, and the land system is responsible for it.' He demanded a thorough reform of the system, ensuring a living wage for labourers, allotments for those who wanted them, the demolition of rural slums, an end to 'capricious eviction', protection against rent increases arising out of improvements made by tenants, and protection against destruction of crops by game preserved only for landlords' pleasure. 'Labourers had diminished, game had tripled. The landlord was no more necessary to agriculture than a gold chain to a watch.'

Lloyd George remarked in private that the land campaign 'was not a case for speeches alone, the country must be flooded with pamphlets and relevant facts'. 50,000 copies of one such pamphlet by Rowntree were published in May 1914, *The Labourer and the Land* with a preface by Lloyd George. It explained how in general agricultural labourers were the worst paid of all workers, with wages well below the minimum efficiency level. A statutory minimum agricultural wage was needed. Rowntree emphasized the deprivations, material and mental, of working-class country life, concluding his sketch on a stern Quaker note reminiscent of the conclusion, already quoted, to his York survey:

> We are afraid of curtailing our luxuries: it is the curtailment of our ideals we should fear. We are afraid of Germany—we should be afraid of England. We talk about the 'yellow peril'—the real yellow peril is nearer home, it is the greed of gold. We are desperately afraid of self-sacrifice; when we are as much afraid of sacrificing other people, the social problem will be well on the way to solution.

Here very clearly can be heard the middle-class Edwardian social conscience at work. But many working men remained as apathetic about land reform as about earlier Liberal reform proposals. The agricultural labourers themselves were traditionally slow thinking and slow moving, the harder to rouse and organize because of their dispersed circumstances. An American observer described the English rustic as 'uneducated, inarticulate, inaudible and grotesquely awkward, both mentally and physically. But he has his small political value for he is always and unalterably for no change!' This was far from wholly true, and the land campaign does seem to have made some impact upon a number of rural voters. The swing against the Liberals in 1912 by-elections was 5.2 per cent in non-agricultural seats, only 2.8 per cent in agricultural; for 1913 the figures were 5 per cent and 2 per cent respectively. But such containment of unpopularity could hardly be claimed as an upsurge of favourable opinion. Nevertheless, Lloyd George was still hoping to make land reform the dominant issue in a 1915 general election. He did

British dreadnoughts at sea.

Territorials going to war 1914.

Committee on Physical Deterioration: (above) Lant St. Board
School (Southwark), 1875, lowest type; (below) the same
school in 1902 showing great improvement.

recognize, however, the importance of proving to urban voters how agricultural conditions and wages directly affected conditions and wages in the towns; and how prosperity in the countryside would greatly increase the demand for town-made goods. But suddenly in August 1914 his energies were to be diverted from making war against the landlords to making war against the Germans.[26]

CHAPTER SEVEN

Trade Union Unrest

'Social peace! A country without strikes! Co-partnership and co-operation of worker and employer! How delightful, and how soothing to the troubled social conscience! . . . Let it be understood once and for all that the interests of Capital and Labour are diametrically opposed, and that although it may be necessary for Labour sometimes to acquiesce in "social peace", such peace is only the lull before the storm.' So asserted G. D. H. Cole (1889–1959), socialist intellectual and historian, in *The World of Labour* (1913). Industrial disturbances and threats of disturbance were widespread during the last Edwardian years, even though not all British industry fell into turmoil, as some alarmed contemporaries seemed to assume. The engineering, iron and steel, and shipbuilding industries, for example, all escaped major strikes. But unsettlement became continuous in coal mining and on the railways, and among unskilled and low paid workers generally. Sir George Askwith (1861–1942), the leading Edwardian industrial conciliator, gave 'the gloomiest reports' about the possible course of the transport and dock workers on strike in 1912. 'If they were severely pinched by cessation of work they would take to looting.' Austen Chamberlain, the Conservative politician, heard how one wholesale armourer had sold out his stock of revolvers, such was the extent of middle- and upper-class alarm. The prolonged 1912 national coal strike produced disruptive effects upon both industry and domestic hearths. 'More works are being closed down every day', wrote Chamberlain. 'More trains are being taken off the railways. The whole machinery of national life is slowly stopping.' Nonetheless he advised firmness in resisting 'blackmailing of the nation'.

Politicians and public were the more alarmed because they were baffled by what was happening. 'We are living in a new world', admitted Chamberlain, 'and the past gives us little guidance for the present.' Seebohm Rowntree, the social analyst and himself a large-scale employer, remarked that people found it hard to understand 'how the vast machinery of production, creating the wealth which maintains the greatest empire the world has seen, should rest on so insecure a foundation'. The public was amazed that apparently minor causes could produce such extensive damage. 'The triviality of the apparent "casus belli" has astounded the casual observer.' But Rowntree knew that surface pretexts masked deeper discontents. 'The superficial cause—the desire for a small addition to the wage in one place, unwillingness to undertake a certain class of work in another, the protection of a penalized fellow worker in a third—was merely like the touching of a spring that sets a huge machine in motion.' The most general influence behind the late-Edwardian strike wave was the extensive fall in real wages already noticed, resulting from price rises unmatched by wage rises. Another factor was loss of faith by working men in the effectiveness of the Labour Party in Parliament, which seemed to have become hesitant, perhaps even irrelevant, in the quest for further social improvement. A third influence, as Rowntree emphasized, was increased working-class awareness 'though gleaned from fiction and the evening paper, with what life may be under more favourable circumstances'. Churchill summed up 'the general mood of industrial democracy' as 'not towards inadequate hours of work, but towards sufficient hours of leisure'. Workmen were 'not content that their lives should remain mere alternations between bed and the factory. They demand time to look about them, time to see their homes by daylight, to see their children, time to think and read and cultivate their gardens—time, in short, to live.' H. G. Wells, in a *Daily Mail* series on 'What the Worker Wants' emphasized the influence of improved education. 'The working man of today reads, talks, has general ideas and a sense of the world; he is far nearer to the ruler of today in knowledge and intellectual range than he is to the working man of fifty years ago. . . . The old workman might and did quarrel very vigorously with his specific employer, but he never set out to arraign all employers.' Many of these influences had been accumulating for years, before finally producing an outburst of labour unrest just before 1914 when unemployment touched its Edwardian low point. Men could most readily defy their bosses when the potential supply of blacklegs was at its lowest. These strike-breakers had been organized by employers on a countrywide basis in a National Free Labour Association. Though masters in settled relations with trade unions rarely tried to replace strikers with blacklegs, employers who wanted to break the unions still tried to use black labour freely, adding greatly thereby to Edwardian industrial tension.[1]

Industrial crisis engulfed the Edwardians in part because of their lack of sophisticated government machinery for smoothing industrial relations. During the nineteenth century, overriding all opposition from employers, Parliament had elaborated detailed codes for the regulation of conditions in factories and mines. Yet the legislature had never provided any means of imposing a settlement in disputes between employers and employed over wages, hours and working arrangements, matters often just as important for the well-being of operatives as their physical conditions of work. In the ten years up to 1914 well over half of all industrial disputes (whether ending in strike action or not) were about wages, the remainder being over trade union recognition, hours of labour, working arrangements, and the employment of particular categories of persons. The Conciliation Act of 1896 had done no more than allow the Board of Trade to appoint an arbitrator if both sides to a dispute wanted one, or a conciliator if either party asked for one, and these feeble facilities were little used. Fundamentally the Act accepted that industrial relations were to be regulated by free negotiations between capital and labour, without State participation and with the strike weapon as the main armament on the workers' side. Yet at the outset of the Edwardian era the whole effectiveness of trade union strike action was in danger. The Law Lords had delivered the 1901 Taff Vale Decision, arising out of a case of picketing by the Amalgamated Society of Railway Servants intended to hinder the Taff Vale Railway Company in the use of blackleg labour supplied through the National Free Labour Association. The Taff Vale Decision undermined union power to call a strike by making union funds liable to meet the damages, to any amount, arising out of an actionable wrong committed by a trade union officer or member. The right to strike was not entirely denied, for a stoppage was still conceivable in which no breach of contract or obstructive picketing occurred, and in which the only object was the advancement of the legitimate interests of the strikers. But such conditions could never be guaranteed, and the Taff Vale Railway Company eventually recovered £23,000 damages from the ASRS. The unions now looked to Parliament for legislation to restore their freedom of action, but not until 1906 was the Trade Disputes Act passed. Moreover, this Liberal measure was only made acceptable to the trade unions under heavy pressure from Labour members. The Liberal position on trade union matters was always ambiguous, divided between care for the interests of the capitalists who provided the party with money and of the workers who provided it with votes. 'They will give you Insurance Bills, they will give you all kinds of soothing syrups', exclaimed Keir Hardie during the 1911 strikes, 'but in the end your Liberal Party, just like your Tory Party, is the party of the rich, and exists to protect the rich when Labour and Capital come into conflict.' The 1906 Bill in its original form remedied the Taff Vale Decision only to the limited extent of allowing that an action could not lie against a trade union unless committed with the authority of the union executive. But eventually under Labour pressure Campbell–Bannerman conceded complete immunity to the unions, an immunity the stronger because it was now made explicit rather than merely implicit in law. An act committed by two or more persons in furtherance of a trade dispute was not to become the basis of a civil action unless an action could be brought if the act had been committed by one person. The right to picket was extended by allowing picketers to attempt to persuade other persons not to work, as well as simply to get or to give information. Action in furtherance of a trade dispute could not become the basis of a civil action merely because it induced another person to break a contract of employment or because it interfered with the trade or employment of other persons. Trade unions could not be sued for tortious acts committed by them, though any form of violence in a dispute remained illegal. In this same year the right to compensation was extended alongside the right to strike. The Workmen's

Compensation Act gave a further 6 million workers protection from injury at work.

Legal opinion remained suspicious of trade union privileges, and in 1909 this suspicion led to another hostile decision by the Law Lords, the Osborne Judgment. W. V. Osborne, a member of the Amalgamated Society of Railway Servants and also of the Liberal Party, brought an action to restrain his union from contributing to the Labour Party. On appeal to the Lords he was granted an injunction forbidding the union from raising a political levy. Here was a serious threat to Labour Members of Parliament financed by the trade unions. The Liberal Government responded by introducing payment of members in 1911; but its 1913 Trade Union Act, though allowing political levies, did not completely reverse the Osborne Judgment. Union members were to be allowed to contract out of payment, and union political funds were to be kept separate from other funds. These limitations, irritating to trade unionists, were the price that had to be paid to appease the intensified suspicion of trade union intentions felt by middle-class Liberals after the great strikes of 1911-12.

During the first half of the Edwardian period the trade unions had remained relatively quiet. Between 1901 and 1907 the number of working days lost through strikes in the United Kingdom fluctuated only between the modest levels of 1.5 million and rather more than 4 million days. Between 1908 and 1913, by contrast, only the 1909 figure kept within this limit. 1908, 1910 and 1911 averaged about 10 or 11 million days, 1913 exceeded 11 million, and 1912 (because of the coal strike) saw the total reach nearly 41 million. In 1905 it was still possible for an observer to emphasize how 'moderation of aim still remains the characteristic of union policy taken as a whole. The Collectivist Utopia, and the even more chimerical ideals of Social Democracy, have been preached to them in vain; they go on steadily amassing capital in their benefit funds; the members build their own houses, and provide for their own old age.' Such was the spirit of craft trade unionism, continuing from mid-Victorian times. The craft unions varied greatly in size, but in 1906 three of the six biggest unions were craft combinations: the engineers with 90,000 members, the carpenters with 60,000, and the boiler makers with 50,000. A second type of Edwardian trade union consisted of more or less skilled operatives in one trade, often organized by locality. The coal miners' unions fell into this category, headed by the South Wales Miners' Federation, the largest of all unions, with over 100,000 members in 1906. A third group of unions embraced a mixed sector of general and transport workers, who had begun to organize during the wave of 'new unionism' at the end of the eighties. The prototype was the Gas Workers' Union with some 30,000 members in 1906. In total the number of trade unionists in Great Britain and Northern Ireland more than doubled between 1901 and 1913, from just over 2 million to over 4.1 million. Half this increase dated from 1911 and after, in part a consequence of the upsurge of union activity but in large part also because Lloyd George's new insurance system obliged workers in many industries each to choose an 'approved society', which could be a trade union.

One feature of the late-Edwardian strike wave followed from the growth in trade union size. As national leaders inevitably grew remote from local union membership they were liable to lose awareness and control, and become almost as much objects of rank-and-file criticism as the employers themselves. 'Unofficial' strikes now became familiar to the British public. As early as 1910 *Punch* carried a cartoon showing workmen parading with a banner inscribed 'Down with Authority'; the men had left a trade union official lying on the road plaintively exclaiming 'Steady on there, wait for your leader! When I gave you that banner I didn't mean down with *my* authority.' But two militant veterans of the great 1889 dock strike, Tom Mann (1856–1941) and Ben Tillett (1860–1943), both powerful outdoor speakers, did retain the support of the workers.

The sequence of major Edwardian industrial crises began in 1907 when the railwaymen demanded a general wage increase. The railway companies were adamant in their rejection, refusing (with one exception) even to recognize the existence of the railway trade unions. The railway directors had some justification in that they were bound by legislation not to increase railway rates, despite increasing costs. The men's justification was the rising cost of living. Under the threat of the first-ever national railway stoppage Lloyd George intervened on behalf of the Government, acting with decision even though well aware of the slightness of his powers under the 1896 Conciliation Act. The directors persisted in refusing direct negotiations with the union leaders, and Lloyd George had to serve as an intermediary. In the end it was agreed to form a board of conciliation for each railway and for each grade of employee on each railway, on which both management and workers would be represented; but the workmen's spokesmen were to be chosen by direct vote, thus avoiding any suggestion of recognition of the unions by the companies. On this compromise basis a national railway strike was averted, but only for four years.

In the summer of 1911 it proved impossible to avoid a shutdown of the railways. Though lasting only two days (18th and 19th August), this first national railway strike added greatly to the tensions of a summer full of crises. The suffragettes were agitating vociferously; the Parliament Bill had only just completed its uncertain passage through Parliament; and the Agadir crisis had erupted with Germany. The railwaymen were incensed by lagging wages, the ineffectiveness of the 1907 machinery, the continuing non-recognition of their unions, and by the Osborne Judgment. Emphasizing the danger of war with Germany, Lloyd George persuaded representatives of the railway companies to meet union leaders, and a modified conciliation scheme was ultimately accepted. As part of the settlement, the Railway Traffic Act of 1913 permitted the rises in rates needed to meet the cost of improved labour conditions.

The seamen and dockers were also noisily on strike during 1911; but the stoppage which had first caught the headlines was the Cambrian strike in South Wales. As with the railway directors, the coal employers were not without a genuine case for tightness in respect of wages. In many areas output per man had been falling and costs rising, mainly because of exhaustion of the best coal seams. The Liberal Government had conceded the miners' demand for a statutory eight-hour day in 1908, but the consequent re-arrangement of working practices had actually meant that for a time this significant piece of State intervention on behalf of the workers had produced as much discontent as satisfaction. The miners, moreover, still demanded legislation to fix a minimum wage. The

South Wales miners were the most militant. Late in 1910 those
working in pits controlled by the Cambrian combine refused
to accept new rates for difficult working, even though these
had been negotiated by W. Abraham (1842–1922), the much
respected chairman of the South Wales Miners' Federation
and Member of Parliament for the Rhondda Valley. In
November the men began a ten-month strike marked by
rioting, the despatch of police reinforcements from London,
troop movements, and one fatal casualty at Tonypandy, for
which Churchill, as Home Secretary, was long unfairly blamed,
by Keir Hardie among others. 'The troops are let loose upon
the people to shoot them down if need be whilst they are
fighting for their legitimate rights. My friends and comrades,
you cannot mix oil and water. There are some men in the
meeting who are half Liberal half Labour—who want to be
friends with both parties. The thing cannot be done.'

1912 proved to be the worst of all Edwardian years for industrial stoppages, dominated by a national coal strike from
February to April in support of a minimum wage demand. A
committee of four Ministers, headed by the Prime Minister,
reluctantly intervened, and eventually the Government sponsored legislation establishing district boards to fix wages. This
was not the minimum wage demanded, but after an inconclusive ballot the miners' leaders called off the stoppage. Next
came a bitter strike of London lightermen, dockers and carters
in the summer of 1912. Its failure emphasized the limitations of
sectional pressure, and during 1913–14 the idea of a 'triple
alliance' of miners, railwaymen and port workers was under
discussion.[2]

Larger unions, organized over a whole industry on the
American model, were beginning to be seen as necessary to
increase pressure upon employers, though only the railwaymen
had come near to achieving such unity by 1914. The amal-
gamation movement was regarded by some militant leaders as
only a first step towards syndicalism, a theory of industrial
organization developed especially in France. Syndicalist ideas
became influential chiefly among the Welsh miners and among
the dock workers. The best known syndicalist publication in
Britain was a pamphlet issued by a group of South Wales
miners in 1912, *The Miners' Next Step*. This advocated the

centralization of the miners' unions to create a national union, which would then ally with similar national unions created in other industries to press for workers' control of all industry. It repudiated traditional forms of working-class leadership, both industrial and political. 'They, the leaders, become "gentlemen", they become M.P.s, and have considerable prestige because of this power. Now, when any man or men assume power of this description, we have a right to ask them to be infallible. This is the penalty, a just one too, of autocracy.' The pamphlet wanted to reduce the state to a Central Production Board which 'with a statistical department to ascertain the needs of the people, will issue its demands on the different departments of industry, leaving to the men themselves to determine under what conditions and how the work should be done. This would mean real democracy in real life.'

To achieve this transformation *The Miners' Next Step* openly advocated 'extremely drastic and militant' action. The 'irritation strike' and the go-slow were recommended to reduce profits and to make capitalists more amenable to their own elimination. A general strike represented a further stage in pressure. These objectives and methods, intended to be applied not only in South Wales and not only in the coal-mining industry but throughout the country, caused great concern in the press and in Parliament. Many people of property feared that the strike wave was much more than a demand for better wages or hours, that it marked the beginning of an attempted revolution. One Conservative moved a motion in the Commons in March 1912 'that, in the opinion of this House, the growth and advocacy by certain labour agitators of an anti-social policy of Syndicalism based upon class warfare and incitement to mutiny constitute a grave danger to the State and the welfare of the community'. He then proceeded to quote at length from *The Miners' Next Step*. The ultra-Conservative *Morning Post* was to cite the pamphlet for years, gloating over it 'with the anticipatory leers and shudders of the Fat Boy in Pickwick'.

The syndicalists certainly hoped that the late-Edwardian labour unrest would lead to a social and industrial transformation, but their real influence proved to be slight. The extremism of their policies reflected the unsettlement of the times, the disillusionment with traditional methods and the hostility towards autocratic employers who refused even to recognize trade unions. But though discontent ran deep this did not mean that most British workers really wanted to commit themselves to revolutionary change, either violent or peaceful. Syndicalism made some appeal as a protest, less as a policy. Philip Snowden, one Labour politician otherwise very critical of the syndicalists, gave them credit for showing how workmen were now insisting upon a respected place in industry, instead of treatment as mere 'hands':

> By some means or other an industrial system must be devised which will give the workman a direct interest in his work, which will give him the maximum amount of control over his labour consistent with the maintenance of the maximum efficiency of production. . . . Socialism has been so much concerned about the community that it has neglected the individual to some extent. Syndicalism comes to urge that aspect of the social problem.[3]

Various interpretations of syndicalism were being discussed among left-wing intellectuals up to 1914. An Anglicized version which came to appeal to many of them (including G. D. H. Cole) was 'guild socialism', an ingenious synthesis of political socialism and industrial syndicalism. Guild socialists viewed the State with less suspicion than pure syndicalists, but they were still opposed to the centralized bureaucracy admired by the Fabian socialists. Under a guild socialist system the State retained ultimate power, but delegated most of it to various industrial guilds, each guild paying a single tax or rent to the State. In the best spirit of medieval guild craftsmen guild responsibility would include the maintenance of high standards of workmanship. Every guild member would be assured of continuous wages, full medical cover, and a pension, without the government being burdened with the administration of these social services. Like the syndicalists, guild socialists were convinced that if only the workers would stand together in demanding workers' control they would prove irresistible. 'Against the united decision of labour never again to sell itself as a commodity how can they contend?'[4]

Guild socialists were confident that they had found 'the solution of the problems now vexing one-twentieth of our population and ruining the remainder'. But both the propertied Edwardian one-twentieth and the labouring 'remainder' were much more attracted by less ambitious remedies. In this spirit the cry for 'the living wage' ran through the strike movement, a demand which could be reconciled with the continuance of the capitalist wage system. In *The Living Wage* (1913) Snowden defined poverty as 'knowledge of reasonable wants unsatisfied'. This still set labour's target well above the level of a wage merely sufficient for physical survival; it thought in terms of enjoyment as well as of existence. Even the Conservative *Times* in a 1911 editorial on 'Labour's Share' admitted the reasonableness of such aspirations, while rejecting the old socialist claim to 'the whole product of labour':

> All the social and political movements which distinguish our age—trade unions, strikes, labour legislation, the advance of democracy, innumerable 'isms', societies and organizations, investigations and inquiries public and private, the collection of statistics, modern forms of administration— all these, and a vast number of other things included in the comprehensive term 'social reform' are merely aspects or manifestations of the tremendous process of change that is going on and making for the redistribution of wealth.

But how much redistribution would be fair in order to secure 'the living wage'? *The Times* ended its well-meaning analysis with an answer despairingly without meaning. 'What, then, is labour's share? We do not know; but it cannot be so large that less than enough is left for the others.' This failed to answer the crucial question of what was 'enough' either for men or for masters. Nevertheless, we have seen how the Edwardians were beginning to respond to this question at least in extreme cases, through minimum wages indirectly provided by law in certain sweated trades and for the miners.[5]

Middle- and upper-class Edwardian opinion was not sympathetic to the idea of a general 'living wage' fixed by legislation; but it was sufficiently concerned to contemplate various other proposals for ensuring a more even balance between labour and capital. Extension of conciliation and arbitration procedures seemed one hopeful line of development. Hundreds of local trade disputes were settled annually through voluntary local boards of conciliation. Could, and should, this machinery be made compulsory for all disputes, as in Australia and New Zealand? Cole and other socialists denounced such enforcement of 'social peace' as implying State support for employers. 'Organized Labour must, at all costs, preserve its right to strike.' The Trades Union Congress also resisted proposals for compulsory arbitration, chiefly because of union leaders' distrust of the dilatory and expensive legal system and of the judiciary, which had shown itself prejudiced against trade unionism. The Liberal Government went no further than the creation in 1911 of an Industrial Council, a body of prominent employers and union officials who could be invited to hear disputes and recommend terms of settlement. But this body proved clumsy in operation, and after 1913 it was allowed to wither away.[6]

Co-partnership was another idea for improving labour relations which was repudiated by the Edwardian trade unions. This again was seen as a device to ensure the continuing predominance of the capitalists and their profits. 'The premium bonus system and the shop piece-work system are spread beautifully beside profit-sharing, tastefully tricked out as "Labour Co-partnership", on the festive board. The sole drawback is that these red herrings, unlike the honest herring that we love, are not intended to whet the worker's appetite for more.'[7]

Distrusted by the trade unions, these devices had therefore achieved little by 1914 in reducing what had come to be called 'industrial warfare'. Yet the main sufferers in the battle of labour against capital were often the men on strike. They could be affected severely even if they eventually won their claims, which was always far from certain. Board of Trade figures showed that only about a quarter of all Edwardian trade disputes (whether involving strike action or not) were settled in favour of the men; much the same number ended in favour of the employers, and about half concluded in compromise. One sensitive employer gave a penetrating account of the mixture of suffering and uplift in the minds of workmen on strike:

Imagine what your feeling would be, if you believed (as if it were the Gospel) that you had a prescriptive right to certain work, of which you were being unjustly deprived, and if you knew that your wife was selling or pawning your furniture, that all your savings were spent and debts being incurred which you could never hope to pay; if you were kept in enforced idleness and bound to report yourself in person every forenoon at the union offices, if your children complained that they had not enough to eat, if awful visions of the workhouse were looming up, and your wife was perhaps being *helped* by kind ladies (curse their condescension!) and that all the while the masters, so far as you could judge, in no way changed their way of life; imagine all this, and you will be able to believe the story that a workman once died of joy when a strike ended. Unless you first realize that the men during a strike grow to look upon themselves as martyrs, and to feel a martyr's exultation, you will never be able to understand how strikes last as long as they do, long after the struggle is evidently hopeless. . . . It is as if one side appealed to the Bible, and the other to the Koran.

Sir Hubert von Herkomer's (1849–1914) painting 'On Strike' (1891) showed a workman standing grimly idle at his doorstep, his wife leaning on his shoulder, a baby in her arms, a child hanging anxiously behind. Ramsey MacDonald observed that this painting might as well have been entitled 'Unemployment': 'the strike must be exceptionally prolonged and exceptionally bitter that entails more suffering on the working classes than one of the periodic depressions of trade. The damage of the strike must be measured in terms of the everyday experiences of the class upon whose lives it falls.' But the fact that the suffering occasioned by strikes had to be added to the even greater suffering brought by unemployment was only the more regrettable.[8]

The Liberal Government, as we have seen, had ventured upon the beginnings of an unemployment policy. But it had not attempted an overall labour policy. Ministerial intervention in the railway and coal disputes certainly showed the government, in extreme instances, taking the ultimate determination of industrial affairs out of the hands of employers. But such intervention was reluctant, and has remained so under all subsequent peacetime governments. Sidney Webb was impressed by what he thought to be a changed mood when he returned from a world tour in 1912. 'The historian of the future will notice that in March 1912, it appeared to everybody quite a simple matter for the Government to impose on every coal-owner in the Kingdom, without compensation, and as a condition of being allowed to use his own property at all, the obligation of paying a Legal Minimum Wage, over the fixing of which, even though it might stop his income and destroy the value of his mine, he had individually and personally no control. And in marked contrast with every piece of Factory Legislation for a hundred years, there was practically no opposition.' Webb contended that 'Regulation of Industry' had now displaced 'Relief of the Unemployed or the Under-employed' as 'the dominant idea'. But this was claiming far too much, valuable and unprecedented though the Liberal Government's interventions certainly were.

Nor was it the wish of the major trade unions that Ministers should go as far as Webb suggested. Confident now of their acceptance in law, the unions were becoming increasingly hopeful of winning the battle of labour versus capital for themselves. Ever since 1913 they have remained hostile to legislative intervention in collective bargaining and firm believers in the autonomy of industrial forces. They have been eager for organized labour and organized management to contest together undisturbed, content with conditions of what one expert observer has paradoxically named 'collective *laissez faire*'. In this spirit on the brink of war in 1914 the 'triple alliance' of miners, railwaymen and port workers was forming for another round of industrial conflict. Sir George Askwith forecast in November 1913 'movements in this country coming to a head of which recent events have been a small foreshadowing'. Such huge industrial struggles were indeed to come in Britain, delayed only by the four-year interruption caused by the First World War.[9]

CHAPTER EIGHT

Women's Rights

Emancipation

The suffragettes had added their shrill voices to the pre-war discord. The cry of 'votes for women' was one aspect of a wider demand for female emancipation and sex equality which had built up from mid-Victorian times, when John Stuart Mill had been its most distinguished advocate. A woman's place was no longer only in the home, even though Edwardian anti-feminists still proclaimed this to be her only proper sphere. Women had come to play an essential part in shops and offices and had entered the professions, albeit still in small numbers outside teaching. Working-class women had provided factory labour since the earliest days of the Industrial Revolution. Females were already allowed to vote in local elections, and in 1907 a Liberal Act allowed them also to serve upon county and county borough councils. Such local participation could be differentiated from the Parliamentary franchise on the ground that local government impinged directly upon women's domestic pre-occupations. But the *Manchester Guardian* emphasized in 1910 how 'almost every statute now directly or indirectly touches the home'. Mrs Philip Snowden's book on *The Feminist Movement* (1913) turned the old anti-suffrage argument on its head: 'because the special sphere of woman is the home, women ought to have the vote'.[1]

Middle-class Edwardian women had come to feel that they could claim a status quite apart from the traditional feminine role of wife and mother. Those who were married were producing fewer children than their mothers, and were consequently less burdened by pregnancies and family cares and more free to look to social and political affairs. A significant number of Edwardian women, moreover, could not hope to

Ulster Volunteers in training. Machine guns spoke louder than words.

Bonar Law at Blenheim Palace, 29 July 1912.

. . PROGRAMME . .

Proprietors . . "THE DAILY BIOSCOPE" SYNDICATE
Business Manager . Mr. G. F. Salas

I.
SAN FRANCISCO DISASTER.

Showing the Sections of the City Devastated.

PANORAMA OF 4th AND MARKET STREETS.

PANORAMA, from Motor Car. DOWN MARKET ST.,
ending at Palace Hotel and Call Building.

PANORAMA NEAR PALACE HOTEL,
showing President Roosevelt in a carriage.

PANORAMA OF UNION SQUARE,
showing thousands of people in this spot. Were it not for the
flags this would readily pass for an actual scene showing confusion incidental to the earthquake.

PANORAMA OF CLIFF HOUSE.

All of the Sections shown have been destroyed either by the Earthquake or by
the Fire.
Actual Scenes of the ruin and devastation in this beautiful City, as it appears to-day,
have been taken for us by our American Agents, and are now on the way to England.

II.
LOST! A LEG OF MUTTON.

Hungry Willie, who has not tasted food for some days, espies
a jolly leg of mutton hanging outside a butcher's shop, and
puts the matter's back is turned he snatches it off the hook and
flies down the street. The fun now commences, and the chase
... some of the finest yet produced. New obstacles are
... and the scenes evoke long laugh from beginning to
...

A SCREAMING COMIC.

III.
THE OLYMPIC GAMES AT ATHENS.

*We were appointed Official Cinematographers to H.M. The
King of Greece, and held the sole and exclusive Cinematograph Rights for*

**THE GREATEST SPORTING EVENT
IN THE WORLD'S HISTORY.**

ARRIVAL OF H.M. KING EDWARD.
ENTRY OF ROYALTIES INTO ARENA.
ROYALTIES TAKING THEIR SEATS.
GRAND MARCH PAST OF COMPETITORS.
THE DANISH TEAMS, including Ladies.
THE SWEDISH AND GERMAN TEAMS.
HEAVY WEIGHT LIFTING.
ROPE CLIMBING EXTRAORDINARY,
And other Events.

IV.
A NAVAL ENGAGEMENT.

P.C. Green and Jack Tar have very nearly a stand up fight over
Mary Jane, who is busy beating a carpet in her master's garden.
A serious disaster is averted by Jack offering to toss the Bobby for
the girl. The jolly sailor wins and immediately interviews Mary
Jane, much to Green's annoyance, who decides not to let Jack Tar
have it all his own way. The poor Bobby gets a hot time for
poking his nose where it is not wanted, and the subject, which is
... an extremely funny one, finishes with a great roar when Constable
Green gets mixed up in the carpet.

Both original and clever humour.

This Programme is subject to change without notice.

SPECIAL CHILDREN'S MATINEES: Every Saturday Afternoon, commencing at 3 o'clock.

XVII   *The programme at the London Gaumont 1906—two newsreels,
two short comedies.*

*Amusement in the home. Possession of a piano had become a
lower-middle-class status symbol.*

marry because of the excess of females over males. By 1913 this was estimated at 1,200,000 in England and Wales, 18,887,000 females outnumbering 17,687,000 males. These 'redundant women', as one mid-Victorian had named them (when they numbered only half the Edwardian total) were now refusing to accept themselves as supernumeraries, and were joining with married women in demanding full electoral recognition. A sympathetic male journalist summed up the new spirit in 1908:

> In Victorian England she was the graceful decoration of life, a symbol of sweetness and innocence, a creature with pretty, kittenlike ways, but having no relevance to the business of the world. Today she is emerging into sex consciousness and beating at the bars of circumstance. The cage is enlarged; but it is still a cage. She goes to the University and is bracketed with the Senior Wrangler; but she is denied her degree. She qualifies for the Bar, as Christabel Pankhurst did, but she is denied the right to practice. She enters the inferior walks of life, and finds that there is one standard of payment for men and an immeasurably inferior one for women. She falls, and finds that society has smiles for her betrayer and the flaming sword for his victim. . . . She cannot have equality of treatment. She cannot have simple justice, for she is a women in a world made by men. 'Madame', said Charles XI of Sweden to his wife . . . 'I married you to give me children, not to give me advice.' That was said a long time ago; but behind all the changes of the centuries, it still represents much of the thought of men in relation to women.[2]

Recognition of women's rights in law had indeed been gradually extending since the passing of the 1857 Matrimonial Causes Act, which for the first time had made divorce available to persons of less than large means. Yet whereas a husband could divorce his wife for adultery alone, in the case of an erring husband the law still required proof of incest, rape, bigamy with a married woman, an unnatural offence, or adultery accompanied by cruelty and desertion. The Divorce Law Reform Association (1906) joined in pressure which eventually led to the appointment of a Royal Commission on

Divorce and Matrimonial Causes (1909-12). The work of this body, conducted against a background of suffragette outrages and of increasing freedom in writing about sex relations, attracted considerable attention and emotion. It recommended that women be allowed equality with men before the law with respect to grounds for divorce, also that divorce should be made less costly so that poorer people were not excluded from using the courts. A majority further advised that desertion for more than three years, cruelty, incurable insanity, incurable drunkenness, and imprisonment under commuted death sentence should constitute grounds for divorce. A minority of three, headed by the Archbishop of York, opposed any such extension of grounds. The liberating influence of the First World War was destined, however, to assist the enactment of many of the majority proposals during the nineteen twenties.[3]

Thirteen years after the Matrimonial Causes Act of 1857 came the Married Women's Property Act (1870), another step towards sex equality. The 1857 Act had given a wife who obtained a judicial separation the enjoyment of civil rights independent of her husband; the 1870 Act, as developed by amendments into the Edwardian period, allowed a married woman to retain ownership of her property even while she continued to live with her husband. He no longer automatically gained control of her estate on marriage. Even this, however, was not sufficient for all Edwardian feminists. They demanded that part of a husband's income be credited to his wife as wages for work performed at home. 'Equal pay for equal work' was here the feminist slogan, whether for work performed as a housewife or as an employee. Mrs Snowden noted with satisfaction how the newly appointed men and women Insurance Commissioners were being paid identical salaries, 'the only case of equal pay for equal work in any department of Government'.[4]

But were women physically and psychologically capable of bearing the responsibilities which must accompany such extensions of their rights? Some eminent Edwardian medical men said not. One such was Sir Almroth E. Wright (1861-1947), a distinguished bacteriologist and one of the founders of modern immunology, who in March 1912 sent a letter to *The Times* which aroused widespread controversy. In 1913 he reiterated his views at greater length in a book entitled *The Unexpurgated Case Against Women's Suffrage*. Sir Almroth argued that 'the mind of woman is always threatened with danger from the reverberations of her physiological emergencies'. He contended that the militant suffragettes were sexually and intellectually embittered. They comprised the excess female population, 'that million which had better long ago have gone out to mate with its complement of men beyond the sea'. He gave it as his considered medical opinion that men and women could never work together side by side as equals. The quality of men's work would always be undermined by the presence of women. 'Their programme is to convert the whole world into an epicene institution . . . in which man and woman shall everywhere work side by side at the selfsame tasks for the selfsame pay.' Furthermore, claimed Wright, government ultimately depended upon physical force, and women were physically weak; it also required intellectual stability, in which again women were deficient; finally, it needed appreciation of standards of abstract morality, whereas women thought only subjectively. In short, Wright's arguments gave medical stiffening to the simple old anti-female suffrage prejudice, cited for example in a 1903 *Handbook to Political Questions of the Day*, that 'women *are* women'.

In a Commons debate Wright's arguments were variously described as 'extraordinarily able' and as an 'insult'. Perhaps the most effective answer came in a bantering letter to *The Times* from 'C.S.C.', Mrs Winston Churchill (b. 1885):

After reading Sir Almroth Wright's able and weighty exposition of women as he knows them the question seems no longer to be 'Should women have votes?' but 'Ought women not to be abolished altogether?' . . . We learn from him that in their youth they are unbalanced, that from time to time they suffer from unreasonableness and hypersensitiveness, and that their presence is distracting and irritating to men in their daily lives and pursuits. If they take up a profession, the indelicacy of their minds makes them undesirable partners for their male colleagues. Later on in life they are subject to grave and long-continued mental disorders, and, if not quite insane, many of them have to be shut up. . . . Cannot science give us some assurance, or at least some ground of hope, that we are on the eve of the greatest discovery of all—i.e., how to maintain a race of males by purely scientific means?[5]

The Edwardians were the first generation to begin to learn scientifically about sex. Sigmund Freud's (1856–1939) psychological work was just becoming known outside specialist circles on the eve of the First World War, though the first English translation of *The Interpretation of Dreams* (1913) still contained a publisher's note limiting its sale to members of the medical, scholastic, legal and clerical professions. Havelock Ellis's (1859–1939) *Studies in the Psychology of Sex* appeared between 1897 and 1928; all but the first volume, however, had to be published in the United States. In *Man and Woman* (1894), which had reached its fifth edition by 1914, Ellis succeeded for the first time in English in explaining objectively and readably to non-specialists how and why the sexes differed, yet also how they were equal, female with male. The subject of sex, thanks in important part to his influence, could now be acknowledged to exist, at least in print and among thinking people. Sexual relations could be accepted not as disgusting but as potentially enriching for both men and women. Nevertheless, for ordinary middle-class girls the subject was likely to be still surrounded by a conspiracy of silence. A friend of Vera Brittain's (1896–1970) 'was always afraid of going too far with men because she really didn't know what "too far" was. I was quite unable to enlighten her.' Where information was given about sex it could be dangerously wrong. Sir Lawrence Jones (1885–1969) was one of an undergraduate group which boldly asked one Oxford doctor over their port if women enjoyed sexual intercourse. 'Speaking as a doctor', was the reply, 'nine out of ten women are indifferent to or actively dislike it; the tenth, who enjoys it, will always be a harlot.'[6]

This was not a view shared by leading Edwardian men of letters, as their writings began daringly to reveal. 'The most correct honeymoon', asserted Arnold Bennett, 'is an orgy of lust; and if it isn't, it ought to be.' His novel *Whom God Hath Joined* (1906) was devoted to the theme of divorce, emphasizing the suffering imposed upon innocent and guilty alike by the

existing narrow divorce laws. Wells even more daringly discussed sex outside marriage. He had praised free love for the
elite (including himself) in *A Modern Utopia* (1905), but his
novel *Ann Veronica* (1909) secured much wider notice for his
challenging views. His heroine was a girl both beautiful and
clever who defiantly left home, became a suffragette, fell in
love with an older man, and (not waiting to be seduced)
seduced him, ran off with him to Switzerland, became pregnant,
and yet lived happily ever after. This story, based upon an
affaire of Wells's own, was banned by many libraries. One
clergyman exclaimed that he would rather send his daughter
to a house infected with typhoid fever than let her read *Ann
Veronica*. An attempt was even made to ostracize Wells from
society, but his literary friends rallied round him.

Nevertheless, Sir Edmund Gosse (1848–1928), a not illiberal
literary critic, was grumbling by the end of 1910 about 'the
new craze for introducing into fiction the high-bred maiden
who has a baby'. He had recently read three novels with such
a theme, including no doubt Forster's *Howards End*. In the
same year the *Encyclopedia Britannica* article on 'English
Literature' drew attention to the similar freedom being shown
in the writing of plays. It noted the 'curious reticence' of the
nineteenth century, 'of which the 20th century has already
made uncommonly short work. The new playwrights have
untaught England a shyness which came in about the time of
Southey, Wordsworth and Sir Walter Scott.' A sustained campaign was waged to ease stage censorship, still controlled by the
Lord Chamberlain; and by the later Edwardian years though
the system was not reformed its attitudes were markedly
relaxed. A leading campaigner was Bernard Shaw. His play
Getting Married (1908) called farcically into question conventional views of marriage and divorce. Beatrice Webb found his
Misalliance (1910) 'brilliant but disgusting', 'everyone wishing
to have sexual intercourse with everyone else'. Mrs Webb
rightly emphasized how 'in the quiet intermediate area of
respectably working-class, middle-class and professional life,
and in much gentle society, there is not this over-sexed condition. . . . Let us hope that future historians will not take this
play even of the new school of intellectuals, as really representing English society as a whole at the beginning of the twentieth

century.' But these exaggerations remained significant and influential, promoting easier relations between the sexes, encouraging women perhaps not to the point of licence as portrayed on the stage but at least to the point of greater freedom and wish for freedom.

This emancipation was many-sided, progress on one front often stimulating movement on another, as traditionalists were concernedly aware. For many of them greater sex freedom was seen as part of the advance of 'socialism'. Shaw and Wells were both socialists, and Wells in *Socialism and the Family* (1906) had seemed to threaten the very institution of matrimony. Easier divorce could be regarded as a threat to marriage and to the stability of society. The Divorce Commission minority believed that the majority proposals 'would lead the nation on a downward incline on which it would be vain to expect to be able to stop half way'. And just as conservatives feared that the social balance might be upset through female emancipation, so they feared that 'votes for women' would dangerously disturb the political balance, upsetting the delicate interplay between masculine parties, classes and interests which had operated so fruitfully over two centuries.[7]

'Votes for Women'

'When the long struggle for the enfranchisement of women is over, those who read the history of the movement will wonder at the blindness that led the Government of the day to obstinately resist so simple and so obvious a measure of justice.' So forecast the suffragette leader in 1911. Yet even if the introduction of votes for women was simple in terms of political justice it remained complicated in terms of political practice. Did it mean votes for all women, universal female suffrage? If so, it could never be conceded without simultaneously, or previously, granting votes to all men. Such a completely democratic interpretation of the slogan found the least support in Parliament. Did it mean, alternatively, votes for women on the same restricted terms as currently applied to men? But this must then exclude most wives, for they were not householders. On the other hand, votes for women on present terms would allow some of them plural votes, which the Liberals wanted to abolish entirely. Was then some middle way discoverable? By 1913 many Liberal Members of Parliament had agreed that women householders and householders' wives over a certain age might be enfranchised. But were women also acceptable as candidates for and members of the Commons, in the same way as since 1907 they had been allowed to sit on local councils? Edwardian women who campaigned for the vote were themselves divided over the extent of their ideal demand. Both the militant 'suffragettes' and the non-militant 'suffragists' were ready, however, to be satisfied in practice by votes on 'the same terms as men', even though under the existing franchise this would leave female voters in a marked minority. When first raised in mid-Victorian times the women's demand for the vote referred only to some 300,000–400,000 spinsters or widows; and this Edwardian demand still only embraced some four or five times that number out of an adult female population in England and Wales of well over 11 million by 1911. 'The Women's Social and Political Union are *not* asking for a vote for every woman, but simply that sex shall cease to be a disqualification for the franchise.' The women campaigners' prime concern was for recognition, and in this sense concession of the vote even to a minority would be sufficient. The vote, explained a sympathetic male commentator in 1910, 'has always appeared as a symbol of social worth. So long as it is enjoyed by men, and by them denied to women, so long must women be in a state of subjection.'

For several years about 1870 the demand for women's suffrage had been quite strongly voiced in and out of Parliament; but it had never looked like becoming practical politics. Many Liberals, then and into Edwardian times, though favourable in principle, were discouraged by the expected Conservative bias of middle-class women voters. 'Gladstone spoke in favour, said he would vote against and ran away finally.' Queen Victoria herself had been a sharp anti-feminist, asserting that one mid-Victorian enthusiast (the mother of Bertrand Russell) 'ought to get a *good whipping*'. By the turn of the century, however, activity was reviving. Many self-governing colonies had given the vote to women, and the new Independent Labour Party was inclined to be sympathetic. In 1897 the National Union of Women's Suffrage Societies united all existing organizations. Finally, in 1903 the Women's Social and Political Union was founded by Mrs Emmeline Pankhurst (1858–1928), widow of a radical Manchester barrister, supported by her daughters Christabel (1880–1958) and Sylvia (1882–1960). Mrs Pankhurst was a remarkable woman, good looking, an outstanding public speaker (as was Christabel), and an able organizer. The *Daily Mail* dubbed her followers 'suffragettes' to distinguish them from the non-militant 'suffragists' of the NUWSS. The word 'social' in the WSPU title probably reflected Mrs Pankhurst's initial concern for the improvement of the lot of working-class women. This purpose came out clearly in her speech from the dock in October 1908 on a charge of conduct likely to provoke a breach of the peace. 'We believe that if we get the vote it will mean better conditions for our unfortunate sisters . . . legislation can never be effected until we have the same power as men to bring pressure

Suffragette logic—but the politicians equivocated.
Nobody knew how women would vote.

to bear upon governments.' But Mrs Pankhurst later moved away from her early ILP connections towards Conservatism. Though some working-class activists did emerge—notably

Annie Kenney (1879–1953), a cotton worker—both the suffragette and suffragist organizations were predominantly middle-class, with a spicing of aristocratic supporters of both sexes.

For two years the WSPU attracted little attention. It was ignored by politicians and by the press. To win notice it therefore turned in 1905 to militant action, to the interruption of political meetings. Militancy began at a Liberal meeting in Manchester in October. Sir Edward Grey (1862–1933) was asked if he would support votes for women, and when he declined to answer the question Christabel Pankhurst and Annie Kenney caused a disturbance and had to be forcibly ejected. They were later arrested for trying to hold a protest meeting outside the hall, refused to pay fines, and each spent seven days in prison. This has been claimed as the first imprisonment 'endured by any woman for a political cause in this country'.

The suffragettes wanted to know how much (or little) to expect from the new Liberal Government. Liberal and Conservative leaders and back-benchers were greatly divided on the question of female suffrage. Campbell–Bannerman was inclined to be favourable, Asquith to be hostile. Churchill's attitude fluctuated. Balfour was friendly, Bonar Law rather less so. Even some Labour politicians hesitated, fearful lest the grant of votes to some women should damage the prospect of universal suffrage for all men. Lloyd George concluded that the Liberals must either allow universal suffrage for both sexes or nothing, since enfranchisement of only middle-class women would strengthen the Conservative vote. Against this background of difference among political leaders even within the parties it is not surprising that between 1907 and 1912 a succession of private member's bills, though attracting noticeable support, all came to nothing. The suffrage organizations meanwhile continued to grow. The NUWSS increased from only 16 affiliated societies in 1903 to over 300 by 1911. The income of the WSPU rose from £2700 in 1907 to £36,500 in 1914, so that the Home Secretary began to threaten to make 'rich women' members pay for the damage done, 'women who use their wealth against the interests of society, and pay their unfortunate victims to undergo all the horrors of hunger and thirst striking in connection with the commission of crime'. Alongside its 'outrages', the WSPU was sufficiently endowed to conduct a continuous publicity campaign, not only holding (and interrupting) meetings but also publishing pamphlets and leaflets on a large scale. Its penny weekly *Votes for Women* first appeared in 1907, succeeded by *The Suffragette* in 1912.

In 1912 the Liberal Cabinet at last agreed to allow the insertion of women's franchise clauses into a Government Bill abolishing plural voting and extending the male franchise, provided the Commons expressed a wish for such additions on a free vote. But unexpectedly in January 1913 the Speaker ruled that this was inadmissible because it changed the character of the Bill. After this rebuff the NUWSS turned in disillusion from a non-party position to support for Labour, as the only party officially advocating women's suffrage. The suffragettes, for their part, dangerously intensified their campaign of militancy, which had already progressed beyond interruption of meetings to shop window smashing. Systematic arson of churches, railway stations and other places now continued through 1913 and into 1914. Cabinet Ministers were assaulted, and during the 1913 Derby a suffragette was fatally injured when she threw herself under the King's horse. Mrs Pankhurst was sentenced to three years' imprisonment after accepting responsibility for a bomb explosion in a house being built for Lloyd George. Suffragettes in prison had contrived to secure early release by going on hunger strikes. Forcible feeding had aroused widespread criticism, leading the Government to sponsor the 'Cat and Mouse' Act (1913), allowing release of suffragettes for recuperation followed by re-arrest. To such strange lengths had the Pankhursts' extremism driven the legislature. But suffragette fanaticism had begun to dismay even many advocates of the women's cause. The *Manchester Guardian* complained of 'diseased emotionalism'. Mrs Pankhurst asserted in her memoirs, published in 1914, that militancy had been proved right because it had gained notice for the agitation: 'our heckling campaign made women's suffrage a matter of news—it had never been that before. . . . For another thing, we woke up the old suffrage associations.' The limited militancy of the early years could certainly be justified on these grounds, but later excesses evoked not sympathy but anger.

By 1912 the Pankhursts were growing both increasingly dictatorial within their movement and increasingly unconciliatory towards the outside world. Defections of other leaders in 1907 and 1912 had left the WSPU as simply their instrument. Mrs Pankhurst pictured herself as the unquestioned commander-in-chief of an army. 'Autocratic? Quite so. But, you may object, a suffragette organization ought to be democratic. Well the members of the WSPU do not agree with you . . . we don't want anybody to remain in it who does not ardently believe in the policy of the army.' The Pankhursts expected not merely single-mindedness but also unhesitating obedience. Single-mindedness was certainly desirable. Mrs Pankhurst believed that votes for women could have been gained 'years ago' if women had concentrated upon the one basic demand. 'They never did, and even today many English women refuse to adopt it. They are party members first and suffragists afterwards; or they are suffragists part of the time and social theorists the rest of the time.' Single-mindedness had been Cobden's successful policy for the Anti-Corn Law League, and the Pankhursts were seeking to emulate the League, conducting an extra-parliamentary agitation acting above party politics but aiming to persuade politicians of all colours in Parliament of the need for reform. The methods of the WSPU were defined in its constitution:

1 Action entirely independent of all political parties.

2 Opposition to whatever Government is in power until such time as the franchise is granted.

3 Participation in parliamentary elections in opposition to the Government candidates and independently of all other candidates.

4 Vigorous agitation upon lines justified by the position of outlawry to which women are at present condemned.

5 The organizing of women all over the country to enable them to give adequate expression to their desire for political freedom.

6 Education of public opinion by all the usual methods, such as public meetings, demonstrations, debates, distribution

of literature, newspaper correspondence and deputations to public representatives

But the day for successful agitation along such extra-parliamentary lines had passed. Reform could not now be pressed upon Ministers mainly by noisy outside agitation, for parliamentary party allegiances and majorities had become too strong. The woman author of a book called *Towards a Sane Feminism*, published in 1916, was already able to appreciate this weakness in the pre-war suffragette position:

> the initiative of political reforms was no longer with the people. The days of Reform Bill riots and Chartism had given place to the reign of the expert. Today a new remedy for social grievances is elaborated by Mr and Mrs Webb and a committee is formed to boom it, and Sir Leo Chiozza Money writes a testimonial, and by-and-by Mr Lloyd George is pleased by the colour and the sparkle of it and goes to the electorate protesting that he is almost certain that it has practically no taste at all and no unpleasant after-effect. And the electorate swallows the medicine hopefully and —calls in the other party if it regrets the dose too bitterly. . . . A proposal for reform that did not come from the Government or from the Opposition Front Bench appeared to the majority of the electors decidedly frivolous. Quite often they were willing enough to give a theoretical assent to the suffragist dogmas. But it was one thing to sign a petition or join a suffrage society and quite another to vote against one's party. In those pre-war days every voter in the kingdom might have signed a petition for women's enfranchisement and it would still have been possible for Mr Asquith to lie low and say nothing without the smallest fear of weakening his position.

Within this framework of political initiative Lloyd George was, as here suggested, the leading politician most likely to have espoused the cause of female suffrage. Yet instead of encouraging and flattering him, the suffragettes continually harassed him. 'Why don't they go for their enemies?', he asked despairingly on one occasion. While remaining favourable in principle, he became increasingly aware that violence was proving counter-productive, angering instead of converting both politicians and the electorate. 'I don't mind and it doesn't put me out much at meetings or irritate me. I'm used to the rough and tumble and have had to fight my way; so is Churchill (though he is sensitive about his perorations), but it's different with Grey; he isn't accustomed to interruption and can't do with it. What really matters is the effect on the audiences and on the public.'

'They are mad', continued Lloyd George; 'Christabel Pankhurst has lost all sense of proportion and of reality.' In these immediate pre-war years the Pankhursts' tone had certainly become increasingly hysterical. Hostility to all men began to appear as a theme in their speeches and writings. A *Times* letter drew attention in 1912 to some titles of suffragette literature: *Sex War and Women's Suffrage, Women: A Few Shrieks*, and the like. Not merely the superiority of women, but the superfluousness of men began to be asserted. 'Suffrage theology', the correspondent noted, 'teaches us that Adam was made of dust and to dust he will return, but that Eve was not.' Finally, in 1913 Christabel Pankhurst published a widely noticed pamphlet called *The Great Scourge and How to End It*, warning women against marriage because three-quarters or more of men suffered from venereal disease contracted through pre- and extra-marital dissipation with prostitutes. '"Sacrifice yourself, sacrifice yourself", is a cry that has lost its power over women.' The new cry now suggested by Miss Pankhurst was 'Votes for Women and Chastity for Men'.[8]

The non-militant NUWSS refused to follow the Pankhursts along this road towards sex war. Instead, the suffragists emphasized the importance of men and women working together for a reform which would bring mutual advantage. But such moderation could not cancel the damage done by the extreme arguments and actions of the suffragettes. Their excesses gave countenance to those women as well as men who organized in opposition to any extension of female suffrage. Mrs Humphry Ward (1851–1920), the novelist and social worker, played a leading part in forming the Women's Anti-Suffrage League (1908) which in 1911 merged with the Men's League for Opposing Women's Suffrage to become the National League for Opposing Women's Suffrage. Mrs Ward did not want educated women to remain aloof from the world, but she argued that they should concentrate upon serving women and children less fortunate than themselves without clamouring selfishly for 'rights' at the risk of provoking sex war. In this spirit, while opposing votes for women in parliamentary elections or the admission of women to the Commons, Mrs Ward was equally firm in wishing to retain women's votes in local elections and women's membership of municipal and other local bodies. This two-sided approach logically answered Mrs Snowden's charge that 'with a fine disdain of logic they have proclaimed that the sphere of woman is the home, and have come out of the home to prove it'. Many Edwardian women remained indeed well content to centre their whole interests upon the home. Some, though not as many as the popular novelist Marie Corelli (1855–1924) implied in her pamphlet *Woman or—Suffragette?* (1907), centred their lives upon the boudoir: 'the very desire for a vote on the part of a woman is an open confession of weakness . . . if she has the natural heritage of her sex, which is the mystic power to persuade, enthral and subjugate man, she has no need to come down from her throne and mingle in any of his political frays, inasmuch as she is already the very head and front of Government.'[9]

When war came in August 1914 both the suffragettes and the suffragists patriotically stopped their agitations. This saved the Pankhursts from continuing along an increasingly dangerous and futile course. Gradually the contributions made by women to the war effort justified their claim to full citizenship. By November 1915 George Sturt (1863–1927), the rural writer, was remarking how 'the national attitude towards women is undergoing an unobserved but far-reaching development, and they, all unconsciously, are beginning to find a different environment'. 'Time was', admitted the editor of *The Observer* in 1916, 'when I thought that men alone maintained the state. Now I know that men alone never could have maintained it.' The 1918 Representation of the People Act gave the vote to all men and to 8.5 million women over thirty. In the same year women were also allowed to sit in the Commons. The 'flapper vote' for women between twenty-one and thirty had to wait until 1928, and plural voting survived until 1948. But substantially 1918 saw the beginning of electoral democracy in Britain. Since 1928 one fear of Mrs Pankhurst's opponents has been realized—women voters have markedly outnumbered men.[10]

CHAPTER NINE

Irish Home Rule

The Pankhursts justified their intensified militancy during 1913–14 by comparing its still limited character with the threats of civil war in Ireland coming from 'responsible' Conservative politicians. In a Commons speech of June 1914 one such Conservative tried to rebut this comparison by claiming that whereas the suffragettes were encouraging 'anarchy', which was indefensible, the right to rebellion under extreme provocation was traditionally acceptable. Conservatives were again exclaiming 'Ulster will fight and Ulster will be right', the slogan coined by Lord Randolph Churchill in 1886 in opposition to the first Liberal Home Rule Bill, and now revived in opposition to the third Home Rule Bill of 1912–14.[1]

The problem of the past, present and future of Ireland had been transmitted unsolved from the Victorians to the Edwardians. 'Anglo-Irish history', warned one Irishman, 'is for Englishmen to remember, for Irishmen to forget.' But English opinion had long tended to be impatient with Irish complaints. In his play *John Bull's Other Island* (1904) Shaw tried to teach the English about the Irish. 'A conquered nation is like a man with cancer: he can think of nothing else. . . . All demonstrations of the virtues of a foreign government, though often conclusive, are as useless as demonstrations of the superiority of artificial teeth, glass eyes, silver windpipes, and patent wooden legs to the natural product.' Though Shaw's play was successful in terms of theatre, it did little to reduce English incomprehension. The *Handbook to Political Questions of the Day* (1903) listed various Edwardian anti-Home Rule arguments all conceived in this spirit of non-understanding: 'that nobody really wants Home Rule; the desire for Home Rule is merely a

Scarborough 1913. Bathing machines and donkeys.

Chamberlain on tariff reform. Trying to answer the 'little loaf' argument.

A poster issued by the Imperial Tariff Committee Birmingham. Tariff reform and fear of the foreigner.

XIX

at Westminster. Balfour deplored Irish insistence that their nationality required more particular treatment than English or Scottish nationality, both of which continued contentedly within the United Kingdom. 'What is enough for Scotsmen and Englishmen can never be enough for them. To think so would be treason to Ireland.' Balfour argued that this left the British government with only two courses, either to concede complete autonomy (inside or outside the Empire, as the Irish decided) or to maintain the union. A compromise along the lines of Home Rule was impracticable since it meant overthrowing the existing system without fully satisfying Irish aspirations. The Liberals insisted in reply that Home Rule would work, that the Irish would be satisfied with limited independence. When Austen Chamberlain told Churchill in 1913 that his 'root objection' to Home Rule was the idea of 'Ireland a Nation', Churchill chaffed him that this was 'to deny to Irish sentiment any satisfaction in the enjoyment of its Parliament. You are like the R.C. Church which admits the necessity of the marriage bed but holds that you must find no pleasure in the enjoyment of it.' But Churchill went on to add contradictorily that 'there can be no "nation" as long as they accept a subsidy and we can always bring them to book by withholding supplies.' As with State socialism so with Irish nationalism the Edwardian Liberals were trying to discover a middle position, without too much care for logic or contradiction. The Liberals hoped that, just as the English were happily inconsistent in their attitude to State intervention, so the Irish might be equally inconsistent in their attitude to self-government. 'Give them leave to fly a green flag over the Parliament House in College Green and they won't care a pin whether they have a real Parliament or not.' Such was the view of one English Member of Parliament. 'I know all about it because there are a lot of Irish in my constituency.' Balfour and the Conservatives were unimpressed by these Liberal arguments. They were sure that the only course was to continue the union. Fortunately, contended Balfour in 1913, this was likely to prove much easier in the future 'now that all Irish grievances connected with land, religion, and finance have been removed'. This would produce a gradual decline of 'the exclusive and often hostile form which Irish patriotism outside Ulster has assumed'.

The Conservatives at Westminster seemed unwilling to abandon the claim to a Home Rule veto. During the Parliament Bill debates Churchill complained to the King of 'their claim to govern the country whether in office or in opposition and to resort to disorder because they cannot have their way'. Once the Lords' veto had been limited they seemed ready (in another phrase of Churchill's) to substitute the 'veto of violence' for the 'veto of privilege'. In July 1912 Bonar Law, the Leader of the Opposition, ungrammatically and appallingly asserted at a Conservative rally held in the forecourt of Blenheim Palace (a suitably privileged location) that he could 'imagine no length of resistance to which Ulster will go in which they will not be supported by the overwhelming majority of the British people'. *The Times* reported that the audience rose and cheered these sentiments 'for some minutes'. During the next two years Conservative speeches provided, in Asquith's description, 'a complete Grammar of Anarchy'. The Conservatives could not shed the belief that they were the 'natural' ruling party; yet by 1914 they had spent eight frustrating years in opposition. They had convinced themselves that the Liberals had not been given a Home Rule mandate in 1910, and that therefore no such measure should be enacted unless and until a general election had shown public opinion to be favourable. They asserted that the Liberals were only rushing forward with Home Rule in order to retain Irish support and thereby cling on to office. 'We shall use any means to deprive them of the power which they have usurped and to compel them to face the people whom they have deceived. Even if the Home Rule Bill passes through the House of Commons, what then? I said in the House of Commons, I repeat here, that there are things stronger than Parliamentary majorities.' Law's official biographer, Robert Blake, does not try to justify such language. 'Perhaps their insistence upon a fresh General Election proceeded less from a feeling that they had been tricked at the last one than from a conviction that, whatever the mind of the electorate had been in 1910, an appeal to the people in 1912 would result in a Conservative victory.'

The Liberals answered (with good reason) firstly, that Home Rule had indeed been under discussion during the 1910 elections; secondly, that to admit the Conservatives' right to

force another general election would be to admit their continuing right of veto; and thirdly, that even if the Government
won a favourable election verdict Ulster would still threaten
violent resistance to the enforcement of Home Rule. Around
these arguments and counter-arguments language and feelings
grew steadily stronger during 1912–14; and social contact
between Conservative and Liberal politicians became increasingly strained, in some cases to breaking point.

The best argument in Ulster's favour was the claim that
under the unwritten British constitution majorities had generally
respected significant minority rights. Unfortunately, both the
Conservatives and Liberals began by assuming that, for economic reasons, respect for the rights of Ulster implied abandonment of Home Rule for the rest of Ireland. The Liberals
therefore too long tried to ignore Ulster's claim for separate
treatment, while the Conservatives pressed Ulster's case not
only on its own merits but also with the discreditable expectation
of thereby preventing the introduction of Home Rule even in
the rest of Ireland. A handful of reactionary Southern Irish
landlords exercised great influence within the Conservative
hierarchy. Faced with such intransigent opposition, it was im-
material that the Home Rule Bill introduced by Asquith in
April 1912 was extremely limited in its conception of Home Rule.
Only restricted powers were conferred upon a Dublin Parliament, and much financial and other control was reserved to
Westminster. Asquith contended that Home Rule was not a
step towards separation: 'the implication upon a large, I might
say upon a colossal, scale of Imperial credit in the working out
of Land Purchase and in the maintenance of Old Age Pensions
makes the idea of separation between the two islands more
unthinkable than ever it was.' On the other hand, Asquith was
eager to present Home Rule as a step towards more efficient
government through the devolution of some of the powers of the
Imperial Parliament. The idea of 'Home-Rule-all-round', of
separate domestic legislatures for England, Scotland, Wales and
Ireland had been linked with discussion of Home Rule since
Gladstone's day. 'Has any deliberative assembly in the history
of the world', asked Asquith, referring to the multifarious
functions of the Commons, 'ever taken upon itself such a
grotesquely impossible task?' He cited the example of the

Transvaal to prove how the concession of self-rule to Ireland might quickly make loyal friends out of recent enemies. Over a score of self-governing legislatures already owed allegiance to the Crown. 'They have solved, under every diversity of conditions, economic, social, and religious, the problem of reconciling local autonomy with Imperial unity. Are we going to break up the Empire by adding one more?'

In private, though not in public, Ministers were from the first prepared to admit that Ulster might need 'special treatment'; but they long hoped that Ulstermen were only bluffing in their threats of civil war. They were not bluffing, as the Government came gradually to realize. Sir Edward Carson (1854–1935), the Ulster leader, emphasized as early as 1911 in a private letter to Captain Craig (1871–1940), the chief organizer of resistance, how he was 'not for a mere game of bluff'. In September 1912 at a public gathering in Belfast Carson's followers solemnly began signing the Covenant, a pledge to use 'all means which may be found necessary to defeat the present conspiracy to set up a Home Rule Parliament in Ireland'. Almost a quarter of a million Ulstermen signed this threat of armed resistance. By 1914 the Ulster Volunteers, Carson's army, were highly organized, and arms were being landed in only semi-secrecy from Germany. In England a British Covenant was published in March 1914, supporting 'any action' necessary to prevent the enforcement of Home Rule, 'and more particularly to prevent the armed forces of the Crown being used to deprive the people of Ulster of their rights as citizens of the United Kingdom'. Its first signatories included Lord Roberts (1832–1914), the most popular living British soldier, Milner, Kipling, Elgar, and Dicey. Like Roberts, many army officers were Conservatives with Irish connections. Early in 1914 Bonar Law even toyed with the disturbing idea of using his Lords' majority to amend the annual Army Act, upon which all discipline depended, in order to prevent the employment of troops against Ulster, thereby forcing a general election. In March the news that the Government had ordered military movements to meet possible violence in the North provoked a spate of resignations among army officers. This so-called 'Curragh Mutiny' was not a mutiny in the proper sense; but it did demonstrate the unreliability of the army in the excited circumstances of the day. Not many young officers were as perceptive as Archibald Wavell (1883–1950) in deploring this 'political victory': 'how are you to use your Army to keep law and order against strikers once the officers have successfully resisted an attempt to use them to enforce a law which they do not approve?' When Churchill, as First Lord of the Admiralty, sent ships to the Irish coast 'in case of serious disorders arising' he was accused by the Opposition of planning a pogrom of Ulster 'loyalists'. Carson called him 'Lord Randolph's renegade son who wanted to be handed down to posterity as the Belfast butcher who threatened to shoot down those who took his father's advice'. This exaggerated Conservative reaction perhaps reflected a feeling that Churchill's unlimited energy and taunting oratory were vital to the Government's steadfastness during these last months of Irish crisis.

After the Curragh incident Asquith himself became War Secretary. He was still hoping to avoid a complete breakdown, either in Parliament or in Ulster. Moving on 9th March 1914 the second reading of the Home Rule Bill (now on its third circuit), he offered the Opposition an Amending Bill which would have postponed the application of Home Rule to Ulster for six years. This would have interposed two general elections between the beginning of Home Rule and its application in the North. Carson dismissed this gesture as 'sentence of death with stay of execution for six years'. Nevertheless, he and Bonar Law, though not all their followers, were now ready for some compromise. This was demonstrated in July when Carson, Craig, Bonar Law and Lansdowne met Asquith and Lloyd George, plus Redmond and John Dillon (1851–1927), the Irish leaders, in a conference called under royal auspices at Buckingham Palace. The idea of exclusion was now accepted by both sides, but the conference still broke down over the exclusion or inclusion of two Ulster counties with almost equal Protestant/Catholic populations. The Conservatives intended to insist upon the perpetual exclusion of Ulster, but the conference never reached discussion of this second problem.

Both sides had modified their positions since 1912, but because their remaining differences seemed intractable Ireland was on the brink of civil war by the last days of July 1914. The 'English political compromise' appeared to be disintegrating.

Buxton had claimed in the introduction to his *Handbook to Political Questions of the Day* (1903) that differences between Liberals and Conservatives were never asserted as conflicts 'between right and wrong':

> It is frankly acknowledged to be but a conflicting idea, or a dissimilar point of view; a belief on the one side in the beneficial results of action, on the other a dread of the evil results of great changes. . . . The principles advanced by the two parties cannot be reconciled, and may differ fundamentally; but they are, after all, founded on the same basis of supposed right, and the conception and realization of them is but a matter of degree.

This happy restraint now seemed to have been abandoned. The Opposition, in Churchill's words, were not 'playing the

TURNING THE TABLES
(*It is announced that Mr. Winston Churchill is spending Easter in Madrid*).

game' in trying to eject the Government by threatening civil war. 'Had British statesmen and leaders of great parties in the past allowed their thoughts to turn to projects of bloodshed within the bosom of the country, we should have shared the follies of Poland.'

By July 1914 the Catholics of the South were armed and organized to match the Protestants of the North. Yet Asquith still confided to a friend his characteristic 'fixed belief that in politics the expected rarely happens'. And so, indeed, it turned out in this case. Suddenly war erupted on the Continent. On 30th July Asquith and Bonar Law agreed that in the interests of national unity the Government's Amending Bill, which still only proposed the exclusion of Ulster for six years and which was certain to provoke furious scenes in Parliament, should not proceed to a second reading. The Home Rule Bill itself was placed on the statute book in September, but its application was postponed for the duration of the war. Before the return of peace the 1916 Easter rising had added another bitter chapter to the history of Anglo-Irish discord, with the result that after the war a limited measure of Home Rule could no longer even hope to satisfy Southern Irish opinion.[3]

Between 1912 and 1914 alongside the Bill for Irish Home Rule ran another Liberal proposal designed to meet Celtic aspirations, the Welsh Disestablishment Bill. This too was passed at the third attempt in 1914 without the Lords' assent, its application being then postponed because of the war. The Anglican Church in Ireland had been disestablished upon Liberal initiative in 1869, and the Welsh bloc of Liberal Members of Parliament had long been demanding a similar measure as a recognition of Welsh nationality. Nonconformists in Wales outnumbered Welsh Anglicans by nearly three to one. English public opinion was uninterested in the question, but Conservative Churchmen in Parliament fought the Disestablishment Bill as fiercely and obstructively as the Home Rule Bill. Bonar Law even told Asquith in conversation that 'a very much larger number of our Members in the House of Commons would, if they had to choose, prefer Home Rule rather than the disestablishment of the Church'. Conservative Churchmen had convinced themselves that disestablishment would open the floodgates to paganism. F. E. Smith (1872–1930), a leading Conservative protagonist against both Home Rule and Welsh disestablishment, even assured the Commons that the latter

scheme had 'shocked the conscience of every Christian community in Europe'. G. K. Chesterton properly deflated such
exaggeration in verse:

> Are they clinging to their crosses,
> F. E. Smith,
> Where the Breton boat-fleet tosses,
> Are they, Smith?
> . . . .
> If the voice of Cecil falters,
> If McKenna's point has pith,
> Do they tremble for their altars?
> Do they, Smith?

But the exaggerated language of Conservative opposition to
both the Irish and the Welsh policies of the Liberal Government was simply a mirror of the intensely bitter political
antagonism of these last Edwardian years.[4]

CHAPTER TEN

The Coming of War

'Ah 1914! "Oh! that a man might know the end of this year's business ere it come." I see not a patch of blue sky!' When at the year's opening a leading Liberal (Morley) wrote thus to a leading Conservative (Austen Chamberlain) all his fears were concentrated upon Ireland. Up to the last week of July the *Manchester Guardian* was carrying anxious headlines— 'Hopes of a Settlement', 'A Critical Moment'—referring not to Europe but to the Irish crisis. How much, or how little, during the years leading to 4th August 1914 did Edwardians foresee the coming of a major war? Did they expect Britain to be involved in any such conflict if ever it occurred? How did they regard foreigners and foreign affairs? What was the short-term impact of the war? How did the Edwardian era come to an end? These associated questions can be considered separately from a detailed account of British foreign policy in the period.

Foreign policy, indeed, was conducted largely without the knowledge of the Edwardians themselves. '"Foreign affairs",' remembered a contemporary, '—it was typical that we so spoke of international relationships—were matters for experts.' Culturally, awareness of Europe was growing during the last Edwardian years, evidenced by the London Post-Impressionist exhibition of 1910 or the visit of the Russian ballet in 1911; but English insularity was deep-seated, not only among the working classes who rarely travelled overseas (except as servicemen or emigrants) but also among the Edwardian upper and middle classes, who toured the Continent in large numbers. *The Nation* remarked in 1912 how every English tourist 'carries with him a miniature England of his own . . . we dispossess "the natives", and give them the air of strangers and intruders in their own land'. It was a tribute to French adaptability 'that they have formed an *entente* with us, in spite of the British tourist'. Notwithstanding the entente, the Continent was often viewed with distaste. Mrs Wilcox in *Howards End* observed how her husband had 'very little faith in the Continent, and our children have all taken after him'. In relation to the peoples of the Far East the 'Yellow Peril' was a widespread fear. The German Kaiser, who shared and encouraged this bogey, assured Winston Churchill in 1911 that all future wars would be 'racial'.[1]

This, however, was a long-term scare. Germany herself presented more of a challenge for the Edwardian present, in terms first of commercial and increasingly also of naval and political rivalry. A *Daily Mail* survey entitled *Our German Cousins* (1910) complained that what was 'even more astounding than the rise of Germany to success is the indifference with which the epoch-making development of this phenomenal expansion is regarded in England'. When the volume consequently found few buyers, Harmsworth 'boomed' it in the *Mail* as 'The Book That Will Not Sell!', offering a prize to the reader with the most convincing explanation. As a result, 200,000 copies were then bought in a fortnight. The *Mail* had been warning of German rivalry and hostility since its first years, though obviously with little effect. In 1909 H. G. Wells used 'The Coming of Bleriot' as a technological as well as a military warning. 'One meaning, I think, stands out plainly enough, unpalatable enough to our national pride. This thing from first to last was made abroad. . . . In spite of our fleet, this is no longer, from the military point of view, an inaccessible island.'[2]

Commercially the United States was growing even more powerful than Germany. But Edwardian politicians and the Edwardian public were more sympathetically inclined towards the 'Yankees' than towards any Europeans. The Edwardian upper classes were importing American heiresses in increasing numbers. By 1914 at least 130 American girls, including Winston Churchill's mother, had married British peers and sons of peers. Anglo-American diplomatic relations grew warmer as Britain tacitly came to accept American predominance throughout the New World, while noting with satisfaction how the Spanish–American War (1898) had transformed the United States into a fellow imperialist power. Kipling's poem 'The White Man's Burden' was significantly sub-titled 'the United States and the Philippine Islands'. The Edwardians found consolation in the belief that the Americans were of the same Anglo-Saxon 'race' as themselves. Alfred Austin (1835–1913), poet laureate, published eleven stanzas in *The Times* of November 1899 extolling 'The Old Land and the Young Land':

> Then the Old Land said, 'Youth is strong and quick,
> And Wisdom is strong but mild;
> And blood than water is yet more thick,
> And this Young Land is my child,
> I am proud, not jealous, to watch it grow,'
> Thus the Old Land spoke and Smiled.

About the turn of the century Joseph Chamberlain dreamt of an alliance between the Anglo-Saxon powers, linked perhaps with Teutonic Germany. Yet he was really well aware that the Americans were not interested in formal commitments, and perforce he had to rest content with reiterating Austin's cliché. If ever 'Anglo-Saxon liberty and Anglo-Saxon interests' were threatened 'by a great combination of other Powers', declared Chamberlain, 'in that case, whether it be America or whether it be England that is menaced, I hope that blood will be found to be thicker than water.' Here was a leading English politician conceding equality to the United States upon the world stage; but in *The Americanization of the World, or the Trend of the Twentieth Century* (1902) W. T. Stead, a leading journalist, was already willing to admit that Britain would be the junior partner in any alliance. She must be ready to merge her Empire in 'the United States of the English-speaking World' so as 'to realize the Great Ideal of Race Union'.

By the later Edwardian years, however, this emphasis upon 'race' had diminished, influenced perhaps by growing aware-ness that the future of the British Empire would depend not upon Anglo-Saxon predominance but upon keeping the loyalty of its non-white majority, influenced perhaps also by realization that an increasing number of United States citizens were not of Anglo-Saxon stock. In 1906 Sir Edward Grey, the

Liberal Foreign Secretary, played down the 'race' theme in a confidential letter to President Theodore Roosevelt:

> We are really well disposed (though there are perhaps too many sentimentalists), and there is a real friendly feeling towards the United States. Some people call it Anglo-Saxon race feeling. But it is not really that as between us and you. Your Continent is making a new race and a new type, drawn from many sources. . . . So I do not dwell upon race feeling. But common language helps to draw us together, and religion also. . . . But, more than all this, I should say that some generations of freedom on both sides have evolved a type of man and mind that looks at things from a kindred point of view, and a majority that has a hatred for what is not just or free.

Grey was thus disclaiming the 'blood is thicker than water' assumption, though still asserting a 'special relationship'. This same line was repeated in 1907 by James Bryce (1838–1922), speaking in public just before his departure for Washington as British Ambassador. Bryce described American friendship as 'of special value to us', based upon ties 'not only of interest, but what is higher and greater than interest, of sympathy, ties that rest upon community of language, on the possession of the same literature, of the same political institutions, and of the same traditions'. This assumption was reflected in 1912 when *Whitaker's Almanack* removed its section on the United States out of alphabetical order among the foreign powers to a special place immediately after the section on the British Empire.[3]

W. H. Page, the American Ambassador, once remarked of Sir Edward Grey (1862–1934), Foreign Secretary 1905–16, that 'he'd make a good American with the use of very little sandpaper'. In a period when Foreign Secretaries enjoyed great independence, not only from Parliament but also from their Cabinet colleagues, Grey was one of the most powerful men in Edwardian England, with the opportunity to commit his country very far towards peace or war in any present or future crises. Born into a Northumberland landowning family with a tradition of public service, through eleven taxing years he forced his deep love of country pursuits into the background. Gladstone remarked how he had never known a man with 'such aptitude for political life and such disinclination for it'. As a countryman Grey consciously retained for himself (in Wordsworth's words, which meant much to him) a 'central peace at the heart of endless agitation', a calm self-sufficiency unruffled by man-made crises. In the days of Gladstone and Disraeli foreign policy had still been a matter of party difference; but Grey had accepted and developed the policy of his Conservative predecessor, Lord Landsdowne. This had sought to extricate Britain from the exposed position revealed during the Boer War when no major power had offered diplomatic support. The term 'splendid isolation' had been coined in 1896 to describe a situation in which the isolation was already coming to be more felt than the splendour. An Anglo-Japanese alliance was hesitantly concluded in 1902 to protect British interests in the Far East, followed in 1904 by the Anglo-French Entente, on paper simply the settlement of long-standing colonial differences but increasingly in practice something more. In 1907 Grey concluded a similar entente with Russia. This was neither so successful nor so popular; but it did mean that Britain had come to terms with both partners (the Dual Entente) on one side of the European balance, yet not with the Triple Alliance of Germany, Austria and Italy on the other. As early as 1906 Grey sanctioned secret military conversations with France. Most members even of the Cabinet knew nothing of these until 1912. Grey felt that conversations were necessary so that Britain *could* (not necessarily *would*) support France if she were attacked by Germany. He always insisted in public and in private that there was no formal commitment, an entente was not an alliance. But, especially after naval discussions had led in 1913 to the withdrawal of the French fleet to the Mediterranean, Britain's moral obligation was hard to deny. During the 1906 Moroccan crisis provoked by Germany, Grey was already admitting how it would be difficult for Britain to keep out of a Franco-German conflict. 'The *Entente*, and still more the constant and emphatic demonstrations of affection (official, naval, political, commercial, municipal and in the press), have created in France a belief that we should support her in war.' Again in 1911, justifying further military conversations in response to the renewed Moroccan crisis, Grey told Asquith that 'no doubt these conversations and our speeches have given an expectation of support. I do not see how that can be helped.' Over the years the Foreign Secretary had committed Britain very far, mainly upon his own initiative. By temperament he preferred to act alone and in private. But it was the pressure of circumstances plain to all (German recklessness, Austrian disintegration, Balkan turbulence), which had forced his peace-seeking diplomacy to become also preparation for war.

Radical and Labour critics were especially unhappy at the shroud of secrecy surrounding Edwardian diplomatic exchanges, fearful of the extent of British involvement. *Punch* carried a cartoon in 1911 entitled 'The New Diplomacy', showing an 'Advanced Democrat' looking over Grey's shoulder at the diplomatic card table:

'Look here, we've decided that this isn't to be a private room any more; and you're to put your cards on the table and then we can all take a hand.'
'What, and let my opponents see them too?'

Back-bench Members of Parliament were almost as ignorant of the conduct of British foreign policy as the Edwardian man in the street. Reformers argued that parliamentary control could be reconciled with the need for secrecy if a small number of members were appointed to a Foreign Affairs Committee. 'A House which really meant to control foreign affairs would not be content to assert its control over treaties and declarations of war. It is the conduct of affairs between one great crisis and another which ends in the treaty or the war.' So argued H. N. Brailsford only a few weeks before the final crisis in 1914. The radical weekly *Nation* and the daily *Manchester Guardian* persistently but unavailingly tried to establish the full extent of British commitments. On the centenary of John Bright's birth in 1911 *The Nation* complained that he would have denounced 'our Continental entanglements; and he would have thought it the melancholy prelude to a colossal war! But his first question would have been: "What is twentieth century Liberalism doing in this galley?".'[4]

Edward VII

George V when Prince of Wales.

XX

The first payment of old-age pensions 1909.

Winston Churchill and Lloyd George.

Radicals contended that Britain ought to retain freedom of action in foreign affairs for Cobdenite reasons both of high morality and of strict finance. In reality, however, the case for increased defence spending proved irresistible throughout the Edwardian years, expenditure rising from under £35 million in 1890 to over £91 million by 1913. Naval estimates grew especially fast because of the 'naval race' forced by Germany—from almost £31 million in 1901 to £51.5 million by 1914. From the time of her 1898 and 1900 Navy Laws Germany embarked upon the building of a large fleet, and this lay at the heart of the growing, even though fluctuating, Anglo-German tension throughout the Edwardian period. The Germans a serted their sovereign right to build a big navy. They also argued that their commerce and colonies needed protection, a reasonable point but one not compatible with the short range of the new German ships, most of which were clearly built to fight in the North Sea. In the early days of the new naval policy it was possible to justify this emphasis by an honest (if mistaken) belief that the north German coast required defence against a possible British attack. Another German argument stressed the need to build a fleet so large that the British navy would only be able to destroy it at prohibitive cost to itself; it was thought that this prospect could be used to influence British policy in favour of Germany and away from France and Russia. In the event, the only influence exerted by German battleship-building was to make Britain counter-build. Traditionally Britannia had ruled the waves, and almost everyone in Britain, though there were differences over the mathematics of supremacy, agreed that this predominance must be maintained. For Germany a fleet was (in Churchill's word) a 'luxury': for Britain, with her dependence upon imported food and raw materials and with her world Empire, it was a necessity.

Gradually, under the pressure of German building, the two-power standard, under which the British fleet had been maintained at a strength more than equal to the combined strengths of the next two largest navies, was replaced by a standard of sixty per cent superiority over the German navy. From 1905 the construction of the *Dreadnought,* much more powerful than all previous battleships, compelled the rebuilding of all battle fleets from scratch. Britain led the way, but Germany was now not far behind. In 1909 a naval scare swept Britain, in fear that the Germans had secretly accelerated their capital ship construction so that by 1912 they might enjoy numerical superiority. 'We want eight and we won't wait' became the popular cry for the immediate construction of eight rather than four new capital ships. 'We are not yet prepared to turn the face of

COPYRIGHT EXPIRES

GERMAN TAR: ' "*We don't want to fight, but, by jingo, if we do, we've got the ships, we've got the men, we've got the money too.*" '

JOHN BULL: '*I say, that's* my *old song.*'

GERMAN TAR: '*Well, it's mine now.*'

every portrait of Nelson to the wall', exclaimed the *Daily
Telegraph* on 18th March. The Liberal Government, though
reluctant to spend so heavily, eventually did build the eight
vessels, taking account of the entry of Austria and Italy into the
dreadnought race. The fear of German acceleration proved
unfounded, but in the early stages of the war these four extra
ships were to be invaluable in maintaining British naval
supremacy.[5]

The Liberal Government always accepted that the British
fleet would save Britain from invasion. Soldiers would be needed,
argued Haldane, War Secretary 1905–12, only to mop up such
small numbers of enemy troops as slipped through the naval
net. For this purpose he formed the Territorial Army, organized
on a county basis to appeal to local patriotism with an establishment of 300,000 volunteers. They were to undergo annual
training for four years and be liable for service until the age of
thirty. For overseas fighting in a major war Haldane created an
'expeditionary force' of regulars. All party leaders, Conservative as well as Liberal, recognized that the British public
would not accept any army re-organization requiring compulsory military service. Freedom from such service was
tenaciously (albeit erroneously) held to be part of traditional
British liberty. 'I am happy in believing', wrote Gissing in 1903,
'that most English people are affected by it as I am, with the
sickness of dread and of disgust.' In the spring of 1914 Lansdowne, the Conservative leader in the Lords, admitted that
compulsion could only be introduced when backed by 'an
overwhelming body of public opinion . . . I do not believe that
at this moment the condition of public opinion with regard to
compulsory service is such as to justify either Party in attempting to press it upon Parliament. That feeling is common to the
Front Benches on both sides.'

Yet since the time of the Boer War, with its revelation of
British military shortcomings, a campaign had been waged by
the National Service League (1901) to secure, if not conscription in the full sense, at least 'national service'. This involved
compulsory military training for home defence lasting four
months for the infantry, up to six months for other branches.
All able-bodied men aged between eighteen and twenty-one

were to be enlisted 'without distinction of class or wealth'. This basic training was to be followed by annual musketry practice and by a fortnight's instruction in camp for three years. During a decade Lord Roberts led the National Service League's campaign. By 1909 the League had attracted 35,000 members and was publishing large quantities of propaganda literature. Roberts defined its task as 'to hammer away on the anvil of the electorate until we have shaped the sword of public opinion so strong and so sharp, and of such finely tempered steel, that it will carry us to victory.' His early speeches were collected under the title *A Nation in Arms* (1907): 'the nation must identify itself with, and take a practical interest in, the Army, and no longer look upon it as a profession with which it has nothing to do but find the money to defray its cost'.

Haldane planned his army policy on the assumption that the defeat of the navy was unthinkable, since if the fleet could not command the seas Britain must sooner or later starve, even if she had raised a million-strong army. Roberts and his supporters answered by postulating the case of a partial naval defeat, followed by the landing of a large enemy army. If met by a strong home defence force, much stronger than the Territorial Army, national service advocates argued that such an invasion might at least be checked. This would then gain time for a naval recovery, which would cut off the invader's supplies and communications 'To leave the bulk of the manhood of this country without military training at all', concluded Lord Milner, 'to rely solely upon the Navy, is not to use the immense advantage of our insular position but to abuse it—to presume upon it.' Moreover, asked Milner, would not military training be physically good for the youth of Britain? 'War is an evil, and a tremendous evil, but military training is not.' 'Have you thought of the physical improvement conscription would bring about in the manhood of the country?', inquired one military character in a 1905 play. 'What England wants is chest! (he generously inflates his own.) Chest and Discipline. I don't care how it's obtained.' Roberts emphasized the wider social connections of national service in a letter to *The Times* (1911). Social reform and national defence were 'intimately connected, and a satisfactory solution of them must precede any real strengthening of Imperial bonds':

The conditions amid which millions of our people are living appear to me to make it natural that they should not care a straw under what rule they may be called upon to dwell and I can quite understand their want of patriotic feeling . . . with how much more confidence should we be able to appeal to the young men of this nation and the Empire to do their duty as citizen soldiers if we had the certainty that they regarded England, not as a harsh step-mother, but as a true Motherland, sedulously nurturing its youth, and not indifferent to their welfare in manhood or in age?

Roberts then went on to make it plain that he regarded the Conservatives as much more likely to adopt such policies than the Liberals. 'Is it too late to hope that the Unionist Party will come forward to lead the millions that wait for a leader?'

Despite all Roberts's efforts, despite his concern for social service as well as national service, despite the support of *The Times*, the *Daily Telegraph* and the *Daily Mail*, the vast majority of the British people refused to countenance the adoption of compulsory military service in the years before the First World War. 'If the country is not safe with its regular forces at their present size, why not make the Services better worth a man's while to join?' Such was one dismissive working-class rejoinder to all Roberts's appeals.[6]

The nearest the British people came to accepting any scheme of training was within the Boy Scout movement, started in 1908 and attracting over 100,000 members within two years. Its founder, Lieutenant-General Sir Robert Baden-Powell (1857–1941), the hero of the siege of Mafeking, conceived the movement very much in the same spirit as Lord Roberts, his commander-in-chief in South Africa, conceived national service. The Boy Scout motto was 'Be Prepared'. Baden-Powell's *Scouting for Boys* (1908) declared roundly that Britain was 'suffering from the growth of "shirkers" in every class of the community—men who shirk their duties and responsibilities to the State and to others'. Scouts were to be trained in 'energetic patriotism' by mainly outdoor activities. The movement was avowedly non-political, but Conservative bias could not be concealed in the *Scouting for Boys* section on 'Government'. 'The House of Commons is made up of men chosen by the people to make known their wants and to suggest remedies, and the House of Lords sees whether they are equally good for all and for the future of the country.' This was an interpretation of the role of the upper house held also by Roberts, who voted with the 'die-hards' against the Parliament Act.[7]

In a 1966 survey, 34 per cent of the men rolled who were born between 1901 and 1920 claimed to have belonged to the Boy Scouts. The movement therefore probably did make a contribution to the development of Edwardian 'patriotism', crudely conceived, helping to prepare the British people for the 1914–18 war. But had the Edwardians any premonitions of the catastrophe towards which they were moving? They were certainly aware of the mood of violence, present and threatened, circulating within society during the immediate pre-war years. They knew of the competing European alliance systems. 'On the one hand we find the reasoned opinion of Europe declaring itself more and more strongly for peace, and, on the other hand, preparations for war which in their extent and effectiveness suggest that a lust for blood is the actuating principle of modern society.' So complained Campbell-Bannerman. But other British observers reassured themselves by emphasizing that rivalry need not mean war. The Neo-Darwinians, by contrast, were happy to accept that rivalry might well produce violence, a consequence which they regarded as natural and beneficial. 'History shows me one way and one way only, in which a high state of civilization has been produced, namely, the struggle of race with race.' Such was the argument of Professor Karl Pearson's (1857–1936) *National Life from the Standpoint of Science* (1901). Articles entitled 'God's Test by War', and 'A Vindication of War' appeared in the *Nineteenth Century* during 1911, and the *Daily Mirror* spoke in similar terms to a more popular audience: 'That England is always at war shows an amount of energy and superabundant spirits that go a long way to demonstrate that we are not a decaying race. Three little wars going on, and the prospect of a large one looming before us we take quite as a matter of course.' Answers to the Neo-Darwinians came from radicals such as L. T. Hobhouse, who denied that Darwin had shown how the struggle for existence was 'the condition of progress'. The theory of evolution rightly understood, contended Hobhouse, gave predominance to 'the evolution of the mind', thus justifying reformers who wished to encourage the application of ethical principles in both national and international politics.[8]

Was international working-class solidarity likely to act as a safety-valve, preventing capitalist governments from conducting wars with each other? English socialists were divided over this possibility. 'Let us assume the danger of a German invasion to be real', exclaimed Keir Hardie in 1908. 'What is our duty as Socialists and Labour men? Is the German Socialist movement a fraud, and the Socialist Party, with its three and a half million voters, a sham? Is our own Labour Party, with its million and a half Trade Union adherents and its magnificent Socialist backing, a thing of no meaning? Assuredly not!' On the other hand, two other leading Socialists, Hyndman and Blatchford, played an active part in warning of the German danger, which they did not believe the German Socialists could control. In 1909 Blatchford contributed a widely noticed series of articles to the *Daily Mail*, recommending national service and preparation for war as the only hope of preventing its outbreak, by making the German militarists realize that force would not pay. 'I write these articles because I believe that Germany is deliberately preparing to destroy the British Empire, and because I know that we are not ready to defend ourselves against a sudden and formidable attack.' 'Blatchford and Hyndman', replied Keir Hardie, 'seem to have set themselves the task of producing that very feeling of inevitableness than which nothing could more strengthen the hands of the warmongers on both shores of the German Ocean. . . . Is that work worthy of the traditions of Socialism?' After the onset of war G. D. H. Cole was to admit that much of Labour's 'somewhat artificial philosophy of international relations' had proved 'shallow and unreal'.[9]

The most widely noticed of all Edwardian discussions of international relations, read in translation throughout the world, was Norman Angell's (1872–1967) *The Great Illusion*, first published in 1910 and frequently reprinted up to 1914. Angell did not argue, as he was often misrepresented as arguing, that commercial inter-relationships had now made war impossible. What he did claim was that such inter-connections meant that any major war would now prove economically disastrous, for the victors as much as for the vanquished: 'military power is socially and economically futile . . . it is impossible for one nation to seize by force the wealth or trade of another'. Angell hoped that European statesmen would remember such rational economic considerations. Unhappily, the final crisis showed them preoccupied with irrational factors of ambition and prestige.[10]

The *Daily Mail*'s warnings had continued year by year. 'War is a horrible and dreadful thing for everybody, and the only way for England not to have war with Germany is for England to get ready' (July 13 1906). But left-wingers could dismiss such admonitions as merely subscriptions to Harmsworth's maxim that readers liked 'a good hate'. The irresponsibility of the *Mail* seemed confirmed when as early as 1902 it came near to recommending a pre-emptive strike upon the German fleet. If the new German navy constituted a danger, asked the *Mail*, 'does not common sense dictate the propriety of destroying it before the boy becomes a man, or a giant, as will be the case by 1915?' The weekly *John Bull*, conducted by the charlatan Horatio Bottomley (1860–1933) was still more inflammatory and probably still less influential. In 1912 it too recommended an attack upon the German fleet, if the Germans persisted with further construction. 'Today! Tomorrow will be too late.' After the outbreak of war both the *Mail* and *John Bull* published collections of their forecasts of conflict, the latter regretting that its 1912 naval advice had not been taken.[1]

Less strident, and perhaps more persuasive, at least among the thinking public, were the writings of H. G. Wells, some of whose journalism had indeed appeared in the *Daily Mail*. In 1909 Wells was discussing 'The Possible Collapse of Civilization' through waste of resources upon war coupled with underinvestment in social improvement. In May 1914 he published *The World Set Free*, which described the collapse of the social order through the use of atomic bombs in a war beginning with a German invasion of France through Belgium. Here was remarkable foresight, telescoping the events of only a few weeks later at the start of the First World War with events over thirty years later destined to bring the end of the Second World War. A steady succession of warning books and plays had already appeared before 1914. The most widely noticed warnings of a future German invasion were Erskine Childers's (1870–1922) *The Riddle of the Sands* (1903), William Le Queux's (1864–1927) *The Invasion of 1910* (1906), and Guy du Maurier's (1865–1915) play *An Englishman's Home* (1909), said to have encouraged a marked rise in Territorial Army recruiting.[12]

Yet Wells was well aware of the diminishing effect of his own and others' warnings the more often they were repeated. 'A threat that goes on for too long', he was to write after the threat had become the reality of war, 'ceases to have the effect of a threat, and this overhanging possibility had become a fixed and scarcely disturbing feature of the British situation':

> it stimulated a small and not very influential section of the press to a series of reminders that bored Mr Britling acutely, it was the excuse for an agitation that made national service ridiculous. . . . It bored him; there it was a danger, and there was no denying it, and yet he believed firmly that it was a mine that would never be fired.

This was perhaps the typical British attitude right up to the last days of July 1914. The war danger had become too much a commonplace to be taken quite in earnest. When the final crisis was breaking the *Manchester Guardian* admitted revealingly that 'the European war which has been talked about for so long that no one really believed it would ever come is nearer embodiment than any of us can remember'. A *Daily Mail* journalist writing in the privacy of his diary on the day after the British declaration of war perhaps voiced the most representative attitude:

> Today our splash is 'Great Britain declares War on Germany', and there is a recruiting appeal in the paper too—'Your King and country need you'—addressed to all men between eighteen and thirty. The mock warfare of Ulster is already forgotten. People speak of it in whispers of shame . . . The great war that we have had in our innermost thoughts, but have always kept in reserve, in the belief that it would be for our children or our children's children to go through is here, and *we* are to go through it. The country is serious and sober and surprised.

In other words, the British people had vaguely expected a major war some day, but had never prepared themselves to find that the day had actually arrived, as it did on 4th August 1914.[13]

During the first half of 1914, in particular, neither the British public nor the British Government were expecting war. The Balkan crises of 1912–13 had been settled by the Concert of Powers, and this seemed to promise future co-operation between them to maintain peace in times of tension. A remnant of this hope seems to have survived in some circles even a fortnight after the start of hostilities. A *Punch* cartoon (19th August) entitled 'The Old Refrain' showed two old ladies conversing:

> *First Old Lady:* 'My dear, what do you think of this war? Isn't it terrible?'
>
> *Second Old Lady:* 'Awful! But it can't last long; the Powers will surely intervene.'

During July the Cabinet had been pre-occupied with the Irish crisis. Only on the 24th did it hold its first foreign affairs discussion for a month. Ministers were concerned at the prospect of war between the four Continental Powers, but 'happily', concluded Asquith in his diary, 'there seems to be no reason why we should be anything more than spectators'. The Sarajevo assassination (28th June) had evoked little British concern either for the murdered Austrian Archduke, or for the Serbs on whose territory the event had occurred and who were being threatened by the Austrians. Serbia was a backward, disreputable country; the Archduke was unpopular. 'It would be absurd to grieve over it. He was a curious, dumb, reserved, uncomfortable sort of man.' So wrote one Cambridge don, A. C. Benson (1862–1925), in his diary. His vacation routine continued as usual: 'Rupert Brooke came to dine—very handsome, but more mature since his travels.' Each day during the last week of July, however, brought the Cabinet and the country nearer to realization not only that a European war was beginning but that Britain would be under strong pressure from France to participate. Detachment would not be possible. Not to intervene would require a positive decision made in the light of British interests and obligations. Was intervention necessary to maintain the balance of power? *The Times* argued in this sense on 29th July. The *Daily News* and *Manchester Guardian*, both Liberal papers, countered emphatically the next morning:

> 'We have no direct interests at all,' says *The Times*, 'except those of seeing elementary fair play in the quarrel between Vienna and Belgrade.' This is not a British interest at all. Our interest is in fair play in England, and especially in Ancoats and Hulme. But if we had to choose foreign clients we should prefer others than the Servians . . . We have not seen a shred of a reason for thinking that the triumph of Germany in a European war in which we had been neutral would injure a single British interest, however small, whereas the triumph of Russia would create a situation for us really formidable.

British honour, continued the *Guardian*, was not involved with respect to neutrality of Belgium, for in 1870 Gladstone had carefully restricted the British commitment to defend Belgian integrity to the duration solely of the Franco-Prussian War.

But on 4th August Britain declared war, and the country was irretrievably committed to fighting in what immediately became known as the 'Great War'. Liberal and radical journals which had opposed intervention soon transferred their aversion to war-making into support for the war as a crusade to establish permanent peace. H. G. Wells led the way with a series of articles significantly entitled 'The War That Will End War'. 'This, the greatest of all wars, is not just another war—it is the last war.' During the first weeks such idealism could still be linked with some disinterestedness. On 20th August the *Times Literary Supplement* editorial was emphasizing how, with her allies fighting desperately for survival, Britain alone could take a balanced view. 'For the moment the conscience of the world is in our keeping.' But such restraint did not last long as the casualty lists and stories of German 'atrocities' became known. By 22nd October the same paper's editorial was headed 'The Illusions of War'. 'It seemed easy not to hate the Germans when the war began, but it is less easy now that we have borne the strain of war for two months and a half.' The idealistic mood reflected in Rupert Brooke's immensely popular war

sonnets, '1914'—'Now, God be thanked Who has matched us
with His hour'—was soon qualified for both the poet and his
public. 'Not a bad place and time to die, Belgium 1915? . . .
Better than coughing out a civilian soul amid bedclothes and
disinfectant and gulping medicines in 1950.' The extent of
German 'war guilt' began to be assessed. On the eve of war
Gilbert Murray, the classical scholar, had signed a plea for
British neutrality; but the Belgian invasion had changed his
whole view. 'Now I see that on a large part of this question—
by no means the whole of it—I was wrong . . . One is vividly
reminded of Lord Melbourne's famous dictum: "All the sensible men were on one side, and all the d--d fools on the other.
And, egad, Sir, the d--d fools were right!".'[14]

At home the slogan at first was 'business as usual'. A short
war, 'over by Christmas' was expected. But by Christmas
deadlock had been reached in France. Were the British armies
in Flanders to 'chew barbed wire' (in Churchill's phrase), or
should an effort be made to turn the enemy flank via the Baltic
or the Balkans? The outcome was the unsuccessful 1915
Dardenelles diversion. In May quite suddenly a coalition
Government was formed, Asquith remaining Prime Minister.
During 1915 the front in France nowhere moved more than
three miles; yet the cost in casualties was sickening. Asquith's
second son went out in April, and his wife had to make a personal readjustment now being repeated hundreds of thousands
of times. 'It is very difficult to believe that history will interfere
in one's private life to such an extent. Beb going to the front
seems too melodramatic to be true.' Three weeks later she was
noting how London 'looks distinctly more abnormal now—
more soldiers, more bandages and limps, and more nurses—
quite a sensational sense of strain.' 'Total war' meant full
organization of the 'home front', as Sidney Webb eagerly
explained to Bernard Shaw in August 1915:

> If I were in power . . . I should decree *Universal Submission* to
> the National Need—not young men for the trenches only,
> but everyone for what he was fitted; and not persons only
> but also property and possessions—everything to be placed
> at the disposal of the Government against a mere receipt in
> paper—and then let the Government Departments *organize*

what they could in each branch, preparing plans for Munitions, Aircraft, Ships, Transport and what not, with the materials in persons, things and cash thus placed at their disposal.

What Webb desired soon largely came to pass. The State began to dominate life as never before. 'The mass of the people became, for the first time, active citizens.' Conscription, food rationing, control of employment, all proved necessary for victory. The Liberals initiated this policy on patriotic grounds, but the fact of war plus the price of victory undermined their party as a major political force. 'War is fatal to Liberalism', as Churchill had declared before 1914. The traditional Liberal slogan had been 'peace, retrenchment and reform'. Now there was no peace, and the opposite of retrenchment. 'When one thinks of all our schemes of social reform just set going and of those for which plans had been made in this year's Budget, one could weep.' So confided Christopher Addison (1869-1951), Parliamentary Secretary at the Board of Education, to his diary on the first day of war. Free trade, the central Liberal commercial creed, was sacrificed in 1915 when import duties were imposed, limited at first in range and duration but destined never again to disappear. The 1916 Asquith-Lloyd George split greatly added to Liberal difficulties, but the whole position of Liberalism was already weakened before this. Perhaps it was already insecure even before the war. The social reforms of Lloyd George and Churchill had been improvisations, brilliant but uncertain in their intellectual ground, like the two men themselves. The Liberals had expressly repudiated 'socialism', but the rise of the wartime state made socialist methods of government credible. Before the war even the Labour Party had not been explicitly committed to socialism. By 1918 it was ready to offer a fully socialist programme and to become a fully organized national party. Its new 1918 constitution provided for party membership by individuals and for local party machinery. *Labour and the New Social Order* spoke out boldly:

Today no man dares to say that anything is impracticable. The war, which has scared the old political parties right out of their dogmas, has taught every statesman and every Government official, to his enduring surprise, how very much more can be done along the lines that we have laid down than he had ever before thought possible.[15]

The economic dislocation caused by war was becoming apparent by 1915. A book on *The City, its Finance July 1914 to July 1915 and Future* warned that 'it is well to be prepared to see our financial power somewhat reduced at the end of this war'. The book made a call for restraint in personal spending in a spirit which has since become only too familiar. 'Rigid economy and retrenchment in every household—hard strenuous work so organized that every member of the community should get the opportunity of using all his ability for the common cause.' Edwin Montagu (1879-1924), Financial Secretary to the Treasury, wrote concernedly to the Prime Minister in July 1915 about the distorting effects of mass military recruiting upon the British economy:

I cannot understand how the Government is content to go on recruiting and recruiting men of all ages and 'employments. We must increase our export trade by the employment of many more men than at present, not only on munitions but on their normal avocations . . . we can only find the money if we can make more money: and we can only make money by selling abroad, as we alone of the Allies are able to do.

But the large army policy was continued, regardless of its economic consequences, so that by 1916 Britain possessed a land force of Continental proportions for the first time in her history, destined to be shattered on the Somme. 750,000 men from the United Kingdom, and 200,000 from the Empire died in the war. This loss of life and diversion of resources was materially and psychologically very damaging for Britain. One American expert has recently concluded that concentration upon a mass army marked 'the beginning of the end of Britain's long preponderance as a world power'.[16]

Yet it would be wrong to assume that all the effects of war were bad. We have noted its part in gaining 'votes for women'. The war also lessened the gaps between the classes. Taxation fell heavily upon the upper and middle ranks. Income tax, only 1s. 2d. in 1914, had reached 6s. by the end of the war, and even in peace was never again to drop below 4s. Working-class employment remained steady during the war and wages high. Labour was in demand as never before. 'For the first time in the history of this country since the Black Death', Montagu told Asquith, 'the supply of labour has not been equal to the demand, and the working man knows it.' The trade unions were now finally recognized as a vital part of national life. Membership rose from over 4 million in 1914 to nearly 8 million in 1919. Drunkenness was permanently reduced when licensing hours were restricted in the interests of the war effort and as the specific gravity of beer was progressively reduced. The cinema boomed, losing its earlier proletarian associations, and becoming a powerful instrument of all-class entertainment.

By the spring of 1915 peace was definitely at an end for Britain, and with it the Edwardian era. The age would, of course, have ended, was ending, even without the impact of war. 'All the world is changing at once', as Churchill had remarked in 1911. Many restless features that tend to be regarded as entirely products of post-war unsettlement can be traced back before 1914. In music 'ragtime' with its accelerated rhythm crossed the Atlantic in 1912, as J. B. Priestley remembered. 'The syncopated frenzy was something quite new. Shining with sweat, the ragtimers almost hung over the footlights, defying us to resist the rhythm, and drumming us into another kind of life in which anything might happen.' Rupert Brooke saw the review 'Hello Ragtime' no less than ten times. Alongside this noisy new music came new undecorous dances— the turkey trot, the bunny hug, the chicken scramble. The dances encouraged and reflected an easier relationship between the sexes. The tango, it was declared, was 'not a dance but an assault'.[17]

An assault on the Edwardian imagination had been launched by the Post-Impressionist exhibition in London at the end of 1910, organized by Roger Fry (1866-1934). The conventional art public was at first shocked by what it took to be either a bad joke or attempted fraud, but the exhibition was influential in beginning the break-up of old attitudes too long continued.

British painting had suffered an insular Victorian hangover up to 1910. By 1914 Post-Impressionism had been followed from the Continent by Cubism, Futurism and other innovations. Painters like Henri Matisse (1869–1954) and Pablo Picasso (b. 1881), composers like Claude Debussy (1862–1918) and Igor Stravinsky (1882–1971), a ballet dancer such as Vaslov Nijinsky (1890–1950), and designers like Alexandre Benois (1870–1960) and Léon Bakst (1866–1924) represented an often aggressive new approach in the arts. 'Advanced' opinion responded first and most consciously to these new stimuli, but by 1914 even ordinary Edwardian Englishmen (and women) had begun to widen the limits of what they accepted as proper and possible both in the arts and in human relationships. Sergei Diaghilev (1872–1929), the ballet impresario and an open homosexual, was lionized by Edwardian society only some fifteen years after Oscar Wilde (1856–1900) had been imprisoned and ostracized for much less public activity. The change in atmosphere became so marked that, looking back from 1924, Virginia Woolf was to claim that 'in or about December 1910 human character changed'. She meant that attitudes not only to art but to life and relationships were becoming less rigid during the years just before 1914:

> The first signs of it are recorded in the books of Samuel Butler, in *The Way of All Flesh* in particular: the plays of Bernard Shaw continue to record it. In life one can see the change, if I may use a homely illustration, in the character of one's cook. The Victorian cook lived like a leviathan in the lower depths, formidable, silent, obscure, inscrutable; the Georgian cook is a creature of sunshine and fresh air; in and out of the drawing-room, now to borrow the *Daily Herald*, now to ask advice about a hat . . . All human relations have shifted—those between masters and servants, husbands and wives, parents and children. And when human relations change there is at the same time a change in religion, conduct, politics, and literature. Let us agree to place one of these changes about the year 1910.[18]

In other words, an atmosphere recognizable (albeit remotely) as that of 'modern times' was emerging in these last

Edwardian years. Visual evidence of this can be found in the
late-Edwardian transformation in women's dress. For nearly a
century the basic shape of women's clothes had consisted of

A DECADE'S PROGRESS

I.   *Mrs. Browne, Mrs. Browne junior, and Mrs. Browne junior's little girl as
     they were in 1901 and—*
II. *As they are today.*

more or less ample angles and curves. Then quite suddenly in 1910 a decisively vertical line became established, and women's costume with its high waistband became shaped like a letter 'H', almost masculine. Ankles began to show. Women's dress, in short, was reflecting women's wish to find greater freedom. 1911 saw a rage for violent colours, replacing the pastel shades of Edward's reign, perhaps a symptom of the restless tendencies of the times. A 1911 *Punch* cartoon (see p.257) called 'A Decade's Progress' summed up this whole trend, showing a grandmother, mother and daughter as they had been dressed in 1901 and as they were now attired in 1911. The dowdy voluminous clothes of the earlier date, making the grandmother an old lady and the mother seem plain, had been replaced by much simpler looser wear producing a sense of release for all three females. The 'flapper', the characteristic young woman of the nineteen twenties, had already been so named by 1914:

Florrie was a flapper, she was dainty, she was dapper,
And her dancing was the limit, or the lid.

This song was first heard just weeks before the outbreak of war. A month before the catastrophe *Punch* (July 8th) was criticizing the brevity of women's bathing costumes. '*She*: "Herbert, I can't find my bathing-dress anywhere!" *He:* "See if you've got it on." ' And three weeks later *Punch* was grumbling about the increasing use of cosmetics by 'the girl of the period'. A little known writer on rural problems remarked early in 1914 how 'the first quarter of the twentieth century will go down to posterity as a period full of the true material of historians, who watch not for the actual happenings or epochs in the lives of kings or states, but for the beginnings of movements destined to change the whole fabric of society.' These words were written even before the impact of the 'deluge'. 'This country has arrived at a crucial period in its history. The future is obscure and one false step may easily mean disaster; for gestation is giving place to birth.' These remarks may be left to sum up the sense of change which was characterizing the later Edwardian years, change which was coming even before the addition of the terrible, overwhelming stimulus of world war.[19]

References

CHAPTER ONE

1. W. S. Churchill, *Liberalism and the Social Problem* (1909), 317; R. S. Churchill, *Winston S. Churchill*, I (1966), 546.
2. C. F. G. Masterman et. al., *The Heart of the Empire* (1902), vii; R. D. Blumenfeld, *R.D.B.'s Diary 1887–1914* (1930), 191–2.
3. *The Nation*, 7th May 1910, 18th February, 1st July 1911; H. Ellis, *Impressions and Comments* (1926), 227–8
4. A. White, *Efficiency and Empire* (1901), viii–ix; *Fortnightly Review*, LXXX (1906), 871; J. A. Hobson, *The Crisis of Liberalism* (1909), 271; A. Birrell, *Collected Essays and Addresses* (1922), I, 363; M. Holroyd, *Lytton Strachey*, I (1967), 13, II (1968), 66–7, 230.
5. Lucy Masterman (ed.), *Mary Gladstone, Her Diaries and Letters* (1930) 480–1.
6. C. C. Gillespie, 'The Work of Elie Halévy', *Journal of Modern History*, XXII (1950), esp. 246–8; E. Halévy, *Imperialism and the Rise of Labour* (2nd ed., 1951), viii–x; E. Halévy, *The Rule of Democracy* (2nd ed., 1952), v-vi; Alain, *Correspondence avec Elie et Florence Halévy* (Paris 1958), esp. 270, 359, 372; E. Halévy, *The Era of Tyrannies*, trans. R. K. Webb (1965).
7. G. M. Trevelyan, *English Social History* (3rd ed., 1946), ix.
8. C. F. G. Masterman, *The Condition of England* (1911 ed.), 11.

CHAPTER TWO

1. Unless otherwise indicated, statistics in this book are taken from the *Census of England and Wales 1911, General Report with Appendices*, Cd. 8491 (1917); A. R. Prest, *Consumers' Expenditure in the United Kingdom 1900–1919* (1954); A. T. Peacock and J. Wiseman, *The Growth of Public Expenditure in the United Kingdom* (1961); B. R. Mitchell, *Abstract of British Historical Statistics* (1962); D. C. Marsh, *The Changing Social Structure of England and Wales 1871–1916* (2nd ed. 1965); Phyllis Deane and W. A. Cole, *British Economic Growth 1688–1959* (2nd ed., 1967); D. Butler and Jennie Freeman, *British Political Facts 1900–1967* (2nd ed., 1968).
2. K. Pearson, *National Life from the Standpoint of Science* (2nd ed., 1905); T. H. C. Stevenson, 'The Fertility of Various Social Classes in England and Wales from the Middle of the Nineteenth Century to 1911', *Journal of the Royal Statistical Society*, LXXXIII (1920), esp. 416–18, 431–2.

3. J. W. Robertson Scott, *The Life and Death of a Newspaper* (1952), ch. XIX.

4. E. M. Forster, *Howard's End* (1910), ch. VI; *The Times*, 31st October 1913; Ethel M. Elderton, *Report on the English Birthrate* (1914); National Birth-Rate Commission, *The Declining Birth-Rate, its Causes and Effects*, (2nd ed., 1917), 21, 37; P. Fryer, *The Birth Controllers* (1965), 185–9; *The Hard Way Up, The Autobiography of Hannah Mitchell, Suffragette and Rebel* (1968), 101–2.

5. S. C. Johnson, *A History of Emigration* (1913), ch. XIV; B. Thomas, *Migration and Economic Growth* (1954), esp. ch. V, 153–4.

6. 1911 Census, *General Report*, 62.

7. *Report on the Decline in the Agricultural Population of Great Britain 1821–1906*, *Cd.*3273 (1906); B. S. Rowntree and May Kendall, *How the Labourer Lives* (1913), esp. 22–3, 30; Mrs. Cobden Unwin, *The Land Hunger, Life under Monopoly, Descriptive Letters and other Testimonies from Those Who Have Suffered* (1913), 68–71; M. Fordham, *A Short History of English Rural Life* (1916), vii–ix, 161–62; A. K. Cairncross, *Home and Foreign Investment 1870–1913* (1953), ch. IV; J. Saville, *Rural Depopulation in England and Wales 1851–1951* (1957); Lord Ernle, *English Farming Past and Present* (6th ed., 1961), ch. XVIII; J. D. Chambers and G. E. Mingay, *The Agricultural Revolution 1750–1880* (1966) esp. 179–81, 185–6, 197, 209–10.

8. G. M. Young, 'Government' in E. Barker (ed.), *The Character of England* (1947), 102, 105–6.

9. R. Vaughan, *The Age of Great Cities* (1843), esp. 152; A. Briggs, *Victorian Cities* (1963), esp. chs. I, II.

10. A. W. Dale, *Life of R. W. Dale* (1899), 136.

11. P. Geddes, *Cities in Evolution* (1915), 34.

12. *Census of England and Wales 1901, General Report with Appendices, Cd.* 2174 (1904), 40.

13. R. L. Bray, *The Town Child* (1907), vii.

14. C. F. G. Masterman (ed.), *The Heart of the Empire, Discussions of Problems of Modern City Life in England* (1902 ed.), 7–9; B. S. Rowntree and May Kendall, *How the Labourer Lives* (1913), 14–15; B. S. Rowntree, *Poverty A Study of Town Life* (1914 ed.), esp. 150–1, 256–62, 356–9; T. S. and M. B. Simey, *Charles Booth, Social Scientist* (1960); A. Briggs, *Social Thought and Social Action, A Study of the Work of Seebohm Rowntree 1871–1954* (1961), esp. chs. I–III; H. W. Pfautz, *Charles Booth on the City* (1967); A. Fried and R. M. Elman (eds.), *Charles Booth's London* (1969).

15. *O.E.D.*, under 'suburbia'; W. Ashworth, *The Genesis of Modern British Town Planning* (1954), 11–12, ch. VI; W. Ashworth, 'Types of Social and Economic Development in Suburban Essex' in Ruth Glass (ed.), *London, Aspects of Change* (1964).

16. A. F. Weber, *The Growth of Cities in the Nineteenth Century* (1899), 475; *The Times*, 25th June 1904.

17. L. T. Hobhouse, *Democracy and Reaction* (1904), 68–9; T. W. H. Crossley, *The Suburbans* (1905), 79–80; C. F. G. Masterman, *The Condition of England*, esp. ch. III.

18. *Birmingham Daily Mail*, 26th November 1903; A. Briggs, *History of Birmingham* (1952), II, ch. V; D. Read, *The English Provinces c. 1760–1960* (1964), 234–5.

19. G. R. Sims (ed.), *Living London*, I (1902), 296; *The Times*, 18th September 1908; S. and Beatrice Webb, *The Story of the King's Highway* (1913), ch. X; H. G. Wells, *An Englishman Looks at the World* (1914), 1–21; *Punch*, 28th July 1914; C. E. R. Sherrington, *A Hundred Years of Inland Transport 1830–1933* (1934), chs. IX–X; R. Jeffreys, *The King's Highway* (1949), chs. I–IV; R. Hoggart, *The Uses of Literacy* (1959), 116; J. Simmons, *Transport* (1962), 55–63; T. C. Barker and M. Robbins, *History of London Transport*, I (1963), chs. VII, VIII, X; H. Pollins, 'Transport Lines and Social Divisions' in Ruth Glass (ed.), *London*; H. Penrose, *British Aviation, the Pioneer Years 1903–1914* (1967), esp. 178–80; J. R. Kellett, *The Impact of Railways on Victorian Cities* (1969), esp. ch. XI.

20. *O.E.D.*, under 'Town Planning'.

21. E. Howard, *Garden Cities of To-Morrow* (1902), 42, 45–7, 127, 155–6; G. B. Shaw, *John Bull's Other Island* (1904), act I; H. G. Wells, *Anticipations of the Reaction of Mechanical and Scientific Progress upon Human Life and Thought* (1904 ed.), 25–7; T. C. Horsfall, *The Improvement of the Dwellings and Surroundings of the People, the Example of Germany* (2nd ed., 1905), esp. 21, 161–72; E. R. Dewsnup, *The Housing Problem in England* (1907); T. C. Horsfall, *The Relation of Town Planning to the National Life* (1908), esp. 12–14; *Parliamentary Debates*, fourth series, CLXXXVIII (1908), 947–68; *The Times*, 18th September 1908; R. Unwin, *Town Planning in Practice* (1909), ch. I; J. S. Nettlefold, *Practical Town Planning: A Land and Housing Policy* (1914); C. B. Purdom, *The Building of Satellite Towns* (2nd ed., 1949), parts I, II; A. Briggs, *History of Birmingham*, II, ch. V; A. K. Cairncross, *Home and Foreign Investment*, 145–58; W. Ashworth, *The Genesis of Modern British Town Planning*, chs. V–VIII; B. Weber, 'A New Index of Residential Construction and Long Cycles in House Building in Great Britain, 1838–1950', *Scottish Journal of Political Economy*, II (1955); P. Mathias, *The First Industrial Nation* (1969), 376; G. E. Cherry, 'Influences on the Development of Town Planning in Britain', *Journal of Contemporary History*, vol. 4 (1969).

22. G. Haw (ed.), *Christianity and the Working Classes* (1906), 90; H. G. Wells, *Tono-Bungay* (1909), book 2, ch. I; *Punch*, 4th May 1910; P. Laslett, *The World We Have Lost* (1968), 200–10.

23. W. Booth, *In Darkest England and the Way Out* (1890), part I, ch. I; *Sociological Review*, III (1910), 270–1; E. M. Forster, *Howards End*, ch. VI; D. Read, *Cobden and Bright* (1967), 165; R. S. Churchill, *Winston S. Churchill*, II, Companion part 2 (1969), 755.

24. Sir W. Lawson, 'The Classes, the Masses, and the Glasses', *Nineteenth Century*, XX (1886), 795–6; *The Times*, 29th June 1886; G. Gissing, *The Private Papers of Henry Ryecroft* (1903), 122–4; T. W. H. Crosland, *The Beautiful Teetotaller* (1907), 155; S. Reynolds and Bob and Tom Woolley, *Seems So! A Working Class View of Politics* (1911), xviii–ix.

25. E. J. Hobsbawm, *Labouring Men* (1968), ch. 15; H. Pelling, *Popular Politics and Society in Late Victorian Britain* (1968), ch. 3.
26. G. and W. Grossmith, *The Diary of a Nobody* (1894); C. F. G. Masterman (ed.), *The Heart of the Empire* (1902 ed.), 263–4; G. S. Street, *Books and Things* (1905), part 2, ch. VII; S. F. Bullock, *Robert Thorne* (1907), 247–50; Clementina Black, *Sweated Industry and the Minimum Wage* (1910), 64–5; G. Routh, *Occupation and Pay in Great Britain 1906–60* (1965), esp. ch. II; H. W. Pfautz, *Charles Booth on the City*, 139–40.
27. *A Commentary* (1908), 81–4; G. B. Shaw, *Fanny's First Play* (1911), act III; *Books and Persons* (1920), 67–70; T. Clarke, *My Northcliffe Diary* (1931), 49; A. L. Bowley, *Wages and Income since 1860* (1937), 91–2, · 127–36; G. Orwell, *The Road to Wigan Pier* (1937), ch. 8; T. Clarke, *Northcliffe in History* (1950), 152–3; G. Routh, *Occupation and Pay in Great Britain*, 52; P. Laslett, *The World We Have Lost*, 210–19.
28. Helen Bosanquet, *The Standard of Life* (2nd ed., 1906), 8; 1911 Census, *General Report*, 103–4; *New Statesman*, 25th September, 2th October 1915, 21st, 28th April 1917; Inge to Shaw, 11th March 1948 (B. M. Add. Mss. 50538); Katharine Chorley, *Manchester Made Them* (1950), esp. ch. 16; A. Tropp, *The School Teachers* (1957), esp. 273; W. J. Reader, *Professional Men* (1966), esp. 184, appendix I.
29. T. Veblen, *The Theory of the Leisure Class* (1899), esp. ch. IV; Lady Dorothy Nevill, *Reminiscences* (1906), ch. VIII; E. J. Urwick, *Luxury and Waste of Life* (1908), esp. 190–1; *Punch*, 19th July 1911; H. G. Wells, *What the Worker Wants* (1912), 12; *Manchester Guardian*, 11th April 1912; *Daily Herald*, 22nd April 1912; *The Times*, 17th April 1912, 1st January 1913; *Transactions of the Manchester Statistical Society*, 1913–1914, 6; J. Gore, *Edwardian Scrapbook* (1951), ch. 4; R. S. Churchill, *Lord Derby* (1959), ch. 5; R. N. Maciver and C. H. Page, *Society* (1961), 360–1; *Brewer's Dictionary of Phrase and Fable* (8th ed., 1963), 515; F. M. L. Thompson, *English Landed Society in the Nineteenth Century* (1963), ch. XI; R. Pound, 'High Life before 1914' in J. Canning (ed.), *Living History: 1914* (1967); S. Hynes, *The Edwardian Turn of Mind* (1968), 60–1; H. J. Perkin, *The Origins of Modern English Society 1780–1880* (1969), 428–37, 452–4; *Yesterday's Shopping, The Army and Navy Stores Catalogue 1907* (1969), esp. 1228; G. Marcus, *The Maiden Voyage* (1969), esp. 194, 205–8, 210–11, ch. 20.
30. L. G. Chiozza Money, *Riches and Poverty* (1905), frontispiece; C. Watney and J. A. Little, *Industrial Welfare* (1912), 2–3; P. Snowden, *The Living Wage* (1913), 65–6; A. L. Bowley, *The Change in the Distribution of the National Income 1880–1913* (1920); J. L. Hammond, *The Growth of Common Enjoyment* (1933); A. L. Bowley, *Wages and Income in the United Kingdom since 1860*, esp. xiii, ch. II, 94–5; Q. Crewe, *The Frontiers of Privilege* (1961), 68, 73; A. J. Taylor, 'The Economy', in S. Nowell-Smith (ed.), *Edwardian England* (1964); R. S. Churchill, *Winston S. Churchill*, volume II, companion part 2 (1969), 924–6.
31. J. Rowntree and A. Sherwell, *The Temperance Problem and Social Reform* (9th ed., 1901), xv-vi, xviii-ix, 22–3, 598–601; *Report from the Select Committee of the House of Lords on Betting*, Parliamentary Papers 1902

(389) v. 445; B. S. Rowntree (ed.), *Betting and Gambling, a National Evil* (1905), esp. 170–88, appendices 1, 2, 3; T. C. Horsfall, *The Example of Germany*, 21; H. Caine, *Drink, a Love Story on a Great Question* (n.d.), 7–8; T. W. H. Crosland, *The Beautiful Teetotaller* (1907), esp. 147–8; Lady Bell, *At the Works* (1911 ed.), ch. X; *Notes and Queries*, twelfth series, IX (1921), 90, 177; R. C. K. Ensor, *England 1870–1914* (1949), 360–1, 408–9; J. Canning, *Living History: 1914*, 142; P. Rowland, *The Last Liberal Governments*, I (1968), 3, 144–5; *Times Literary Supplement*, 6th February 1969.

32. C. Edwardes, 'The New Football Mania', *Nineteenth Century*, XXXII (1892); E. Ensor, 'The Football Madness', *Contemporary Review*, LXXIV (1898); *England: A Nation* (1904), 32; *Punch*, 15th July 1914; Lady Bell, *At the Works*, ch. VI; M. Marples, *History of Football* (1954), esp. chs. XI, XII.

33. C. F. G. Masterman et. al., *Heart of the Empire*, 269–70; R. Blatchford, *God and My Neighbour* (1903), ix, 192–3; R. Mudie-Smith (ed.), *The Religious Life of London* (1904), ch. II; C. Noel, *The Labour Party, What It Is and What It Wants* (1906), 101–2; G. Haw (ed.), *Christianity and the Working Classes*, esp. introduction, ch. 5; H. D. Traill and J. S. Mann (eds.), *The Building of Britain and the Empire* (illustrated ed., n.d.), 1026; R. C. K. Ensor, *England 1870–1914*, 304–10, 527–31; G. K. A. Bell, *Randall Davidson* (1935), I, 488–9; R. Lloyd, *The Church of England in the Twentieth Century* (1946), I, chs. 3, 8; Katharine Chorley, *Manchester Made Them*, esp. ch. 10; L. Thompson, *Robert Blatchford* (1951), ch. XIII; G. S. Spinks (ed.), *Religion in Britain since 1900* (1952), ch. IV; K. S. Inglis, *Churches and the Working Classes in Victorian England* (1963), chs. 5–7; H. Pelling, *The Origins of the Labour Party 1880–1900* (2nd ed., 1965) ch. VII; R. Tressell, *The Ragged Trousered Philanthropists* (1965 ed.), 153–4; S. Mayor, *The Churches and the Labour Movement* (1967), esp. chs. 6, 7; H. W. Pfautz, *Charles Booth on the City*, 151–6, 290–6, 305–12; H. Pelling, *Popular Politics and Society in Late Victorian Britain*, ch. 2; O. Chadwick *The Victorian Church*, part II (1970), esp. chs. V, VIII.

34. H. J. Palmer, 'The March of the Advertiser', *Nineteenth Century*, XLI (1897); *Mitchell's Newspaper Press Directory* (1905), 8–9; A. Shadwell, *Industrial Efficiency* (1909), 527; Lady Bell, *At the Works*, ch. VII; Lord Northcliffe, 'Price of Newspapers', *Encyclopedia Britannica* (11th ed., 1911), vol. 19, 550; *The Nation*, 18th May 1912; F. W. Hirst, *The Six Panics* (1913), 142–64; R. A. Scott-James, *The Influence of the Press* (1913), esp. ch. XI, 252–3; K. Jones, *Fleet Street and Downing Street* (1920), esp. section III; W. B. Thomas, *The Story of the Spectator* (1928), 102; Amy Strachey, *St Loe Strachey* (1930), esp. part II; H. Hamilton Fyfe, *Northcliffe* (1930), esp. chs. IV, V; T. Clarke, *My Northcliffe Diary*, esp. 195–205; J. L. Hammond, *C. P. Scott of the Manchester Guardian* (1934), esp. chs. V–XI; *History of The Times*, III (1947), IV (1952); H. H. Cudlipp, *Publish and be Damned!* (1953), chs. 2–4; J. B. Jeffreys, *Retail Trading in Britain 1850–1950* (1954), ch. 1; A. P. Wadsworth, 'Newspaper Circulations, 1800–1954', *Transactions of the Manchester*

Statistical Society, 1955; J. W. Robertson Scott, '*We*' *and Me* (1956); A. Briggs, *Friends of the People* (1956), esp. ch. VI; H. J. Perkin, 'The Origins of the Popular Press', *History Today*, VII (1957); F. Williams, *Dangerous Estate* (1957), chs. IX, X; E. Field, *Advertising, the Forgotten Years* (1959); R. Pound and G. Harmsworth, *Northcliffe* (1959); A. M. R. Pound and G. Harmsworth, *Northcliffe* (1959); A. M. Gollin, '*The Observer*' *and J. L. Garvin* (1960), esp. 6, 344; A. Briggs, *Mass Entertainment: the Origins of a Modern Industry* (1961), esp. 9–10; E. Hyams, *The New Statesman* (1963), chs. 1–3; A. J. P. Taylor, *Politics in Wartime* (1964), ch. X; E. S. Turner, *The Shocking History of Advertising* (1965), ch. 6; J. C. Wood and B. J. McCormick, 'Hours of Work', *Chambers's Encylopedia* (1966 ed.), vol. 7, 250–3; D. Ayerst, *Guardian: Biography of a Newspaper* (1971), chs. 20–25.

35. *The Times*, 14th January 1909; F. M. Hueffer, *The Critical Attitude* (1911), chs. III, IV; H. G. Wells, *An Englishman Looks at the World* (1914), 167–9; A. Compton-Rickett, *A History of English Literature* (1918), 664–5; A. Bennett, *Books and Persons* (1920), 81–6, 117–21; W. S. Brown, *The Life and Genius of T. W. H. Crosland* (1928), 74–6; A. Bennett, *Journals* (1932), II, 52; H. G. Wells, *Experiment in Autobiography* (1934), 494–6; A. E. Wilson, *Edwardian Theatre* (1951); K. Martin, *Editor* (1968), ch. 4; J. B. Priestley, *Literature and Western Man* (1969), chs. 19, 20; J. Gross, *The Rise and Fall of the Man of Letters* (1969), ch. 8; 'H. G. and G. B. S.', *Times Literary Supplement*, 27th November 1969; L. Dickson, *H. G. Wells* (1969).

36. Rupert Brooke, 'Sonnet Reversed' (1911); F. Swinnerton, *Autobiography* (1937), 213–14; J. Baines, *Joseph Conrad* (1960), 381–9; R. H. Ross, *The Georgian Revolt* (1967), esp. ch. I, 259–61.

37. R. de Cordova, 'Illustrated Interviews. Dr Edward Elgar', *Strand Magazine*, XXVII (1904); W. Mellers, *Music and Society* (1950), 156–9; F. Howes, 'Music', in S. Nowell-Smith (ed.), *Edwardian England*; M. Kennedy, *Portrait of Elgar* (1968), esp. part II.

38. C. Booth, *Life and Labour of the People in London* (1902), 53–5; Clarke, *My Northcliffe Diary*, 67; J. M. Bulloch, 'Peers who have Married Players', *Notes and Queries*, CLXIX (1935); A. E. Wilson, *Edwardian Theatre*, chs. XIX, XX; L. Baily, *BBC Scrapbooks*, I (1966), 96–101, 169–70; J. Canning, *Living History: 1914*, 113–17.

39. A. Briggs, *Mass Entertainment*, 14–18; Lady Bell, *At the Works* (1911 ed.), 185–6; C. Chaplin, *My Autobiography* (1964), ch. X; L. Baily, *BBC Scrapbooks*, I, 179–81.

40. A. Briggs, *Mass Entertainment*, 13–14; L. P. Jacks, *Life and Letters of Stopford Brooke* (1917), II, 503; L. Baily, *BBC Scrapbooks*, I, 66.

41. C. T. King, *The Asquith Parliament* (1910), 340.

42. Knollys to Campbell-Bannerman, 1st November 1906 (B.M. Add. Mss. 52513); A. V. Dicey, *Introduction to the Study of the Law of the Constitution* (8th ed., 1915), l–li, xci, ci–ii; *Life and Letters of Walter H. Page* (1923), I, 48–51; H. Nicolson, *Lord Carnock* (1930), 270–1; J. A. Spender and C. Asquith, *Life of Herbert Henry Asquith, Lord Oxford and Asquith* (1932), I, 261–2, 305–6; R. C. K. Ensor, *England 1870–1914*, 567–9; E. Halévy,

The Rule of Democracy, 123–4; W. C. Costin and J. S. Watson, *The Law and Working of the Constitution* (1952), II, 451–64; H. Nicolson, *King George the Fifth* (1952), chs. VIII–X, 196–7, 220–9; R. Jenkins, *Mr Balfour's Poodle* (1954), 118–25; G. W. Monger, *The End of Isolation* (1963), 261–4; Sir P. Magnus, *King Edward the Seventh* (1964), esp. ch. 15, 353; R. Fulford, 'The King', in S. Nowell-Smith, *Edwardian England;* R. Jenkins, *Asquith* (1964), esp. 185–7, ch. XV, 235, 282–7, appendix B; R. S. Churchill, *Winston S. Churchill*, II, 647–54; P. Rowland, *Last Liberal Governments*, I, 81, 83–4, 349–50; J. P. Mackintosh, *The British Cabinet* (2nd ed., 1968), ch. 9; F. Hardie, *The Political Influence of the British Monarchy, 1868–1952* (1970), chs. 4, 5.

43. A. Ponsonby, *The Decline of Aristocracy* (1912); A. L. Lowell, *The Government of England* (1912 ed.), esp. chs. XXII, XXXIV, LXIII, LXVI; A. V. Dicey, *Lectures on the Relation between Law and Public Opinion in England* (2nd ed., 1914), 57–9; S. Low, *The Governance of England* (2nd ed., 1914), xxvii–xxxi, ch. X; H. J. Laski, 'The Personnel of the English Cabinet, 1801–1924', *American Political Science Quarterly*, vol. 22 (1928); W. L. Guttman, *The British Political Elite* (1968), ch. 4, 225–32, ch. 12.

44. W. S. McKechnie, *The Reform of the House of Lords* (1909); 'Parliament', 'Parliament Act', *Everyman's Encyclopedia* (1913), vol. 10, 160–1, 167–9; S. Low, *Governance of England*, ch. XIII; *Life and Letters of Walter H. Page*, I, 58; E. Halévy, *The Rule of Democracy*, 312–14, 334; R. Blake, *The Unknown Prime Minister, the Life and Times of Andrew Bonar Law* (1955), 100; R. E. Pumphrey, 'The Introduction of Industrialists into the British Peerage', *American Historical Review*, LXV (1959); H. J. Hanham, 'The Sale of Honours in Late Victorian England', *Victorian Studies*, III (1960); F. M. L. Thompson, *English Landed Society in the Nineteenth Century*, ch. XI; C. C. Westen, 'The Liberal Leadership and the Lords' Veto, 1907–1910', *Historical Journal*, XI (1968); H. J. Perkin, *The Origins of Modern English Society*, 428–37; H. J. Hanham, *The Nineteenth Century Constitution* (1969), 170, 254–6. N. Blewett, *The Peers, the Parties and the People : the General Elections of 1910* (1972), ch. 14.

45. A. L. Lowell, *Government of England*, ch. IX; *O.E.D.*, under 'Mandate'; D. E. Butler, *The Electoral System in Britain since 1918* (2nd ed., 1963), 5–7; N. Blewett, 'The Franchise in the United Kingdom 1885–1918', *Past & Present*, no. 32 (1965); Grace A. Jones, 'Further Thoughts on the Franchise 1885–1918', ibid, no. 34 (1966); H. J. Hanham, 'Politics and Community Life in Victorian and Edwardian Britain', *Folk Life*, vol. 4 (1966); H. J. Hanham, *The Reform Electoral System in Great Britain, 1832–1914* (1968); H. J. Hanham, *The Nineteenth Century Constitution*, esp. ch. 4; N. Blewett, *The Peers, The Parties and the People* ch. 17.

46. 'Parliament', *Everyman's Encyclopedia*, vol 10, 161; J. A. Thomas, *The House of Commons 1906–1911* (1958); J. Cornford, 'The Transformation of Conservatism in the Late Nineteenth Century', *Victorian Studies*, VII (1963).

47. Lord Elton, *Life of James Ramsay Macdonald* (1939), 152–3; E. Halévy,

The Rule of Democracy, 93; C. O'Leary, *The Elimination of Corrupt Practices in British Elections 1868–1911* (1962); W. B. Gwyn, *Democracy and the Cost of Politics in Britain* (1962); H. J. Hanham, *The Nineteenth Century Constitution*, 155–6.

48. *Parliamentary Debates*, fourth series, CXXXVII (1904), 358–9; 'The Congestion of Business in the House of Commons', *Round Table*, II (1911–12); A. L. Lowell, *The Government of England*, chs. XVII, XXIII, XXXV; 'Cabinet'. *Everyman's Encyclopedia*, vol 3, 176–8; A. V. Dicey, *Law of the Constitution*, esp. introduction, 483–4; S. Low, *Governance of England*, introduction, ch. V; *Letters of Queen Victoria*, third series (1930), I, 510; J. P. Mackintosh, *British Cabinet*, part four.

49. M. Ostrogorski, *Democracy and the Organization of Political Parties* (1902), I, 304–5; W. S. MacKechnie, *House of Lords*, ch. VII; J. A. Hobson, *Crisis of Liberalism*, part I; A. V. Dicey, *Law of the Constitution*, xcvii–c; J. L. Garvin, *Life of Joseph Chamberlain*, II (1933), 191; D. Sommer, *Haldane of Cloan* (1960), 77; A. P. Thornton, *The Habit of Authority* (1966), chs. V, VI.

50. *Royal Commission on the Civil Service, Fourth Report*, Cd. 7338 (1914); R. Moses, *The Civil Service of Great Britain* (1914); S. Low, *Governance of England*, xxxii–iii; K. B. Smellie, *A Hundred Years of English Government* (2nd ed., 1950), ch. VI; M. Abramovitz and Vera F. Eliasberg, *The Growth of Public Employment in Great Britain* (1957), ch. 3; D. N. Chester and F. M. G. Willson, *The Organization of British Central Government 1914–1964* (2nd ed., 1968), 19–23, 143–7.

51. *The Times*, 19th August–11th November 1902; J. Redlich and F. W. Hirst, *Local Government in England* (1903); T. C. Horsfall, *The Example of Germany*, 11–15; Lord Avebury, *On Municipal and National Trading* (1906), 174–6; *Birmingham Daily Mail*, 27th April 1907; G. B. Shaw, *The Commonsense of Municipal Trading* (2nd ed., 1908), 1–5; G. M. Harris (ed.), *Problems of Local Government* (1911); A. L. Lowell, *Government of England*, part III; D. Knoop, *Principles and Methods of Municipal Trading* (1912); 'Municipal Trade', *Everyman's Encyclopedia*, vol 9, 393–9; *Final Report of the Departmental Committee on Local Taxation, Cd.* 7315 (1914); E. S. Griffith, *The Modern Development of City Government in the United Kingdom and the United States* (1927), chs. VI, XI, appendices B, L; Beatrice Webb, *Our Partnership* (1948), 160–2; Katharine Chorley, *Manchester Made Them*, 139–40; E. Halévy, *Rule of Democracy*, 512–13, 519; A. Briggs, *History of Birmingham*, II, 127–9; Ursula K. Hicks, *British Public Finances* (1954), chs. I, IV; K. B. Smellie, *A History of Local Government* (3rd ed., 1957), ch. V; A. M. McBriar, *Fabian Socialism and English Politics 1884–1918* (1962), ch. VIII; A. Briggs, *Victorian Cities*, ch. VIII; P. Thompson, *Socialists, Liberals and Labour, the Struggle for London 1885–1914* (1967); R. S. Churchill, *Winston S. Churchill* (1969), volume II, Companion part 2, 761–2.

CHAPTER THREE

1. S. Webb, *Socialism: True and False* (1894), 5; S. Webb et al., *The Basis and Policy of Socialism* (1908), esp. 76–8; J. H. Muirhead, *The Service of*

the State (1908), esp. lecture IV; H. Jones, *The Working Faith of the Social Reformer* (1910), 104–5, 107–14, 278–80; S. Webb, 'Social Movements', ch. XXIII of the *Cambridge Modern History*, vol. XII (1910); E. Barker, *Political Thought in England from Herbert Spencer to the Present Day* (1915), esp. 23, 175–83; Beatrice Webb, *Our Partnership*, 220–4; M. Ginsberg, 'The Growth of Social Responsibility' in Ginsberg (ed.), *Law and Opinion in England in the 20th Century* (1959).

2. H. G. Wells, *New Worlds for Old*, esp. 22–3, 53–5, 88–9, 163–4; R. C. K. Ensor (ed.), *Modern Socialism* (1907), xxvii-ix; [A. Shadwell], 'The Socialist Movement in Great Britain', *The Times*, 7th–19th January 1909; B. Villiers, *The Socialist Movement in England* (2nd ed., 1910), part III; ch. V; C. F. G. Masterman, *Condition of England*, 200.

3. *The Times*, 21st October 1907; R. C. K. Ensor, *Modern Socialism* (2nd ed., 1907), xxvi; *Fabian Essays in Socialism* (1908 ed.), 185; J. Bryce, *The Hindrances to Good Citizenship* (1909), 132; S. Reynolds et. al., *Seems So!* 169–72; H. du Parcq, *Life of David Lloyd George* (1913), IV, 637; *Parliamentary Debates*, House of Commons, fifth series, LXIII (1914), 2050–1; W. H. Mallock, *Social Reform* (1914), esp. 3; E. Townshend (ed.), *Keeling Letters and Recollections* (1918), 155; Lucy Masterman, *C. F. G. Masterman* (1939), 115–16; H. Cudlipp, *Publish and be Damned!* 15; R. Tressell, *The Ragged Trousered Philanthropists* (1955 ed.), esp. 29; R. Hoggart, *Uses of Literacy*, ch. 3; H. Pelling, *Popular Politics and Society*, ch. 1; P. A. Welsby (ed.), *Sermons and Society* (1970), 326–9.

4. R. C. K. Ensor (ed.), *Modern Socialism* (1907), 351–5; G. R. S. Taylor, *Leaders of Socialism* (1908), esp. 17; B. Villiers, *The Socialist Movement in England*, esp. 160–1; H. M. Hyndman, *Further Reminiscences* (1912); C. Tsuzuki, *H. M. Hyndman and British Socialism* (1961), esp. chs. V–X; W. Kendall, *The Revolutionary Socialist Movement in Britain 1900–21* (1969), chs. 1–5.

5. B. Villiers, *The Socialist Movement in England*, esp. 114–15, 171–4, 179–81; R. C. K. Ensor (ed.), *Modern Socialism* (1907), 351–5; E. Hughes, *Keir Hardie's Speeches and Writings* (3rd ed., 1928), 109, 118–21; H. Pelling, *Origins of the Labour Party*; R. E. Dowse, *Left in the Centre, the Independent Labour Party 1893–1940* (1966), ch. 1.

6. S. Webb, *Basis and Policy of Socialism*, esp. 82–3; R. C. K. Ensor (ed.), *Modern Socialism* (1907), 351–5; *Fabian Essays in Socialism* (1908 ed.), viii–ix; *The Times*, 16th January 1909; B. Villiers, *The Socialist Movement in England*, esp. 117; S. and Beatrice Webb, *Industrial Democracy* (1911 ed.), 766–84; Beatrice Webb, *Our Partnership*, esp. 231; Margaret Cole, *The Story of Fabian Socialism* (1961); D. H. Laurence (ed.), *Platform and Pulpit, Bernard Shaw* (1962), 93–6; A. M. McBriar, *Fabian Socialism and English Politics*.

7. R. C. K. Ensor (ed.), *Modern Socialism* (1907), 364–8; V. Grayson and G. R. S. Taylor, *The Problem of Parliament* (1909), esp. ch. VI; J. R. MacDonald, *The Socialist Movement* (1911), esp. xi, 235; *Punch*, 20th March 1912; J. R. MacDonald, *The Social Unrest* (1913), 32–3; H. G. Wells, *An Englishman Looks at the World*, 179; S. and Beatrice Webb,

History of Trade Unionism (1920 ed.), 688–9; F. Bealey, 'Documents relating to the Negotiations for an Electoral Arrangement between the Liberal Party and the Labour Representation Committee', *Bulletin of the Institute of Historical Research*, XXVIII (1955); J. H. S. Reid, *The Origins of the British Labour Party* (1955); P. P. Poirier, *The Advent of the Labour Party* (1958); F. Bealey and H. Pelling, *Labour and Politics 1900–1906* (1958); H. Pelling, *Short History of the Labour Party* (1961), ch. II; *The Labour Party Foundation Conference and Annual Conference Reports 1900–1905* (Hammersmith Reprints of Scarce Documents, no. 3, 1967); N. Blewett, *The Peers, the Parties and the People*, ch. 12, 389–95.

8. *Fortnightly Review*, LXXX (1906), 872–3; 'Liberal Party', *New Encyclopedia of Social Reform* (1908), 708–9; J. A. Hobson, *Crisis of Liberalism*, esp. preface, part II; *Manchester Guardian*, 29th December 1909; L. T. Hobhouse, *Liberalism* (1911), 146–7, 158–62; H. du Parcq, *Life of David Lloyd George* (1913), IV, 629–31; E. Hughes, *Keir Hardie's Speeches and Writings*, 115–17; F. H. Herrick, 'Social Reform and Social Revolution', *Social Forces*, X (1931); F. H. Herrick, British Liberalism and the Idea of Social Justice', *American Journal of Economics and Sociology*, vol. 4 (1944–5); Beatrice Webb, *Diaries 1912–1924* (1952), 8; A. Bullock and M. Shock (eds.), *The Liberal Tradition* (1967), part V; C. L. Mowat, 'Social Legislation in Britain and the United States in the early Twentieth Century', *Historical Studies*, VII (1969).

9. *Parliamentary Debates*, fourth series, CLIV (1906), 1307, CLXVI (1906), 698, House of Commons, fifth series, LXIII (1914), 2050–1, 2092; W. H. Mallock, *A Critical Examination of Socialism* (1908); *New Encyclopedia of Social Reform* (1908), 1248; Lord Hugh Cecil, *Liberty and Authority* (1910); Lord Hugh Cecil, *Conservatism* (1912), esp. chs. III, IV, VI, IX; W. H. Mallock, *Social Reform*, esp. 376–7; F. H. Herrick, 'British Liberalism and the Idea of Social Justice' *American Journal of Economics and Sociology Vol 4*, esp. 75–6; Sir G. Benham, *Benham's Book of Quotations* (1949) ed.), 498; R. J. White (ed.), *The Conservative Tradition* (1950).

10. A. L. Lowell, *Government of England*, II, 116–29; J. A. Spender, *Life of the Right Hon. Sir Henry Campbell-Bannerman* (1923), I, vi; P. Stansky, *Ambitions and Strategies, the Struggle for the Leadership of the Liberal Party in the 1890s* (1964).

11. H. W. Lucy, *Sixty Years in the Wilderness* (1909), ch. II; J. A. Spender, *Life of the Right Hon. Sir Henry Campbell-Bannerman*, esp. ch. XXXVIII; J. Pope-Hennessy, *Lord Crewe* (1955), 60–1; P. Stansky, *Ambitions and Strategies*, 277–99.

12. *The Times*, 21st October, 1907; A. G. Gardiner, *Prophets, Priests and Kings* (1908), 26–33; C. T. King, *The Asquith Parliament*, 22–5; W. S. Blunt, *My Diaries* (1932), 692; Lord Riddell, *More Pages from My Diary 1908–1914* (1934), 78–9, 85, 86, 87, 102, 106, 116–17, 118, 216; Lucy Masterman, *C. F. G. Masterman*, 137; W. S. Churchill, *Great Contemporaries* (1949 ed.), 103–17; Lord Beaverbrook, *Men and Power 1917–1918* (1956), x; Lord Beaverbrook, *Politicians and the War 1914–1916* (1960) 542; Margot Asquith, *Autobiography* (1962 ed.), 306–8; R. Jenkins, *Asquith*, esp. 13,

31, 91, 208, 227–8, 279, 319, 330, ch. XXI, 415, 460–1, 462–3; C. Hazlehurst, 'Asquith as Prime Minister, 1908–1916', *English Historical Review*, LXXXV (1970).

13. A. G. Gardiner, *Prophets, Priests and Kings*, 152–60; C. T. King, *The Asquith Parliament*, 38–40; H. du Parcq, *Lloyd George*, esp. 640; P. Guedalla (ed.), *Slings and Arrows, Sayings chosen from the Speeches of tne Rt Hon. David Lloyd George* (n.d.), esp. 128–9; Lord Riddell, *More Pages from my Diary*, esp. 152, 155; D. Lloyd George, *War Memoirs* (1938), I, 21–3; Lucy Masterman, *C. F. G. Masterman*, 164–5, 170–2; Sir C. Petrie, *Life and Letters of the Right Hon. Sir Austen Chamberlain*, I (1939), 381–8; W. S. Churchill, *Thoughts and Adventures* (1949), 38–40; J. Ehrman, 'Lloyd George and Churchill as War Ministers', *Transactions of the Royal Historical Society*, fifth series, 11 (1961); A. J. P. Taylor, *Politics in Wartime*, chs. I, IX.

14. A. G. Gardiner, *Prophets, Priests and Kings*, 103–11; W. S. Churchill, *Liberalism and the Social Problem*, esp. 79; R. D. Blumenfeld, *R. D. B.'s Diary*, 74–5; J. Buchan, *Memory Hold the Door* (1940), 178; T. Jones, *A Diary with Letters 1931–1950* (1954), 204; W. George, *My Brother and I* (1958), 253; Lord Beaverbrook, *Politicians and the War*, 357; Frances Donaldson, *The Marconi Scandal* (1962), esp. 249–55; R. Jenkins, *Asquith*, 339–40, 361, 426; R. S. Churchill, *Winston S. Churchill*, II, esp. 224–5, 451, 500–1, 574, 576–7, ch. 17.

15. A. G. Gardiner, *Prophets, Priests and Kings*, 213–19; Hardie to Shaw, 14th February 1912 (B. M. Add. Mss. 50538); J. B. Glasier, *James Keir Hardie* (1917); W. Stewart, *J. Keir Hardie* (1921); E. Hughes, *Keir Hardie's Speeches and Writings*, esp. 158–62; P. Snowden, *Autobiography* (1934), I, 125–6, 174; Lord Snell, *Men, Movements and Myself* (1936), 149–50; Margaret Cole, *Makers of the Labour Movement* (1948), 203–26; D. Read, *The English Provinces*, 197–8; R. S. Churchill, *Winston S. Churchill*, II, 262–4; F. Reid, 'Keir Hardie's Biographers', Society for the Study of Labour History, *Bulletin*, no. 16 (1968).

16. Lord Elton, *Life of James Ramsay MacDonald* (1939), esp. chs. V–VIII; B. Sacks, *J. Ramsay MacDonald in Thought and Action* (1952); Beatrice Webb, *Diaries 1912–1924*, 6–7, 10, 17–18; M. Holroyd, *Lytton Strachey*, I, 177; R. I. McKibbin, 'James Ramsay MacDonald and the Problem of the Independence of the Labour Party, 1910–1914', *Journal of Modern History*, vol 42 (1970).

17. Lord Riddell, *More Pages from My Diary*, 59, 69; .A Chamberlain, *Politics from Inside* (1936), 464; Blanche E. C. Dugdale, *Arthur James Balfour* (1939), esp. II, 15; Beatrice Webb, *Our Partnership*, 248–9, 270–1, 290, 309, 382; K. Young, *Arthur James Balfour* (1963), esp. xviii, xx, 126, 214, 314; B. B. Gilbert, *The Evolution of National Insurance in Great Britain* (1966), 97; R. S. Churchill, *Winston S. Churchill*, II, 354; J. P. Cornford, 'The Parliamentary Foundations of the Hotel Cecil', in Robson, *Ideas and Institutions of Victorian Britain*, esp. 296; T. Jones, *Whitehall Diary*, I (1969), 201.

18. Lord Oxford and Asquith, *Memories and Reflections* (1928), I, ch. XXIV; Lucy Masterman, *C. F. G. Masterman*, 218–19; L. S. Amery, *My*

Political Life, I (1953), 387; R. Blake, *The Unknown Prime Minister*, esp. 42, 48–9, 55, 95–6, 139–40; J. M. Keynes, *Essays in Biography* (1961 ed.), 40–4; T. Jones, *Whitehall Diary*, I, 233.
19. J. L. Garvin and J. Amery, *Life of Joseph Chamberlain* (1932–69), esp. I, 202; W. S. Churchill, *Great Contemporaries*, 43–56; A. Briggs, *Victorian Cities*, ch. V; D. Read, *The English Provinces*, ch. IV; R. S. Churchill, *Winston S. Churchill*, I, Companion (1967), 1207.

CHAPTER FOUR

1. L. S. Amery, *My Political Life*, I, 240; J. Amery, *Joseph Chamberlain and the Tariff Reform Campaign* (1969), esp. 219–22.
2. E. E. Williams, *Made in Germany* (2nd ed., 1896), 172–5; *Punch*, 21st August 1901; S. B. Saul, 'The American Impact', *Business History*, III (1961).
3. C. K. Hobson, *The Export of Capital* (1914); R. J. S. Hoffman, *Great Britain and the German Trade Rivalry 1875–1914* (1933), esp. 95–6; A. K. Cairncross, *Home and Foreign Investment*, chs. VI–X; A. R. Hall (ed.), *The Export of Capital from Britain 1870–1914* (1968).
4. *The Times*, 17th April, 20th August 1912; P. W. S. Andrews and Elizabeth Brunner, *Life of Lord Nuffield* (1959), part II; S. B. Saul, 'The Motor Industry in Britain to 1914', *Business History*, V (1962).
5. A. Shadwell, *Industrial Efficiency*, 653; D. H. Aldcroft and H. W. Richardson, *The British Economy 1870–1939* (1969), esp. 101–89.
6. D. H. Aldcroft (ed.), *The Development of British Industry and Foreign Competition 1875–1914* (1968); P. Mathias, *The First Industrial Nation* (1969), part II.
7. E. Burgis, *Perils to British Trade* (1895), viii–ix; *Fabianism and the Fiscal Question*, Fabian Tract no. 116 (1904), esp. 13; Beatrice Webb, *Our Partnership*, 266–7; B. Sacks, *J. Ramsay MacDonald*, esp. 291; N. McCord, *Free Trade* (1970), esp. 138–43, 152.
8. H. W. McCrosty, *The Trust Movement in British Industry* (1907), esp. ch. XIV; H. Levy, *Monopoly and Competition* (1911); D. H. MacGregor, *The Evolution of Industry* (1912), esp. ch. VII; G. R. Carter, *The Tendency towards Industrial Combination* (1913); C. Wilson, *The History of Unilever* (1954), I, ch. VI.
9. B. H. Brown, *The Tariff Reform Movement in Great Britain, 1881–1895* (1943); S. H. Zebel, 'Joseph Chamberlain and the Genesis of Tariff Reform', *Journal of British Studies*, VII (1968).
10. C. W. Boyd (ed.), *Mr Chamberlain's Speeches* (1914), esp. vol II; J. Amery, *Life of Joseph Chamberlain*, volume five (1969), 177–8.
11. H. Cox (ed.), *British Industries under Free Trade* (1903), vii–ix; H. W. Massingham (ed.), *Labour and Protection* (1903), 33–5; *The Times*, 15th August 1903; *Speeches by the Rt. Hon. H. H. Asquith* (1908), 185–6; *Punch*, 5th January 1910; W. J. Ashley, *The Tariff Problem* (3rd ed., 1911), 111–13, 262–3; S. Dark, *Life of Sir Arthur Pearson* (1922), ch. V; A. Marshall, *Official Papers* (1926), 405–6; W. A. S. Hewins, *Apologia of an Imperialist* (1929), vol I; W. K. Hancock, *Survey of British Commonwealth Affairs*, II, part 1 (1942), 72–110; B. Semmel, *Imperialism and Social*

Reform (1960); Margot Asquith, *Autobiography*, 228–9; D. Read, *English Provinces*, 184–90; A. W. Coats, 'The Role of Authority in the Development of British Economics', *Journal of Law and Economics*, VII (1964), 99–103; A. Gollin, *Balfour's Burden, Arthur Balfour and Imperial Preference* (1965); R. Tressell, *The Ragged Trousered Philanthropists* (complete edition, 1965), 21–2; J. Amery, *Joseph Chamberlain*, vols, V, VI.

12. *Manchester Guardian*, 19th January 1906; *The Times*, 30th January 1906; E. Halévy, *Rule of Democracy*, 8–11; J. A. Thomas, *House of Commons*, 6–8; P. Fraser, 'Unionism and Tariff Reform, the Crisis of 1906', *Historical Journal*, V (1962); A. J. P. Taylor, *Politics in Wartime*, 133–5; H. Pelling, *Social Geography of British Elections 1885–1910* (1967), 19–20, 417, 426, 432; N. Blewett, 'Free Fooders, Balfourites, Whole Hoggers, Factionalism within the Unionist Party, 1906–10', *Historical Journal*, XI (1968).

13. A. Chamberlain, *Politics from Inside;* R. Blake, *The Unknown Prime Minister*, chs. IV, VI; J. A. Thomas, *House of Commons*, 8–12; R. S. Churchill, *Lord Derby*, ch. VIII; A. M. Gollin, *'The Observer' and J. L. Garvin*, chs. VIII, XI; K. Young, *Arthur James Balfour*, chs. 12, 13; P. Fraser, *Joseph Chamberlain* (1966), ch. 12; H. Pelling, *Social Geography of British Elections*, 21–7.

14. *Parliamentary Debates*, House of Commons, fifth series, LXII (1914), 56–9; S. B. Saul, *Studies in British Overseas Trade* (1960); W. Ashworth, *A Short History of the International Economy since 1850* (2nd ed., 1962), ch. VII; F. Crouzet, 'Commerce et Empire: L'Experience Britannique du Libre-Echange à la Première Guerre Mondiale', *Annales, Economies, Societes, Civilisations*, vol. 19 (1964); D. H. Aldcroft (ed.), *Development of British Industry*, 77–84.

CHAPTER FIVE

1. 'British Empire', *Everyman's Encyclopedia*, vol. 3, 25–34; E. Sanderson, *The British Empire in the Nineteenth Century* (1899), VI, 352–4; C. W. Boyd (ed.), *Mr Chamberlain's Speeches* (1914), II, 367–72.

2. J. A. Hobson, *The Psychology of Jingoism* (1901), 3–4; H. Newbolt, *Collected Poems 1897–1910* (1910), 131–3; H. G. Wells, *Mr Britling Sees it Through* (1916), book II, ch. I; E. C. Mack, *Public Schools and British Opinion since 1860* (1941), chs. VI–VIII; A. P. Thornton, *The Imperial Idea and Its Enemies* (1959), 88–97; H. Pelling, *Popular Politics and Society*, ch. 5.

3. [Ramsay MacDonald], *Imperialism, its Meaning and Tendency* (1900), esp. 4–5; J. A. Hobson, *Imperialism* (1902), part I, chs. IV, VI, part II, ch. IV; G. Murray, 'Empire and Subject Races', *Sociological Review*, III (1910), esp. 228–9; W. S. Churchill, *The River War* (n.d.), 26–7; J. A. Cramb, *The Origins and Destiny of Imperial Britain* (1915), esp. 219.

4. G. Wallas, *Human Nature in Politics* (1908), 282; 'British Empire', *New Encyclopedia of Social Reform*, 130; Rudyard Kipling, 'The White Man's Burden' in *Rudyard Kipling's Verse* (definitive ed., 1941), 323–4.

5. J. Ramsay Macdonald, *Socialism and Government* (1909), II, 80–91; B. L. Putnam Wheale, *The Conflict of Colour* (1910), esp. 110; G. P. Gooch, *History of Our Time* (1911), 244–5; *Everyman's Encyclopedia*, vol 3, 34; V. G. Kiernan, *The Lords of Human Kind* (1969), 170–2.

6. J. A. Hobson, *Imperialism* (1902), part I, chs. IV, VI, part II, ch. IV; H. N. Brailsford, *The War of Steel and Gold* (4th ed., 1915), 79–82; W. S. Churchill, *The Story of the Malakand Field Force* (1916 ed.), 32; D. K. Fieldhouse, '"Imperialism": an Historiographical Revision', *Economic History Review*, second series, XIV (1961); R. Koebner and H. D. Schmidt, *Imperialism, the Story and Significance of a Political Word 1840–1960* (1964), chs. VII–X; W. H. B. Court, *British Economic History 1870–1914* (1965), ch. 9; B. Porter, *Critics of Empire* (1968); M. E. Chamberlain, *The New Imperialism* (1970).

7. *The Times*, 3rd May 1900; Sir H. Campbell–Bannerman, *Speeches* (1908), 88; *The Times*, 24th May 1911; Lord Milner, *The Nation and the Empire* (1913), 90–1; A. P. Newton, 'The Empire', in F. J. C. Hearnshaw (ed.), *Edwardian England* (1933); W. K. Hancock, *Survey of British Commonwealth Affairs*, I (1937), 53–4; A. B. Keith (ed.,) *Selected Speeches and Documents on British Colonial Policy 1763–1917* (1948), II, 208–29, 240–303; K. Sinclair, *Imperial Federation, a Study of New Zealand Policy and Opinion 1880–1914* (1955); *Cambridge History of the British Empire*, III (1959), ch. X; A. P. Thornton, *The Imperial Idea*, esp. ch. III; B. Semmel, *Imperialism and Social Reform*, ch. VII; D. C. Gordon, *The Dominion Partnership in Imperial Defense 1870–1914* (1965); J. E. Kendle, *The Colonial and Imperial Conferences 1887–1911* (1967), esp. 153–5, 207, 217–30; R. Hyam, *Elgin and Churchill at the Colonial Office 1905–1908* (1968), 319–20; D. Judd, *Balfour and the British Empire* (1968), ch. 10; M. Beloff, *Imperial Sunset* (1969), chs. I–IV.

8. *Parliamentary Debates*, fourth series, CXXXII (1904), 304; B. Porter, *Critics of Empire*, esp. chs. 5, 9; S. E. Koss, *John Morley at the India Office 1905–1910* (1969), 176.

9. *The Times*, 14th May 1906; J. A. Hobson, *The Crisis of Liberalism* (1909), 244–5; *Parliamentary Debates*, House of Commons, fifth series, IX (1909), 951–1058; H. Hamilton Fyfe, *South Africa To-Day* (1911), 43–6; L. M. Thompson, *The Unification of South Africa 1902–1910* (1960); K. Mansergh, *South Africa 1906–1961* (1962); W. K. Hancock, *Smuts, the Sanguine Years 1870–1919* (1962); R. S. Churchill, *Winston S. Churchill*, II, ch. 6; R. Hyam, *Elgin and Churchill*, chs. 4, 11, 13; M. Beloff, *Imperial Sunset*, 122–6; R. Hyam, 'African Interests and the South Africa Act, 1908–1910', *Historical Journal*, XIII (1970).

10. Lord Morley, *Indian Speeches 1907–1909* (1909), 91–2, 96–7; Lord Morley, *Recollections* (1917), book V; S. R. Wasti, *Lord Minto and the Indian Nationalist Movement* (1964), esp. 128, 191; M. N. Das, *India under Morley and Minto* (1964), esp. 183; R. J. Moore, *Liberalism and Indian Politics 1872–1920* (1966), esp. ch. 6; S. A. Wolpert, *Morley and India 1906–1910* (1967); D. Judd, *Balfour and the British Empire*, chs. 14–16; M. Beloff, *Imperial Sunset*, 159–65; S. E. Koss, *Morley at the*

India Office, esp. 201; D. Dilks, *Curzon in India* (1969–70); A. J. Green-berger, *The British Image of India* (1969).

11. Lord Cromer, *Ancient and Modern Imperialism* (1910), 124–7; V. Chirol, *Indian Unrest* (1910), xv–xvi; H. G. Wells, 'Will the Empire Live?' in *An Englishman Looks at the World* (1914), 33–4, 37–41; Lucretius, *The Nature of the Universe* (trans. R. E. Latham, 1951), 62; S. Hynes, *Edwardian Turn of Mind*, 24–6.

CHAPTER SIX

1. H. Gladstone to Campbell-Bannerman, 21st January 1906 (B.M. Add. Mss. 41217 ff. 294–5); Haldane to Shaw, 31st March 1907 (ibid, 50538); P. Rowland, *The Last Liberal Governments*, I, 28.
2. C. Booth, *Life and Labour of the People in London*, volume I (ed. 1902), 166–7; Helen Bosanquet, *The Strength of the People* (1902), 331–2, 339–40; B. S. Rowntree, *Poverty, A Study of Town Life*, esp. 167–72, 350–6, 360–1; E. H. Phelps Brown, *Growth of British Industrial Relations* (1965) ch. 1; T. S. and M. B. Simey, *Charles Booth;* A. Briggs, *Social Thought and Social Action, A Study of the Work of B. Seebohm Rowntree*, chs. I–IV; B. B. Gilbert, *The Evolution of National Insurance in Great Britain*, chs. 1, 2; J. Brown, 'Charles Booth and Labour Colonies, 1889–1905' *Economic History Review*, second series, XXI (1968); D. J. Oddy, 'Working Class Diets in Late Nineteenth Century Britain', ibid, XXIII (1970).
3. G. R. Sims (ed.), *Living London*, III, 203–9; A. Ponsonby, *The Camel and the Needle's Eye* (1910), 144–61.
4. *Report of the Inter-Departmental Committee on Physical Deterioration* (1904), CD. 21751, I, 84–93; A. White, *Efficiency and Empire*, 105; B. Semmel, *Imperialism and Social Reform*, ch. III; B. B. Gilbert, *The Evolution of National Insurance*, ch. II; S. Hynes, *The Edwardian Turn of Mind*, ch. II.
5. B. B. Gilbert, *The Evolution of National Insurance*, 237–45.
6. R. P. Scott (ed.), *What is Secondary Education?* (1899), 6, 56; C. Booth, *Life and Labour of the People of London*, final volume, 202; *The Times*, 15th October 1902; C. T. Bateman, *John Clifford* (1904), 283–5; J. E. Hand (ed.), *Science in Public Affairs* (1906), 94–5; *New Encyclopedia of Social Reform* (1908), 1099–1100; Sir J. Marchant, *Dr John Clifford* (1924), chs. VII, VIII; B. M. Allen, *Sir Robert Morant* (1934), part III; Blanche E. C. Dugdale, *Arthur James Balfour*, I, ch. XV; J. Graves, *Policy and Progress in Secondary Education 1902–1942* (1943), chs. I–XIV; E. Halévy, *Imperialism and the Rise of Labour*, 139–210; J. Floud, 'The Educational Experience of the Adult Population of England and Wales as at July 1949', in D. V. Glass (ed.), *Social Mobility in Britain* (1954); E. Eaglesham, *From School Board to Local Authority* (1956); A. Tropp, *The School Teachers*, chs. 10, 11; D. V. Glass 'Education', in Ginsberg, *Law and Opinion in the 20th Century*; K. Young, *Arthur James Balfour*, 203–7; Marjorie Cruickshank, *Church and State in English Education* (1964), chs. 3–5, appendix C; J. S. Maclure, *Educational Documents England and Wales, 1816–1963* (1965), 140–66; A. M. Kazamias, *Politics, Society and Secondary Education in England* (1966), chs.

I–VIII; B. B. Gilbert, *The Evolution of National Insurance*, 95, 97; E. J. R. Eaglesham, *The Foundations of Twentieth-Century Education in England* (1967).

7. H. G. Wells, *An Englishman Looks at the World*, 72; E. C. Mack, *Public Schools and British Opinion*, 314, 366; D. S. L. Cardwell, *The Organization of Science in England* (1957), ch. VII; K. Martin, *Father Figures* (1966), 54; E. J. R. Eaglesham, *Foundations of Twentieth-Century Education*, ch. VII.

8. A. Mansbridge, *An Adventure in Working-Class Education* (1920); J. F. C. Harrison, *Learning and Living 1790–1960* (1961), esp. ch. VII; T. Kelly, *A History of Adult Education in Great Britain* (1962), chs. 14, 15.

9. J. A. Hobson, *Crisis of Liberalism*, 110; Margaret McMillan, *The Child and the State* (1911), xii–iii, 26–8, 93, 187–8; A. Mansbridge, *Adventure in Working-Class Education*, 31–2.

10. Marjorie Cruickshank, *Church and State in English Education*, ch. 5; P. Rowland, *The Last Liberal Governments*, I, 76–8.

11. *Report of the Inter-Departmental Committee on Physical Deterioration, Cd.* 2210 (1904), II, 372; *The Times*, 2nd January 1905; *Parliamentary Debates*, fourth series, CLII (1906), 1397–8; M. E. Bulkley, *The Feeding of Schoolchildren* (1914); A. V. Dicey, *Law and Opinion*, xlix–l; B. B. Gilbert, *The Evolution of National Insurance*, ch. 3.

12. C. Booth, *Life and Labour of the People in London* (1902), final volume, 143–8; B. S. Rowntree, *Poverty: A Study of Town Life*, 438–41; *Parliamentary Debates*, fourth series, CLXIX (1907), 224, CLXXII, 1190–1, CXC (1908), 618; *Manchester Guardian*, 2nd March 1909; J. L. Garvin, *Life of Joseph Chamberlain*, II, 508–14, III, 625–7; B. Abel-Smith, 'Social Security', in Ginsberg, *Law and Opinion in the 20th Century*; C. L. Mowat, *Charity Organization Society*, 137–44, 158–9; D. Owen, *English Philanthropy 1660–1960* (1964), 504–10; B. B. Gilbert, *The Evolution of National Insurance*, 97, ch. 4; P. Rowland, *The Last Liberal Governments*, I, 156–8; J. Amery, *Joseph Chamberlain*, V, 5–7, 227, 269–70.

13. *Parliamentary Debates*, fourth series, CXC (1908), 585–6; A. G. Gardiner, *Prophets, Priests and Kings*, 32; W. S. Churchill, *Liberalism and the Social Problem*, 155; W. S. Adams, 'Lloyd George and the Labour Movement', *Past & Present*, no. 3 (1953); R. Jenkins, *Asquith*, 166–7; H. Pelling, *Popular Politics and Society*, 144–5; R. S. Churchill, *Winston S. Churchill* (1969), volume II, Companion part 2, 863–4.

14. *Report of the Royal Commission on the Poor Laws and Relief of Distress Cd.* 4499 (1909), part IX, 617, 643–4; W. S. Churchill, *Liberalism and the Social Problem*, 189–210; Mrs S. Webb, 'The Poor Law and How We Can Get Rid of It', in H. Carter (ed.), *The Social Outlook* (1910); S. and Beatrice Webb, *The Prevention of Destitution* (1911); *Encyclopedia Britannica*, XXVII, 578; B. S. Rowntree, *The Way to Industrial Peace and the Problem of Unemployment* (1914), esp. 127–35; S. and Beatrice Webb, *English Poor Law History, Part II, the Last Hundred Years* (1929), vol II; Beatrice Webb, *Our Partnership*, chs. VII, VIII; T. W. Hutchison, *A Review of Economic Doctrines 1870–1929* (1953), 409–17; C. L. Mowat, *Charity Organization Society*, 159–66; D. Owen, *English Philanthropy*,

510–20; B. Rodgers, *The Battle Against Poverty*, I (1968); ch. 6; K. D. Brown, *Labour and Unemployment 1900–1914* (1971).

15. Lord Beveridge, *Unemployment*, esp. 102–10, 148–9, 190–1, 201–8; W. S. Churchill, *Liberalism and the Social Problem*, 253–73, 377–9; H. Carter, *The Social Outlook*, 87; Lord Beveridge, *Power and Influence* (1953), 44–79; B. B. Gilbert, 'Winston Churchill versus the Webbs: the Origins of British Unemployment Insurance', *American Historical Review*, vol. 71 (1966); B. B. Gilbert, *The Evolution of National Insurance*, 233–65; R. S. Churchill, *Winston S. Churchill*, II, ch. 9; R. S. Churchill, *Winston S. Churchill*, II, companion, 851–4.

16. Clementina Black, *Sweated Industry and the Minimum Wage* (1907); W. S. Churchill. *Liberalism and the Social Problem*, 239–52; R. H. Tawney, *The Establishment of Minimum Rates in the Tailoring Industry under the Trade Boards Act of 1909* (1915); S. and Beatrice Webb, *History of Trade Unionism*, 494–5; E. H. Phelps Brown, *Growth of British Industrial Relations*, 197–209, 309–10; W. H. B. Court, *British Economic History*, 385–95; R. S. Churchill, *Winston S. Churchill*, II, 296–300.

17. *Punch*, 5th August 1908; D. Lloyd George, *The People's Budget* (1909); W. S. Blunt, *My Diaries*, 689; Lucy Masterman, *C. F. G. Masterman*, ch. 6; R. Jenkins, *Mr Balfour's Poodle* (1954), 39-48; R. Jenkins, *Asquith*, 195-8.

18. W. S. Churchill, *Liberalism and the Social Problem*, part III; W. S. Churchill, *The People's Rights* (1909); *The Times*, 18th November 1909; 11th December 1909; H. du Parcq, *Lloyd George*, IV, 697–765; Lord Newton, *Lord Lansdowne* (1929), ch. XVI; A. Chamberlain, *Politics from Inside*, 196–200; Blanche E. C. Dugdale, *A. J. Balfour*, II, 40–2; R. Jenkins, *Mr Balfour's Poodle*, 48–57, chs. V, VI; A. M. Gollin, '*The Observer*' *and J. L. Garvin*, ch. IV; K. Young, *A. J. Balfour*, 289–96; R. S. Churchill, *Winston S. Churchill*, II, 340–61; P. Rowland, *The Last Liberal Governments*, I, ch. 12; N. Blewett, *The Peers, the Parties and the People*, esp. chs. 5–7.

19. A. V. Dicey, *Lectures on the Relation between Law and Public Opinion in England* (2nd ed., 1914), 57–9; R. Jenkins, *Mr Balfour's Poodle*, ch. VII; R. Jenkins, *Asquith*, 204–11; C. C. Weston, The Liberal Leadership and the Lords' Veto', *Historical Journal*, XI.

20. *The Times*, 11th August 1911; Lord Newton, *Lord Lansdowne*, ch. XVII; A. Chamberlain, *Politics from Inside*, 200-345; *Blanche E. C. Dugdale, A. J. Balfour*, II, 45-61; Lucy Masterman, *C. F. G. Masterman*, 200-2; R. Jenkins, *Mr Balfour's Poodle*, chs. VIII-XIII, appendix C; A. M. Gollin, '*The Observer*' *and J. L. Garvin*, ch. X; R. Jenkins, *Asquith*, 212-32; R. S. Churchill, *Winston S. Churchill*, II, 340-61; P. Rowland, *The Last Liberal Governments*, I, chs. 13, 15-17; C. C. Weston, 'The Liberal Leadership and the Lords' Veto', *Historical Journal*, XI; N. Blewett, *The Peers, the Parties and the People*, ch. 8–10.

21. H. du Parcq, *Life of David Lloyd George* (1913), IV, 792–3; W. S. Churchill, *Liberalism and the Social Problem*, 265–73, part III; Lord Beveridge, *Unemployment*, 223-30; Lord Beveridge, *Power and Influence*, 80-92; B. B. Gilbert, *The Evolution of National Insurance*, ch. 5.

22. *The Times*, 30th November 1911; Lucy Masterman, *C. F. G. Masterman*, ch. 9; W. J. Braithwaite, *Lloyd George's Ambulance Wagon* (1957); P. Vaughan, *Doctor's Commons* (1959), 196–210; E. R. Turner, *What the Butler Saw* (1962), 254–60; B. B. Gilbert, *The Evolution of National Insurance*, ch. 6.

23. Balfour to A. Chamberlain, 17th October 1911 (B. M. Add. Mss. 49736); A. Chamberlain, *Politics from Inside*, 338; R. Blake, *The Unknown Prime Minister*, 139-40; K. Young, *A. J. Balfour*, 333; B. B. Gilbert, *The Evolution of National Insurance*, 371-3.

24. *Parliamentary Debates, House of Commons*, fifth series, XXVII (1911), 1393–1400; P. Snowdon, *Autobiography*, I, 228–9; J. H. S. Reid, *Origins of the British Labour Party*, 164–5; H. Pelling, *Short History of the Labour Party*, 27–8; A. Briggs, 'The Welfare State in Historical Perspective', *European Journal of Sociology*, II (1961), esp. 228–32; B. B. Gilbert, *The Evolution of National Insurance*, esp. 287–8, 451–2; A. Marwick, 'The Labour Party and the Welfare State in Britain, 1900–1948', *American Historical Review*, LXXIII (1967), 385–6.

25. H. Belloc, *The Servile State* (1912), esp. section IX; R. Speaight, *Life of Hilaire Belloc* (1957), 315-20.

26. P. Collier, *England and the English* (1909), 346–50; D. Lloyd George, *The Rural Land Problem* (1913); Lloyd George/C. P. Scott conversation on the land campaign, 16th January 1913 (British Museum Add. Mss. 50901); *The Land: The Report of the Land Inquiry Committee* (1913–14); B. S. Rowntree, *The Labourer and the Land* (1914), esp. 57; Lord Riddell, *More Pages from My Diary*, esp. 63–4, 70, ch. XX; T. Jones, *Lloyd George* (1951), 45; E. Halévy, *Rule of Democracy*, 468–72; A. Briggs, 62–78; B. B. Gilbert, *The Evolution of National Insurance*, 445–6; M. Kinnear, *The British Voter* (1968), 34; H. V. Emy, 'The Land Campaign: Lloyd George as a Social Reformer', in A. J. P. Taylor (ed.), *Lloyd George Twelve Essays* (1971).

CHAPTER SEVEN

1. W. S. Churchill, *Liberalism and the Social Problem*, 181-2; B. S. Rowntree, *The Way to Industrial Peace*, esp. 2, 4–5, 8–12; H. G. Wells, 'The Labour Unrest' in *What the Worker Wants* (1912), 9–11; G. D. H. Cole, *The World of Labour* (1913), 285–8; A. Chamberlain, *Politics from Inside*, 443–5; H. Pelling, *Popular Politics and Society*, ch. 9.

2. G. Drage, *Trade Unions* (1905), esp. 183; *1910, The Law Reports, House of Lords* (1910), 94, 97, 114–15; *Punch*, 17th August 1910; C. Watney and J. A. Little, *Industrial Warfare* (1912); C. Booth, *Industrial Unrest and Trade Union Policy* (1913); W. T. Layton, *Capital and Labour* (1914), esp. 214-15; S. and Beatrice Webb, *History of Trade Unionism*, chs. IX-XI; Lord Askwith, *Industrial Problems and Disputes* (1920); E. Hughes, *Keir Hardie's' Speeches and Writings*, 146; E. Halévy, *The Rule of Democracy*, 444-86; R. Page Arnot, *The Miners: Years of Struggle* (1953), chs. III-V; R. V. Sires, 'Labor Unrest in England, 1910-1914', *Journal of Economic History*, XV (1955); B. C. Roberts ,*The Trades Union Congress 1868-1921* (1958), chs. V-VII; E. H. Phelps Brown, *Growth of*

British Industrial Relations; P. S. Bagwell, *The Railwaymen* (1963), chs. VIII-XIII; H. Pelling, *History of British Trade Unionism* (1963), ch. 9; H. A. Clegg, A. Fox and A. F. Thompson, *History of British Trade Unionism since 1889,* I (1964); R. S. Churchill, *Winston S. Churchill,* II, 367-86.

3. *The Miners' Next Step,* 8; *Parliamentary Debates,* House of Commons, fifth series, XXXVI (1912), 535-59; P. Snowden, *Socialism and Syndicalism* (1913), esp. 243-4; R. Page Arnot, *The Miners,* 115-18; R. Page Arnot, *The South Wales Miners* (1967), 327.

4. S. G. Hobson, *National Guilds* (1914); A. R. Orage (ed.), *National Guilds, an Inquiry into the Wage System and the Way Out* (1914), v-vi, 281–3; S. and Beatrice Webb, *History of Trade Unionism,* 660–1; M. Wallace, *The 'New Age' under Orage* (1967), 208–9.

5. P. Snowden, *The Living Wage,* esp. 54–5; *The Times,* 11th September 1911.

6. 'Arbitration and Conciliation', *Encyclopedia Britannica,* (11th ed., 1910); G. D. H. Cole, *The World of Labour,* ch. IX; W. T. Layton, *Capital and Labour,* ch. XVI.

7. A. Williams, *Co-Partnership and Profit-Sharing* (1913); G. D. H. Cole, *The World of Labour,* ch. X; A. Briggs, *Social Thought and Social Action, A Study of the work of Seebohm Rowntree,* chs. 4, 5.

8. *Memoirs of John Wigham Richardson* (p.p., 1911), 326–7, 330; J. Ramsay MacDonald, *The Social Unrest* (2nd ed., 1924), 65–6; W. T. Layton, *Capital and Labour,* ch. XV; E. H. Phelps Brown, *Growth of British Industrial Relations,* 159–60.

9. *National Conference on the Prevention of Destitution* (1912), 392-3; O. Kahn-Freud, 'Labour Law', in Ginsberg, *Law and Opinion in England in the 20th Century.*

CHAPTER EIGHT

1. *Manchester Guardian,* 12th July 1910; Mrs Philip Snowden, *The Feminist Movement* (1913), 16, 188-9.

2. A. G. Gardiner, *Prophets, Priests, and Kings,* 261-2; O. R. McGregor, *Divorce in England* (1957), ch. III.

3. *Report of the Royal Commission on Divorce and Matrimonial Causes, Cd.* 6478 (1912); O. R. McGregor, *Divorce in England,* ch. I; S. Hynes, *The Edwardian Turn of Mind,* ch. VI.

4. Mrs Philip Snowden, *Feminist Movement,* esp. 137-8; E. Halévy, *The Rule of Democracy,* 494-8.

5. S. Buxton, *Handbook to Political Questions,* 79; *The Times,* 28th March, 1st April 1912; *Parliamentary Debates,* House of Commons, fifth series, XXXVI (1912), 642, 652; R. S. Churchill, *Winston S. Churchill,* II, companion, 1483.

6. Vera Brittain, *Testament of Youth* (1948), 31-2; L. E. Jones, *An Edwardian Youth* (1956), 162-3.

7. *Encyclopedia Britannica* (11th ed., 1910), IX, 645; *Report of the Royal Commission on Divorce,* 185; A. Bennett, *Books and Persons,* 85, 105-6; E. Charteris, *Life and Letters of Sir Edmund Gosse* (1931), 323-4; Beatrice

Webb, *Our Partnership*, 359-60, 447-9; S. Unwin, *Truth About a Publisher*, 93; S. Hynes, *Edwardian Turn of Mind*, chs. VI-VIII; L. Dickinson, *H. G. Wells*, 51-2, ch. 11.

8. Mrs Pankhurst, *The Importance of the Vote* (1908); W. L. Blease, *The Emancipation of English Women* (1910), 170–2; Lloyd-George/C. P. Scott conversation on the suffragettes, 2nd December 1911 (British Museum Add. Mss. 50901); *The Times*, 7th August 1912; Christabel Pankhurst, *The Great Scourge and How to End It* (1913), vi-x, 99–100; *Manchester Guardian*, 12th July 1910, 9th June 1913; E. Sylvia Pankhurst, *The Suffragette* (1911); *Parliamentary Debates*, House of Commons, fifth series LXIII (1914) 531–2; Emmeline Pankhurst, *My Own Story* (1914), book I, ch. IV; Wilma Meikle, *Towards a Sane Feminism* (1916), esp. 46–7; E. Halévy, *The Rule of Democracy*, 490–527; R. Fulford, *Votes for Women* (1957), esp. 75, 91, 128; Christabel Pankhurst, *Unshackled, the Story of How We Won the Vote* (1959); R. Jenkins, *Asquith*, 245–50; N. Blewett, 'The Franchise in the United Kingdom '*Past and Present*, no. 32; 54–6; L. Baily, *BBC Scrapbooks*, I (1966), 143; Constance Rover, *Women's Suffrage and Party Politics in Britain 1866–1914* (1967); R. S. Churchill, *Winston S. Churchill*, II, 393–407; W. L. O'Neill, *The Woman Movement* (1969).

9. Marie Corelli, *Woman or —Suffragette?* (1907), esp. 3–7, 14–15; Mrs Philip Snowden, *Feminist Movement*, ch. IX; Janet Penrose Trevelyan, *Life of Mrs Humphry Ward* (1923), ch. XII; Constance Rover, *Woman's Suffrage and Party Politics*, ch. IX.

10. H. W. Nevison, *More Changes, More Chances* (1925), 36-7; D. E. Butler, *Electoral System in Britain*, 6-13, 38, 144-6; D. Mitchell, *Women on the Warpath, the Story of Women in the First World War* (1966); *The Journals of George Sturt 1890-1927* (1967) ,vol. 2, 735-6; A. Marwick, *Britain in the Century of Total War*, 105-111.

CHAPTER NINE

1. Sir H. Plunkett, *Ireland in the New Century* (1904), 26; *Parliamentary Debates*, House of Commons, fifth series, LXIII (1914), 510-11; Emmeline Pankhurst, *My Own Story*, 266; Christabel Pankhurst, *Unshackled*, 207, 229.

2. S. Buxton, *Handbook to Political Questions*, 151; E. Mason and R. Ellman (eds.), *The Critical Writings of James Joyce* (1959), 213; H. Pelling, *Social Geography of British Elections*, 19-20, 21-2; M. Kinnear, *The British Voter*, 28, 31, 32.

3. *Parliamentary Debates*, fourth series, CLXXIV (1907), 114–15; S. Buxton, *Handbook to Political Questions*, xviii–ix; *Parliamentary Debates*, House of Commons, fifth series (1912), XXXVI, 1399–1426; G. A. Birmingham, *The Lighter Side of Irish Life* (1912), 4; *The Times*, 29th July 1912, 30th September 1912; *The Times*, 3rd March 1914, 16th March 1914, 27th July 1914; Lord Balfour, *Opinions and Argument* (1927), section II, ch. 2; E. Halévy, *Rule of Democracy*, 527–66; A. Chamberlain, *Politics from Inside*, 567–647; *Rudyard Kipling's Verse* (definitive ed. 1941), 232–3; St J. Ervine, *Craigavon, Ulsterman* (1949), esp. 185;

R. Blake, *The Unknown Prime Minister*, chs. VII, IX-XIII; A. P. Ryan, *Mutiny at the Curragh* (1956); J. Joyce, *Critical Writings*, 212; H. W. McCready, 'Home Rule and the Liberal Party, 1899–1906', *Irish Historical Studies*, XIII (1962–3); R. Jenkins, *Asquith*, esp. chs. XVIII, XIX; J. Connell, *Wavell, Scholar and Soldier* (1964), 87–8; Sir J. Fergusson, *The Curragh Incident* (1964); N. Mansergh, *The Irish Question 1840-1921* (1965), esp. chs. V-VIII; J. R. Fanning, 'The Unionist Party and Ireland, 1906-1910', *Irish Historical Studies*, XV (1966-7); P. J. Buckland, 'The Southern Irish Unionists, the Irish Question, and British Politics, 1906-14', ibid; A. T. Q. Stewart, *The Ulster Crisis* (1967); R. S. Churchill, *Winston S. Churchill*, II, 431-2, chs. 12, 13; F. S. L. Lyons, *John Dillon* (1968), chs. 10-12.

4. *Parliamentary Debates*, House of Commons, fifth series, XXXVIII (1912), 801-20; G. K. Chesterton, *Collected Poems*, 152-4; K. O. Morgan, *Wales in British Politics 1868-1922* (1963), esp. ch. VI; P. M. H. Bell, *Disestablishment in Ireland and Wales* (1969), chs. 7-9.

CHAPTER TEN

1. P. Collier, *England and the English*, 305-6; E. M. Forster, *Howards End*, ch. IX; *The Nation*, 31st August 1912; *Manchester Guardian*, 3rd, 18th July 1914; A. Chamberlain, *Politics from Inside*, 599; Mary Agnes Hamilton, *Remembering My Good Friends* (1944), 63-5; R. S. Churchill, *Winston S. Churchill*, II, companion, 1107-8.

2. Daily Mail, *Our German Cousins* (1910), esp. 7; H. G. Wells, *An Englishman Looks at the World*, ch. I; R. Pound and G. Harmsworth, *Northcliffe*, 389-90; T. Brex (ed.), *'Scaremongerings' from the Daily Mail, 1896–1914* (1914), 16-18.

3. *Parliamentary Debates*, fourth series, LVIII (1898), 1437-8; W. T. Stead, *The Americanisation of the World or the Trend of the Twentieth Century* (1902), preface; *The Times*, 25th November 1899, 28th January 1907; G. M. Trevelyan, *Grey of Fallodon* (1937), 116; R. H. Heindel, *The American Impact on Great Britain 1898-1914* (1940); *Rudyard Kipling's Verse* (definitive ed., 1941), 323; H. C. Allen, *Great Britain and the United States* (1954), ch. 15; M. Beloff, 'The Special Relationship: an Anglo-American Myth', in M. Gilbert (ed.), *A Century of Conflict* (1966); B. Perkins, *The Great Rapprochement, England and the United States 1895-1914* (1969).

4. A. G. Gardiner, *Priests, Prophets and Kings*, 88-95; C. T. King, *The Asquith Parliament*, 25-6; *The Nation*, 11th November 1911; *Punch*, 22nd November 1911; S. Low, *Governance of England*, 297-303; H. N. Brailsford, *War of Steel and Gold*, esp. ch. VII; Lord Grey of Fallodon, *Twenty-Five Years* (1925), esp. I, 95-6; Lord Grey of Fallodon, *Fallodon Papers* (1926), 83, ch. VII; G. P. Gooch and H. Temperley (eds.), *British Documents on the Origins of the War*, III (1928), no. 299; J. L. Hammond, *C. P. Scott*, chs. X, XI; G. M. Trevelyan, *Grey of Fallodon*, esp. 40, 67; A. J. P. Taylor, *The Trouble Makers*, ch. IV; G. W. Monger, *The End of Isolation*, esp. 233-5, chs. 9-12, 329-31; R. S. Churchill, *Winston S. Churchill*, II, 596-8; C. H. D. Howard, *Splendid Isolation* (1967); Zara S. Steiner, *The Foreign Office and Foreign Policy, 1898-1914* (1969), chs.

3, 4; R. S. Churchill, *Winston S. Churchill*, II, companion, 1359-61.
5. *Daily Graphic*, 26th July 1909; *British Documents*, VI (1930), 784; E. L. Woodward, *Great Britain and the German Navy* (1935); A. J. Mardar, *From the Dreadnought to Scapa Flow, the Royal Navy in the Fisher Era 1904–1919*, I (1961); R. S. Churchill, *Winston S. Churchill*, II, chs. 14-18.
6. G. Gissing, *Private Papers of Henry Ryecroft*, 55-6; *The Decline and Fall of the British Empire*, 56-9; S. Reynolds, *Seems So!*, 82-4; Lord Roberts, *A Nation in Arms* (1907), 143-5; General Sir I. Hamilton, *Compulsory Service* (1910), 33-4; *The Times*, 9th October 1911; Lord Milner, *The Nation and the Empire* (1913), 469-78; *Parliamentary Debates*, House of Lords, fifth series, XV (1914), 590; E. Halévy, *The Rule of Democracy*, 154-93; D. Hayes, *Conscription Conflict* (1949), chs. 1-11; D. James, *Lord Roberts* (1954), ch. XIV; B. Semmel, *Imperialism and Social Reform*, ch. XII; M. E. Howard, *Lord Haldane and the Territorial Army* (1966); S. Hynes, *Edwardian Turn of Mind*, 39-44; S. E. Koss, *Lord Haldane, Scapegoat for Liberalism* (1969), chs. II-IV; C. Barnett, *Britain and Her Army 1509-1970* (1970), ch. 15.
7. Sir R. Baden-Powell, *Scouting for Boys* (3rd ed., 1910), esp. 196-7, 285, 290, 295; A. Comfort, *The Anxiety Makers* (1967), ch. 3; S. Hynes, *Edwardian Turn of Mind*, 26-9, 166-71; P. Wilkinson, 'English Youth Movements 1908-30', *Journal of Contemporary History*, vol. 4 (1969).
8. K. Pearson, *National Life from the Standpoint of Science* (1901), esp. 109; L. T. Hobhouse, *Democracy and Reaction*, 115-16; H. Campbell-Bannerman, *Speeches*, 205; H. Cudlipp, *Publish and be Damned!*, 14.
9. E. Hughes, *Keir Hardie's Speeches and Writings*, 136; R. Blatchford, *Germany and England* (1910); H. M. Hyndman, *Further Reminiscences*, ch. XVII; T. Brex, *'Scaremongerings' from the Daily Mail* (1914), 55, 66-9; G. D. H. Cole, *Labour in War Time* (1915), 2; L. Thompson, *Robert Blatchford*, ch. XVI; C. Tzuzuki, *H. M. Hyndman*, ch. X.
10. N. Angell, *The Great Illusion* (ed. 1913), vii-viii; Sir N. Angell, *After All* (1951), part II, chs. I-VI.
11. T. Brex, *'Scaremongerings' from the Daily Mail*, esp. 30; Irene C. Willis, *How We Went Into The War* (1918), 19-25; Caroline E. Playne, *The Pre-War Mind in Britain* (1928), 139; R. Pound and G. Harmsworth, *Northcliffe* 232, 252, 326, 332, 366, 368, 388-9, 443, 454, 455.
12. H. G. Wells, *An Englishman Looks at the World*, ch. 23; H. G. Wells, *Autobiography*, II, 665-6; I. F. Clarke, *Voices Prophesying War 1763-1984* (1966), ch. 3; S. Hynes, *Edwardian Turn of Mind*, 34-53.
13. H. G. Wells, *Mr Britling Sees it Through*, ch. 5; T. Clarke, *My Northcliffe Diary*, 64.
14. H. G. Wells, *The War That Will End War* (1914), 7-8, 10-11; G. Murray, *The Foreign Policy of Sir Edward Grey 1906-1915* (1915), 9-11; Irene C. Willis, *How We Went Into The War*, esp. chs. II, III; *The Diary of Arthur Christopher Benson* (n.d.), 273, 275; R. Jenkins, *Asquith*, ch. XX; A. Marwick, *The Deluge*, ch. 1; *Letters of Rupert Brooke* (1968), 654-5.
15. W. S. Churchill, *Liberalism and the Social Problem*, 67; Webb to Shaw, 18th August 1915 (B. M. Add. Mss. 50553); Lord, Oxford and Asquith, *Memories and Reflections*, II, 51-2; C. Addison, *Four and a Half Years* (1934),

I, 35; G. D. H. Cole, *History of the Labour Party from 1914* (1948), chs. I, II; S. J. Hurwitz, *State Intervention in Great Britain, a Study of Economic Control and Social Response 1914-1919* (1949); J. H. S. Reid, *Origins of the British Labour Party*, chs. 14, 15; C. F. Brand, *The British Labour Party* (1964), chs. 3, 4; A. Marwick, *The Deluge*; A. J. P. Taylor, *English History 1914-1945* (1965), 2; T. Wilson, *Downfall of the Liberal Party*, 15-131; B. McGill, 'Asquith's Predicament', *Journal of Modern History*, vol. 39 (1967); Lady Cynthia Asquith, *Diaries 1915-1918* (1968), 6, 17; A. Marwick, 'The Impact of the First World War on British Society', *Journal of Contemporary History*, vol. 3 (1968); A. Marwick, *Britain in the Century of Total War*, ch. 3; J. Terraine, *Impacts of War 1914 and 1918* (1970).

16. H. C. Sonne, *The City* (1915), esp. 121-2; H. Baldwin, *World War I* (1962), 12, 73, 160; R. Jenkins, *Asquith*, 394-5; S. D. Waley, *Edwin Montagu* (1964), 72-5.

17. L. Baily, *BBC Scrapbooks*, I, 170-4; R. S. Churchill, *Winston S. Churchill*, II, 1361.

18. A. Bennett, *Books and Persons*, 200-3; Virginia Woolf, *Roger Fry*, chs. VII, VIII; R. Fry, *Vision and Design* (1961 ed.), 188-93, 226-31; Virginia Woolf, *Collected Essays* (1966), I, 320-1; S. Hynes, *Edwardian Turn of the Mind*, ch. IX, appendix D.

19. *Punch*, 13th December 1911; H. Aronson, *The Land and the Labourer* (1914) xi-ii; C. W. Cunnington, *The Perfect Lady* (1948), 70-2; J. Laver, *Costume* (1963), 114; L. Baily, *BBC Scrapbooks*, I, 177.

Index